D1566260

The Heart of
Female Same-Sex
Attraction

A Comprehensive Counseling Resource

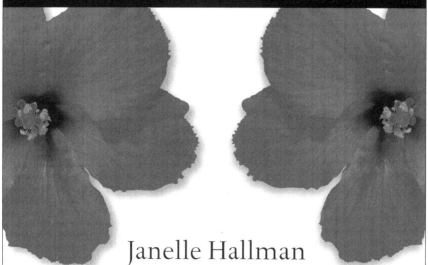

Janelle Hallman

IVP Books

An imprint of InterVarsity Press
Downers Grove, Illinois

InterVarsity Press
P.O. Box 1400, Downers Grove, IL 60515-1426
World Wide Web: www.ivpress.com
E-mail: email@ivpress.com

InterVarsity Press® is the book-publishing division of InterVarsity Christian Fellowship/USA®, a student movement active on campus at hundreds of universities, colleges and schools of nursing in the United States of America, and a member movement of the International Fellowship of Evangelical Students. For information about local and regional activities, write Public Relations Dept., InterVarsity Christian Fellowship/USA, 6400 Schroeder Rd., P.O. Box 7895, Madison, WI 53707-7895, or visit the IVCF website at <www.intervarsity.org>.

Design: Cindy Kiple
Images: Steve Dibblee/iStockphoto

ISBN 978-0-8308-3429-7

Printed in the United States of America ∞

Library of Congress Cataloging-in-Publication Data

Hallman, Janelle M., 1956-
   The heart of female same-sex attraction: a comprehensive counseling
resource / Janelle M. Hallman.
      p. cm.
   Includes bibliographical references and index.
   ISBN 978-0-8308-3429-7 (pbk.: alk. paper)
   1. Lesbians—Mental health. 2. Lesbians—Counseling of. 3.
Lesbianism—Religious aspects—Christianity. 4. Psychotherapy. I.
Title.
   RC451.4.G39H34 2008
   616.890086'643—dc22

                                                                              2007049467

P   22   21   20   19   18   17   16   15   14   13   12   11   10   9   8
Y   26   25   24   23   22   21   20   19   18   17   16   15

To the women who know the struggle and have had the integrity and courage to dig deep for personal truth. This is to the texture, color and beauty of your created and re-created lives.

To my husband and daughter, for the many years of their perseverance and patience while this project consumed our home and lives.

Contents

Acknowledgments 9

Prologue 11

PART ONE: THE BUILDING BLOCKS: *Understanding Their Stories* . 15

  1 The Women and Their Right to Choose 17

  2 The Therapist and Professional Competency 36

  3 Missing a "Home": *Attachment and Self* 50

  4 Lost in Confusion: *Gender Nonconformity and Socialization* . 73

  5 Looking for Home: *Depending on You for Me* 98

PART TWO: THE WORK OF RESTORATION: *Leading Them Home* . 115

  6 Securing the Foundation: *Acceptance and Attunement* 117

  7 Rebuilding on a Corrective Relationship:
    Trust and Empathy 138

  8 Four Basic Blueprints: *Understanding the Various Profiles* . . . 158

  9 Discovering Her Own Home:
    Opening Doors to Healthy Intimacy 181

 10 Leaving the Home of Another:
    Dealing with Same-Sex Attractions 206

 11 Forgotten Rooms: *Transference and Countertransference* . . . 232

 12 Finding the Feminine Within 258

 13 Venturing Out: *The World of Men and Closure* 280

Epilogue 293

Appendix A: Group Therapy 295

Appendix B: Male Therapists 301

References 304

Acknowledgments

If it hadn't been for the hundreds of people who contributed their time, money and prayers, this daunting project would have never materialized. There were many times that I despaired of the monumental task before me. It was in those exact moments that a supporter or friend would drop me an email, encouraging me to simply take the next step—and to never give up. So it was one step at a time that this manuscript neared completion after six years of arduous labor and of receiving support from a team of amazing people.

Thank you to all of my clients. This book was formed in those many hours, weeks, months and years that you allowed me into your lives. I am forever grateful. Thank you to all of the women who agreed to be interviewed and who permitted me to share your words and stories. Thank you to Deloris, Roxanna, Rick and Susan for your dedication to transcribing the hundreds of hours of interview material. Thank you to Jerry and his research assistant, Wanda, Rachel, Karen and Bobbie Jo for helping me to locate and organize the research literature.

Thank you to Shelly, Amy, Leigh-Ann, John, Carla and Veronica and the many others who reviewed chapters and offered gracious suggestions, refining my thoughts and words. Thank you to Veronica, Ellen and Darla for researching, proofreading, formatting and building the bibliography, and for keeping my spirit alive during those discouraging seasons. Thank you to Linda for offering me your literary expertise. Thank you to Deb for repairing and replacing my many computers. Thank you to Corrine, Patty, Elaine, Penny, and Randy and April for opening your homes for my writing retreats.

Thank you to all of you who financially and prayerfully supported this project across these many years. Thank you to InterVarsity Press for helping to make this dream come true. Thank you to all of you who have played a part and who reflect the undying love and faithfulness of our heavenly Father. He is the one who has shown me *how* to never give up: For it is love that "always protects, always trusts, always hopes, always perseveres" (1 Cor 13:7 NIV).

Prologue

Years ago I listened as two of my female friends explained to our small-group Bible study how their relationship had crossed the typical physical and emotional boundaries of friendship into one that included intimate sexual contact. In an effort to better understand the issue of homosexuality and walk with my friends as they sorted out this new territory, I became involved with a faith-based organization in Denver, Colorado, that existed to help people affected by homosexuality. During the several years that I volunteered as a support-group leader, I watched as many of the women came and went. The men seemed to thrive in a group setting, the women less so. I sensed that the women would benefit from a one-on-one encounter in which they felt safe to share and explore their deepest questions and longings. For that reason I decided to pursue a degree in counseling so that I could offer them a private professional setting.

As I pursued my professional training, I struggled with my theological beliefs about homosexuality, gender and God's broader purposes for sexuality. My orthodoxy has not altered over the years; however, my compassion has grown immensely. In general, I hold to a Judeo-Christian worldview. I believe there is a divine design and transcendent purpose for our sexuality beyond mere temporal pleasure. Specifically, I believe that male and female are created in the unique image of God—equally valuable and essential—and are ordained together, in relationship, to reflect the full character and image of a relational or trinitarian God. I don't believe that homosexuality originates within this divine design. Rather, I believe that it originates from our fall or separation from this design. All aspects of humanity—including genetics, biology, body, mind, emotions and psyche—are fallen. As members of the human race, we are *all* collectively responsible for directly or indirectly contributing to the confusion or brokenness within our sexual and gender identities.

Homosexuality does not form in a vacuum, nor is it solely an individual issue (Rom 1), even though the manifestation of this confusion can be profound in some individuals, weaving into their very neurological and psychological constitution. Therefore a greater level of compassion, extra support and attention, and larger portions of grace should be shown to these individuals. It was from these three platforms that I chose to launch my counseling practice.

When I began my counseling internship in 1993, literature was readily available on male homosexuality, but there were no comprehensive publications for understanding the issues concerning female homosexuality. The bulk of my learning came after graduate school through firsthand experience with my clients. My clients were and are patient and willing to teach me and to let me into the innermost parts of their hearts. For that I am grateful. They have gifted me with glimpses of their world through their words and their stories. It is my privilege to share in this book the understanding I have gained from these courageous women.

◆ ◆ ◆

While it has gained the support and interest of many, *The Heart of Female Same-Sex Attraction* is primarily intended for mental health professionals, educators and pastoral-care counselors who are interested in clinical perspective on the issue. In addition, I have attempted to make this book as reader-friendly as possible so it can serve as an effective tool for clergy, lay counselors, mentors and others involved with helping women who struggle with unwanted same-sex attractions (often abbreviated as SSA).

This book is also for friends and family of women experiencing same-sex feelings. And lastly, but perhaps most importantly, this book is for women who are themselves struggling. However, for these readers, the material presented in this book may stir up difficult emotions, and the stories and framework presented may be initially exposing and challenging. I hope this will not discourage the women who struggle or their family members from continuing to reflect on their own lives.

The book is presented in two parts. Part one introduces the reader to the preliminary and ethical considerations in working with this special population, and to the women themselves. Part two offers treatment guidelines and introduces the salient therapeutic issues and effective counseling protocols for working with women in conflict with same-sex attraction. For those readers interested in additional material related to the historic and current research on a variety of issues related to female homosexuality as well as expanded theoretical frameworks referenced within this text, please refer to the book website at www.ivpress.com. An unabridged bibliography is also included on the website. The bibliography listed at the end of this text contains only those sources from which I have directly quoted.

The material in part two has been limited to clinical processes and techniques apart from spiritual or theological frameworks (excepting chapter 13) and associated processes for two reasons. First, I hope that the principles and recommendations in this book can be applied across a variety of faith-based traditions as well as non-faith-based professional settings. Second, I believe that the spiritual frameworks, at least from a Christ-centered theology, have been adequately covered elsewhere.[1]

However, it is only fair to disclose that spiritual direction, inner healing and discipleship counseling remain essential to my practice with those clients who are desirous of and able to receive these interventions. In fact, much of my clinical framework arises out of my observation of how God works in the lives of emotionally, psychologically and spiritually wounded people in general. It is always my hope that a woman will begin to form a new or expanded picture of God first based on her *experience* of my (albeit imperfect) acceptance, love and faithfulness. Often my clients need to reframe God's attributes within a feminine perspective. In other words, the traditional images of God as power, warrior, king and even redeemer do not resonate with their deepest heart's needs. My clients are more apt to draw closer to God when they see him as comforter, nurturer, lover or friend. I have also found that as a woman's distorted images of God begin to change, she is able to walk in her belovedness, leading to a greater sense of well-being and personal growth. Mere therapeutic measures can never mediate the depth of healing and restoration that are often

---

[1]See Bergner (1995); Comiskey (1989, 2003); Dallas (1991); Davies & Gilbert (2001); Davies & Rentzel (1993); Eldridge (1994); Howard (1991, 2005); McIntyre (1996); Paulk (2003); Payne (1981, 1984, 1991); Rentzel (1990); and Whitehead (2003). See also Exodus International, www.exodus-international.org; Desert Streams and their Living Waters and Cross Current programs, www.desertstream.org; Focus on the Family and the Love Won Out program, www.lovewonout.com; Parents and Friends of ExGays and Gays, www.pfox.org; Pastoral Care Ministries, www.leannepayne.org; Redeemed Lives, www.redeemedlives.org. See also Courage (for Catholics), www.couragerc.net; Transforming Congregations (United Methodist), www.transformingcong.org; Evergreen International (for Latter-day Saints), www.evergreeninternational.org; JONAH (Jews Offering New Alternatives to Homosexuality), www.jonahweb.org.

experienced as a woman relentlessly pursues the Truest Lover of Her Soul.

The observations and therapeutic recommendations made throughout the book are for adult women. Recently, I have started receiving more calls from parents of adolescent or young adult daughters struggling with their sexual identities. Sharon Hersh—a professional counselor specializing in work with adolescent women and author of *Mom, Sex Is No Big Deal* (2006)—is experiencing a similar influx of inquiries. In 2005, Hersh only had a few adolescent female clients facing sexual-identity issues; currently, almost 50% of her existing practice involves these types of cases. Although I hope that most of the observations and recommendations within this book will apply to this younger population, many of the therapeutic techniques and interventions may need to be adapted for adolescents.

◆ ◆ ◆

It is my sincere hope that this book will aid you in your relationships with the women who seek your help to discover their truest, fullest identity. I also hope that this book will serve as a launching pad for further dialogue, future research, and increased understanding and development of effective helping techniques for women with same-sex feelings. Ultimately, it is through healing relationships that these women will be able to stretch out into the broader world of interdependent and non-erotic relationships with other women. May you experience the honor of becoming intimate sojourners with them as they discover and live out of their true, unique identities as beautiful, strong women.

PART ONE

The Building Blocks

Understanding Their Stories

Though no one can go back and make a brand new start,
anyone can start from now and make a brand new ending.

CARL BARD

CHAPTER ONE

The Women and
Their Right to Choose

In the West we have a tendency to be profit-oriented,
where everything is measured according to the results. . . .
The success of love is in the loving—it is not in the result of loving. . . .
The more we can remove this priority for results
the more we can learn about . . . love.

BROTHER GEOFF,
QUOTED IN MOTHER TERESA'S *A SIMPLE PATH*

Karen entered therapy because she was despondent over the recent breakup
of a three-year relationship with a female partner. She said that each time she
broke up with a partner, she felt like her heart was being ripped out of her chest.
She feared she was losing parts of her self and exclaimed she never wanted to
go through that pain again. She believed God wanted something more for her
than the dramatic, tumultuous same-sex relationships she had previously
known. She also admitted that she didn't know how to have "normal" friendships with women. They always became emotionally enmeshed or sexualized.

For the next few years, Karen made a commitment to work on her life and
relationships. Her therapist watched her struggle through deep pain, so severe
that at times she questioned her will to live. Yet Karen had tenacity, determination and courage to fight for the life she had always dreamed of having—one
that included a close community of female friends and perhaps marriage and a
family. In therapy she confronted memories of childhood abuse and challenged
core negative beliefs about herself and God. For instance, Karen realized her
own self-hatred kept her from believing and receiving care and kindness from

God and others. She stopped using some of her defensive behaviors, such as sarcasm and anger, and familiar paths of emotional escape, such as drinking or contemplating suicide whenever she felt pain. She stabilized her personal life by settling into a job and an apartment that she enjoyed, and she stepped out into new opportunities for friendship and community.

Now, Karen reports she has many female friendships free of intense dependency and sexualization. Her relationships are satisfying, fulfilling and reciprocal. Although same-sex feelings still arise from time to time, she nevertheless has an overarching sense of well-being and peace, knowing that she is loveable and valuable. She no longer fears the times when feelings of loneliness surface. She has learned to nurture herself and reach out to others for support. She reports feeling like a totally different person.

When asked what helped her stabilize and make such incredible changes, Karen replied, "My therapist! She was focused on me. She cared about *all* of my life. She showed respect. But even more than that, she was always the same, even when I was wrung out with anxiety and thoughts of hurting myself. She was consistent, attentive and patient. Her calming voice, her strong boundaries, her availability, her listening ears, her gentleness and her femininity all somehow changed me! She never gave up on me. She gave me hope."

As I work with women in conflict with same-sex attraction (SSA), I too have hope. My hope is based not on a woman's ability to completely eliminate same-sex desires or attraction, but on her capacity to heal and to grow into a solid, secure woman within a solid, secure therapeutic relationship. I have hope that a woman can mature in giving and receiving love in all of her relationships and no longer be restricted by destructive relational patterns. I have hope that a woman can be released from the deep core of shame, self-hatred and desperation that prevents her from becoming the woman God intends her to be.

IN PREPARATION FOR THIS BOOK

Over the previous fifteen years, I have collectively counseled, befriended or formally interviewed hundreds of women with SSA and emotional dependency. I have also counseled, consulted and interviewed over fifty mothers of self-identified lesbian daughters. Most of these women gave me permission to include their words and stories in this book in the hopes that their stories could help another woman by first helping a counselor to understand the fears, longings and needs behind female SSA. I am therefore honored to be able to share their exact quotes and anecdotes, even though some of their names and identifying information have been altered to protect their anonymity.

The vast majority of the women with whom I have been personally acquainted come from a very special subpopulation of women with SSA. These women are

- between 25 and 55 years old
- part of a *faith tradition*
- *conflicted*[1] about or desire to change or manage their *same-sex feelings and behaviors* in a way that is congruent with their religious beliefs about sexual chastity and purity
- *pursuing help* from professional counselors, nonclinical support groups or spiritual discipleship organizations in reaching their goals

I have not, however, had the same honor of working with women who are not from a faith tradition or who are not in conflict with their lesbian orientation or identity. Additionally, I have limited experience in working with the next generation of adolescent and young adult women, all of whom have grown up within a very different culture than those women raised before the 1980s. Therefore, it is possible that my perspectives or insights do not apply to *all* women who experience SSA. Nevertheless, I believe it is still valuable to present my observations and understanding of the histories and clinical dynamics of women of faith *in therapy* or support-group settings who have spent years communicating their personal insights to me as they grow and heal.

I have also interviewed many seasoned psychotherapists who specialize in helping women in conflict with SSA and reviewed most of the research and academic literature focusing on etiology, demographics, mental health and clinical considerations of female homosexuality. This includes gay-affirmative literature as well as most of the relevant historical and scientific literature from the 1950s to the present. This book therefore reflects the collective experiences, scientific inquiry and clinical frameworks of many professionals as well as the insights and stories of the women themselves.

Finally, I humbly acknowledge that I have much more to learn about this

---

[1]Women in conflict with their same-sex feelings are, clinically speaking, *ego-dystonic*. The *Comprehensive Glossary of Psychiatry and Psychology* defines *ego-dystonic* as "denoting aspects of a person's personality that are viewed as repugnant, unacceptable or inconsistent with the rest of the personality" (Kaplan & Sadock, 1991, p. 63).

complex area of human experience. I therefore offer my perspectives with a spirit of openness. This book is not intended to serve as ammunition to judge, explain away or otherwise dismiss homosexual women who desire to live peaceful lives free of contempt and condemnation from fellow human beings. On the contrary, I hope this book stirs compassion and a desire within each reader to build relationships with all women, regardless of the beliefs or intentions surrounding their sexual identity.

A NEED FOR RELATIONSHIP

As psychiatrist and author Irvin Yalom, M.D., stresses in his book *The Gift of Therapy*, "Therapy should not be theory-driven but relationship-driven" (2002, p. xviii). He suggests a client can be helped purely through experiencing an intimate relationship with their therapists. This couldn't be truer than for female clients with SSA. When I asked more than 20 women who struggle with unwanted SSA what affected them most about psychotherapy or lay counseling, their answer was unanimous: the relationship. Not one alluded to counseling techniques, insights received or even things learned. Admittedly, they did benefit from these aspects, but they emphasized that the love, acceptance and commitment of their therapist, pastor or friend made the deepest impact on them. In fact, most women with SSA will not progress markedly in their individual process of growth, development and healing apart from a loving, curative relationship with either a professional or a layperson who can provide safe and nurturing support.

A NEED FOR SAFETY AND TRUST

I discovered fairly early on in my counseling practice, however, that many of my clients first needed to feel safe before they could begin to feel loved. Without safety and security, trust cannot be established. Without trust, loving relationships cannot be built. For many women with SSA, safety is still a preeminent need.

This is not always or solely because of childhood losses or trauma; it is also because many women haven't found safe places as adults. They are all too aware of the relentless and pervading controversies surrounding homosexuality in political, legal (adoption and marriage), theological, ecumenical, psychological, scientific, medical and educational realms. Even though homosexuality for them is very personal and often shameful, they must continue to endure public misunderstanding, dogmatic opinions and endless debates, especially when it comes to the issue of "change." Some former homosexuals say that life as a gay person is not satisfying and that "change" is possible. Others say that the "change" they experienced didn't last and now believe once gay always gay. Some say that you will be harmed if you try to change your homosexuality; others say you will be harmed if you do not.

These women long for a safe, quiet place to simply *be*. They are exhausted and often overwhelmed by this combative and confusing milieu. They want to be known as a person, not just as a woman with SSA. They are so much more than the sum of their sexual expression, yet—like all women—need a place to explore and ask personal heartfelt questions about life, love, sexuality, gender and God without being rejected or worrying about political correctness. They need a safe place.

THE STRUGGLE: NO TWO ARE ALIKE

Every woman with SSA is unique—not only in personality, family history, and talents and abilities but in how she experiences her same-sex attraction. For example, consider some of the women who are currently in my therapy group.

Cathy is 37 years old, married with two children. She has had three nonsexual emotionally dependent relationships with women. Although she longs for a woman's touch and comfort, she does not identify herself as homosexual.

Tina, who is 35 and single, has had two long-term same-sex relationships. Many of her friends have embraced a lesbian identity and encourage her to do the same. She believes she would be happier as a lesbian but is torn because of her religious beliefs.

Rebecca was surprised to find herself in the arms of one of her female friends three years ago, at the age of 22. Although the closeness and affection felt great, she does not want to further explore or pursue a same-sex relationship. She has always wanted to marry and have a family.

Danielle, 45, lived with one lesbian lover for over a decade. She believes God has called her out of lesbian relationships but has little hope she can ever relate to a man.

Lisa, who is 55 years old, has tried to have a same-sex relationship but struggles with knowing how to build any kind of relationship, with either a man or a woman. She doubts anyone really wants to be with her.

Based on these vignettes, not to mention the myriads of others I could have presented, it seems inappropriate to assign the term *female homosexual* to every woman with SSA. Additionally, many women say they would be offended or humiliated if they were labeled as homosexual or lesbian. These terms can incite fear and often imply the existence of certain behaviors, attitudes and feelings that are simply not present within their particular experience or identity. Yet, to be sure, they all admit to experiencing some level of same-sex attraction or emotional dependency, or both, as defined here:

Same-sex attraction. Same-sex attraction includes any desire toward another woman, in reality or fantasy, that may involve erotic feelings, sexually charged sensations or a strong preoccupation with nonsexual physical affection such as being held, hugged, casually touched or cuddled. The presence of SSA does not preclude the presence of opposite-sex attraction or behaviors.[2]

Same-sex emotional dependency. Same-sex emotional dependency is the state of a same-sex relationship wherein one or both of the women become intensely emotionally and psychologically dependent on the other for a sense of self, attachment, identity, purpose, security or well-being. This dependency often thwarts the woman's opportunity to appropriate these essential aspects of life through her own autonomous individual growth and development. The dependency is emotionally based and therefore may or may not include physical or sexual involvement or activity.

Same-sex sexual behavior. Same-sex sexual behavior should be distinguished from both same-sex attraction and same-sex emotional dependency. It is possible for women to experience same-sex attraction without acting on it in sexual behavior with another woman. Likewise, it is possible for women to engage in same-sex behavior without any underlying same-sex attraction or desire.[3] This latter phenomenon is illustrated in the cultural trend of young women publicly kissing or petting as a means to arouse young men (Stepp, 2004) or participating in same- and opposite-sex petting groups referred to as "cuddle puddles" (Morris, 2006). Many young women are also now proclaim-

---

[2]Many researchers note that "homosexuality and heterosexuality are dimensions and not air-tight categories" (Goode & Haber, 1977, p. 20) and therefore are "best conceptualized as being on a continuum" (Schneider, Brown & Glassgold, 2002, p. 266; see also Epstein, 2006). Further, many researchers observe that female sexuality, in general, is extremely fluid or flexible rather than static along this continuum (Diamond, 1998, 2000; Nichols, 1988b; Shechter, 2004; Sophie, 1986).

[3]The insights and observations offered in this book are focused on women who experience unwanted same-sex feelings, not on women who are casually choosing same-sex behaviors.

ing themselves "lesbians until graduation" or experimenting with both sexes since bisexuality is considered culturally exotic or cool ("Confessions of a LUG," 1999). It remains to be seen how these adolescent behaviors and disintegrating cultural sexual ethics will affect the sexual desires, orientations or identities of these women as adults.

Sexual orientation. The term *sexual orientation* needs to be distinguished from all of the above terms. Sexual orientation is typically assessed by evaluating one's sexual arousal patterns, attractions, fantasies, yearnings, behaviors and identity.[4] If a woman reports most of these factors as being predominantly associated with other women, especially across her life span, she would be said to have a predominant homosexual or same-sex orientation. I believe that most of the women with whom I work have a same-sex or bisexual sexual orientation, yet many do *not* integrate this orientation into their broader identity. They believe their same-sex feelings and behaviors are not harmonious or consistent with their true self or fundamental identity. In other words, they do not assume a same-sex sexual identity or refer to themselves as homosexual, bisexual or lesbian.[5]

There are also women with same-sex feelings and desires who do not have a same-sex sexual orientation. For example, some women consistently struggle with same-sex emotional dependency yet do not desire or fantasize about sexual involvement with women. Instead, they may fantasize about or desire a romantic relationship with a man but often face obstacles to developing heterosexual relationships. There are also many older women who find themselves in a same-sex relationship because of the powerful nature of the love and connection between themselves and *one* particular woman. Their same-sex desire and involvement does not globalize to other women, nor does their heterosexual orientation wane.

Given the variations of how each woman experiences, acts on or identifies

---

[4]Researchers Byne and Parsons (1993) highlight the subjective element of sexual orientation and therefore its potential to change or evolve: "We use the term *sexual orientation* to signify a cognitive identification and subjective emotional sense of oneself on a continuum of homosexual/bisexual/heterosexual identity. This definition allows for a spectrum of thoughts and feelings and even for a discrepancy between one's actions and one's thoughts and fantasies. Furthermore, it allows for the possibility that one's sexual orientation may change over time" (p. 229). See also Gonsiorek, Sell & Weinrich (1995).

[5]Based on a comprehensive survey of Americans' sexual practices, it is estimated that 13% of 150 women surveyed who desire to have and do have sex with other women do not consider themselves lesbians (Michael, Gagnon, Laumann & Kolata, 1994, p. 177).

with same-sex feelings, and considering the shame and initial mistrust a woman may experience in the opening stages of therapy, I have learned to be patient, allowing my client the time she needs to find her own language to unfold her experiences, beliefs, identities and therapeutic goals. I have also discovered that a woman's *experience* of my patience and respect in this regard is, in and of itself, therapeutically curative. However, for purposes of brevity within this book, I will rely on the acronym "SSA" to encapsulate all of these broader definitions and possible struggles and identities within a woman's life.

THE NATURE OF CHANGE

Few women enter therapy with the single request to "change" their sexual orientation. Typically, a woman will initially want to address difficulties related to one or more of these issues:

- the crisis of a recently terminated same-sex relationship
- generalized depression, anxiety or mistrust
- chronic feelings of emptiness, toxic shame or a lack of a basic sense of self
- loneliness and isolation
- a pattern of emotional dependency or enmeshment with female friends
- self-hatred
- dealing with men

At the beginning of treatment, most of my clients are unclear about what is realistic in terms of changing their SSA. They may be unsure of how much of their life they *can* or *want* to change. For many women, same-sex relationships have been the only means by which they have survived an unstable sense of self and weathered deep unmet intimacy needs. Additionally, some women have molded their adult identity around their same-sex feelings and relationships. Even if I could somehow "fix" or quickly "change" these core attractions and drives within a woman, it would be unwise to do so until she has established other organizing principles for her identity, meaning and intimacies.

Therapy is rarely, if ever, focused on the *direct* eradication of a woman's same-sex feelings or orientation. A woman's SSA is not a neatly compartmentalized aspect within her life that can be easily isolated and simply extricated; it is rarely a behaviorally based phenomenon that can be objectively observed, quantified or controlled, although it certainly has behavioral components. Female SSA is an extremely complex multidimensional biological, cognitive, emotional, behavioral and relational *dynamic* that may or may not reach into a woman's core identity.

However, this does not mean that a woman can't experience profound change in many factors of her sexuality. For example, because female sexuality is more emotionally than physically based, sexual arousal and attraction patterns can and do change as a woman's emotional connections change. Core beliefs that often drive a woman's same-sex intimacies—such as the belief that only women are able to emotionally connect—can be challenged and often change. The content and frequency of a woman's sexual fantasies can change. Behavioral aspects of a woman's sexuality, especially if there is a compulsive component, commonly change. Change can occur as a woman heals from sexually abusive experiences. A woman can also change or develop her identity to include a broader definition of her personhood than one solely focused on sexuality. Everybody, including women who struggle with SSA, should have the freedom to challenge and change beliefs, break old vows, alter relational styles and heal from past abuses. We are always in the process of becoming. Change itself is not only a part of our inalienable right as human beings, but also a part of the inherent dynamic of natural human growth and development.

The degree to which a woman with SSA *can* or *will* experience change will be uniquely determined based on several factors:

- the nature of biological influences on her psychosexual differentiation
- her abuse and trauma history
- the degree of exclusivity of her same-sex feelings (i.e., whether she also experiences bisexual feelings)
- the nature and frequency of her same-sex behaviors and patterns of emotional dependency
- the level of identification with homosexuality
- her current circumstances
- her motivation to change

After committing to psychotherapy many women *do* experience a shift in their SSA and relational patterns. However, I have come to learn that change is not necessarily or ultimately defined as a complete cessation of all same-sex feelings or temptations. Change, for most of my clients, ultimately means growing and developing as women—feeling free to take charge of their destiny, so to speak, and choosing to live the life God is directing them to live.[6]

Shari, one of the women I interviewed, said that coming out of lesbianism wasn't about becoming straight: "My general goal was that I would no longer have romantic relationships with women. *But more than that, it was about experiencing peace: peace with God and peace with myself—in my mind and in my heart.* The struggle was difficult, but finally having a restful, peaceful mind was worth every minute of it."

THE CONTROVERSY ABOUT CHANGE

Because of the ongoing public debates about the causes and changeability of homosexuality and the political pressures within certain professional associations and academic environments, many counseling professionals and students fear that they could lose their licensing credentials if they offer what has been coined "reparative therapy" to a man or woman desirous of understanding or altering homosexual feelings or behaviors.[7] These professionals assume that their only option for helping a homosexual client is to offer "gay affirmative therapy."[8] My heart aches over how few therapists have been formally trained or encouraged to support the many women in conflict with their same-sex feelings because of religious beliefs or general disillusionment with same-sex relating.

In response, I will briefly present the primary points of controversy within the psychological community surrounding the scientific, theoretical and clinical bases underlying any therapeutic intervention that is not primarily gay affirmative.

It is often claimed that sexual orientation is inborn (solely genetic or biological)

---

[6]"Indeed, the goal of therapy is not simply to eradicate a problem, but also to help the patient learn how to cope with the existing problem now and in the future, should it reemerge. When a condition of any sort is deeply ingrained (as homosexuality often is), then managing it as it arises is a viable therapeutic goal." (Dallas, 1996, p. 371.)

[7]*Reparative, conversion* or *corrective* therapy are catchall terms for any therapy offered by a therapist who works *in alliance* with a client's desire to explore, change or alter, rather than accept, affirm and identify with, their same-sex feelings and behaviors. Reparative therapy is not defined by a single theoretical orientation, therapeutic sequence or body of techniques.

[8]Gay affirmative therapy (GAT) has emerged to help clients become self-actualized as homosexual persons (Falco, 1991). The gay affirmative therapist "celebrates and advocates the validity of lesbian, gay, and bisexual persons and their relationships" (Tozer & McClanahan, 1999, p. 736). "GAT presumes that dissatisfied homosexuals would be satisfied if they could only be free of the internalized prejudices [homophobia] of society" (Nicolosi, 1993, p. 214). Like reparative therapy, gay affirmative therapy is not, as far as I am aware, defined by a single theoretical orientation, therapeutic sequence or body of techniques.

and therefore is an immutable aspect of a person's core identity. Presently, there is no conclusive evidence that female homosexuality is inborn or solely genetic or biologically based.[9] When asked whether homosexuality is rooted solely in biology, Dean Hamer, Ph.D.—a geneticist and pioneer in the study of the so-called gay gene—replied, "Absolutely not. . . . From twin studies, we already know that half or more of the variability in sexual orientation is *not* [italics added] inherited. Our studies try to pinpoint the genetic factors, not to negate the psychosocial factors" (Toufexis, 1995). J. Michael Bailey, Ph.D., a psychologist and well-known pioneer in the causal research of homosexuality, concludes together with his colleagues that while genetic factors are implicated, familial and environmental factors also contribute to sexual orientation (Bailey, Dunne & Martin, 2000, p. 534). Kenneth Zucker, Ph.D., a psychologist and leading specialist in gender issues, also supports a multifactorial model of sexual orientation differentiation and contends that "future empirical inquiry must continue to invest its efforts" on the transactional nature of *both* psychobiological and psychosocial influences (2001, p. 115). Most seasoned researchers and clinicians in this field now agree that homosexuality arises out of a combination of biological, developmental and environmental influences, although this is rarely acknowledged within popular media.[10]

Further, many contemporary studies support the notions that female sexuality in general is fluid or flexible rather than rigid or fixed and that it is structured differently from male sexuality.[11] While the concept of sexual *fluidity*—the *spontaneous* evolution or transformation of one's sexual attractions, behaviors or identity—is not identical to the concept of *changeability,* which involves *intentional* effort directed toward altering or changing one's sexual attractions or behaviors, it does support the notion that *sexual feelings and behaviors are not absolutely immutable or unchangeable.* It does *not,* however directly translate into proof that *any* woman with SSA can easily change or alter her same-sex attractions or orientation.

---

[9]See Bailey, Dunne & Martin (2000); Banks & Gartrell (1995); Bearman & Bruckner (2002); Byne & Parsons (1993); Jones & Kwee (2005); Jones & Yarhouse (2000); Satinover (1996a, 1996b); Whitehead & Whitehead (1999). For more information on scientific evidence on the etiology of homosexuality, refer to www.ivpress.com.

[10]See also Bem (1996); Byne & Parsons (1993); Friedman & Downey (1993a, 1993b); Pattatucci (1998); Whitehead & Whitehead (1999); Zucker (2001).

[11]Diamond (1998, 2000); Dixon (1985); Henderson (1984); Kinnish, Strassberg & Turner (2005); Lippa & Arad (1997); Nichols (1988b); Schecter (2004); Sophie (1986). For more information on the fluidity of female sexuality, please refer to www.ivpress.com.

It is often claimed that there is no compelling evidence that reparative therapy works or that individuals can change their sexual orientation. Over the past decade, several studies have shown that some women have changed the intensity of same-sex feelings, behaviors and core features of their sexual orientation through participation in religious organizations or therapy.[12] In a recent longitudinal study assessing the possibility of change, Jones and Yarhouse (2007) report, "the most surprising single finding was that the subpopulation from this study that was most likely on average to manifest significant change" was the subpopulation which had been most profoundly and predominately homosexual. Admittedly, the scientific evidence of the efficacy of "reparative therapy" does require bolstering with ongoing research, but so does the evidence supporting the practice of gay affirmative therapy. Presently there is no comprehensive body of research that specifically proves or disproves the efficacy (or harm) of gay affirmative therapies.[13] Neither is there evidence that proves that change is impossible.

Some believe that attempts to change one's homosexuality through the use of reparative therapy are damaging to one's personhood and self-respect. Sadly, some people do experience negative effects of psychotherapy. Specifically, there are studies that show that *some* men and women may have suffered negative effects of reparative therapy.[14] But even these studies, together with several others, show that for *other* men and women, reparative therapy promoted psychological well-being, even when there was not a significant change in the person's same-sex orientation.[15] In the most recent study evaluating if a person's attempt to change their sexual orientation is harmful, Jones and Yarhouse (2007) found that the participants studied experienced a statistically significant decrease in psychological symptoms and distress rather than evidence of harm.

---

[12]MacIntosh (1994); Nicolosi, Byrd & Potts (2000a, 2000b); Schaeffer, Hyde, Kroencke, McCormick, Nottebaum (2000); Schaeffer, Nottebaum, Smith, Dech & Krawczyk (1999); Spitzer (2003); Throckmorton (2002). There is also a historic record of published reports and anecdotal studies by practitioners who observed positive treatment outcomes for women in conflict with homosexual feelings. For more information on the history of treating women with SSA, please refer to the book website at www.ivpress.com.

[13]Bieschke, McClanahan, Tozer, Grzegorek & Park (2000); Cochran (2001); Miville & Ferguson (2004); Nicolosi, Byrd & Potts (2000a); Spitzer (2003).

[14]Beckstead & Morrow (2004); Shidlo & Schroeder (2002); see also chapter 2.

[15]MacIntosh (1994); Nicolosi, Byrd & Potts (2000a, 2000b); Schaeffer, Hyde, Kroencke, McCormick & Nottebaum (2000); Schaeffer, Nottebaum, Smith, Dech & Krawczyk (1999); Spitzer (2003).

It is often alleged that in 1973 the American Psychiatric Association (APA) removed homosexuality as a diagnostic category from its Diagnostic and Statistical Manual of Mental Disorders (DSM) *because of scientific proof that it is not a mental disorder but a healthy variation of human sexuality; therefore, it should not be considered a "treatable" condition.* In 1973, a small group of psychiatrists (members of the Board of Trustees of the APA) did indeed make a decision to remove homosexuality from the DSM.[16] The decision was based on the determination of the Nomenclature Committee that homosexuality was not a mental disorder and should not, therefore, be categorized as one. Generally, a decision of this magnitude would be made based on an overwhelming preponderance of scientific evidence. However, throughout the committee's deliberations, no conclusive scientific evidence was presented or analyzed to prove that homosexuality was inborn or unchangeable, to refute previous findings or experiences of clinicians specializing in the treatment of homosexuality, or to prove that the mental health or overall psychological well-being of homosexuals was the same as nonhomosexuals.[17]

Besides being influenced by extremely well-organized and persuasive gay activist groups, the committee reviewed only a few purportedly scientifically based studies.[18] Further, the psychiatrists involved in the review process neither had an extensive background in the theoretical or clinical dimensions of homosexuality nor were experts on the associated body of research and literature (Bayer, 1987). They failed to recognize (or refused to admit) the limitations and bias of the research presented. Ronald Bayer, a social scientist who investigated this monumental event, suggests that the final decision "was *not a conclusion based on an approximation of the scientific truth as dictated by reason,*

---

[16]Of the 15 board members, 13 voted and 2 abstained.

[17]One study that did exist comparing the psychological adjustment of homosexual and heterosexual women—Saghir, Robins, Walbran & Gentry (1970)—was overlooked, as were many others: see Freedman (1968); Ohlson & Wilson (1974); Thompson, McCandless & Strickland (1971). These studies were not necessarily conclusive but were still part of the developing scientific record at that time. Saghir, Robins, Walbran, and Gentry (1970) found that homosexual women sought out psychotherapy much more often than heterosexual women, had greater levels of depression and alcohol dependence and drug use, and reported a higher number of suicide attempts—findings similar to the current body of research.

[18]The studies examined included the two Kinsey reports (Kinsey, Pomeroy & Martin, 1948; Kinsey, Pomeroy, Martin & Gebhard, 1953), a study on the existence of homosexuality in non-Western cultures (Ford & Beach, 1951), and Evelyn Hooker's (1957) study comparing the results of the Rorschach test (*subjective* in nature) administered to a *nonrandom* sample of 30 homosexuals and 30 nonhomosexuals (Lortie, 2000).

but was instead an action demanded by the ideological temper of the times" (1987, pp. 3-4).[19]

Numerous studies suggest that homosexuality *is* associated with increased risk of mental health problems.[20] Further, the *DSM-IV-TR* still presumes that some clients will experience "persistent and marked distress about sexual orientation" (sec. 302.9, "Sexual Disorder Not Otherwise Specified," p. 582) and will seek services related to this distress. Yarhouse and Throckmorton (2002) emphasize that these negative emotions *are* legitimate mental health concerns and can be responded to by supporting "a client's wish to reorient or confirm one orientation over another" (p. 67).

Some believe that men and women are conflicted over their homosexuality because they have inadvertently internalized society's oppressive homophobic attitudes or heterosexist beliefs; therefore the only ethical form of treatment is gay affirmative therapy. This statement comes dangerously close to neglecting the possibility that a homosexual man or woman may indeed have underlying psychological and emotional issues that would benefit from psychotherapy apart from simply affirming one's sexual orientation. Even Douglas Haldeman, Ph.D., a leading critic of reparative therapy, admits that a genuine conflict between a man or woman's religious identity and their sexual orientation can indeed exist apart from cultural anti-gay sentiment. He therefore supports their right to seek the treatment of their choice. He remarks that it may in fact be "less emotionally disruptive, for an individual to contemplate changing sexual orientation than to disengage from a religious way of life that is seen as completely central to the individual's sense of self and purpose" (2002, p. 262).

In conclusion, neither the American Psychiatric Association (APA) nor the American Psychological Association have officially banned the practice of reparative therapy (Nicolosi, Byrd & Potts, 2000b).[21] They have, however, issued position statements (APA, 1998, 2000) and resolutions (American Psycholog-

---

[19]For more information on this decision and on psychopathology and homosexuality, see the book website on www.ivpress.com.

[20]Biernbaum & Ruscio (2004); Bradford, Ryan & Rothblum (1994); Cochran (2001); Fergusson, Horwood & Beautrais (1999); Fergusson, Horwood, Ridder & Beautrais (2005); Herrell, Goldberg, True, Ramakrishnan, Lyons, Eisen et al. (1999); Sandfort, de Graaf, Bijl & Schnabel (2001); Warner, McKeown, Griffin, Johnson, Ramsay, Cort et al. (2004).

[21]In 2006, the president of the APA, Gerald P. Koocher, stated that the "APA has no conflict with psychologists who help those distressed by unwanted homosexual attraction" and that the client's choice to enter therapy to diminish homosexual attractions must be respected *(NARTH Bulletin, 14*[2], 1-2, 39-40 [2006, Fall]).

ical Association, 1997) stating that the efficacy and ethicality of reparative therapy is still under debate.[22] All three documents emphasize and reiterate common therapeutic principles, offer guidelines and make ethical recommendations to therapists working "with clients who come to treatment with questions about their own sexual orientation or that of a family member" (Schneider, Brown & Glassgold, 2002, p. 265).

Within these position statements,[23] mental health practitioners are exhorted to

- follow all ethical codes for their particular profession
- be informed and sensitive to a client's distress and experiences related to social prejudice or oppression of homosexuality
- respect the client's right to have values, attitudes and opinions different from their own
- not base their services on the a priori assumption that the client *should* change his or her homosexual orientation
- not determine the goal of treatment coercively or through subtle influence
- not make deceptive statements regarding the scientific basis for their services
- make appropriate disclosure and obtain documented informed consent
- not operate outside of their realm of expertise

Every therapist embarking into this challenging work should regularly consider the ethical mandate of do no harm while negotiating a client's evolving therapeutic goals or treatment plan.

When therapy is provided to a women in conflict with same-sex feelings, it should not be done casually.[24] This is a specialized field that requires education, professional training, consultation and supervised experience. Every psychotherapist entering this field must make a commitment to professional competency and to an ongoing openness to study new clinical and scientific findings. *Full disclosure* of the above existing disputes about causes, changeability and efficacy of various therapies for SSA should be made. Each woman

---

[22]See Rosik, 2003; Yarhouse, 1998; Yarhouse & Throckmorton, 2002.

[23]See also American Counseling Association's "Ethical issues related to conversion or reparative therapy." Reviewed in *Counseling Today*, *49*(1), 14-15.

[24]For recent research on psychologists' attitudes on what constitutes ethical practice when working with sexual identity issues, see Liszcz & Yarhouse (2005). See also Nicolosi & Nicolosi (2002), chap. 8.

must also offer her full informed consent before treatment proceeds.[25] All treatment provided should follow the above ethical guidelines and include ongoing assessment of the client's wishes for and ability to proceed with any particular direction of therapy (Throckmorton, 2002).

GRANTING HER THE RIGHT TO CHOOSE

It is indeed the personal right of any woman *in conflict* with her same-sex feelings, behaviors, orientation or identity to seek therapy from mental health professionals in an attempt to grow, heal or change any aspect of her life. This right to choose parallels the personal right of a woman to accept and embrace her same-sex feelings and identity and to seek supportive and affirming therapy.[26] Robert Spitzer, one of the primary psychiatrists involved in removing homosexuality from the DSM, still believes that a woman's right to choose reparative therapy "should be considered fundamental to client autonomy and self-determination" (2003, p. 414) and should therefore not be denied to a woman who expresses a rational, self-directed goal of change.

Even Haldeman (2002) notes that "psychology does not have the right to interfere with individuals' rights to seek the treatments they choose. . . . Psychology's role is to inform the profession and the public, not to legislate against individuals' rights to self-determination" (pp. 262-63). He notes that "the rights of individuals to their diverse experiences of religion and spirituality deserve the same respect accorded sexual orientation" (p. 262).[27]

GRANTING HER UNCONDITIONAL FREEDOM TO GROW AND HEAL

I believe that a woman also deserves the right to grow and heal even if she is unsure about changing her same-sex feelings or identity. Before God, she has

---

[25]On obtaining informed consent, see Yarhouse (1998, 2001). For specific practice guidelines, see Throckmorton & Yarhouse (n.d.).

[26]Dr. Mark Yarhouse—author, clinician and associate professor at Regent University—emphasizes that ethically, psychologists must acknowledge that people are "self-determining agents with respect to their ability to pursue therapy and choose between various treatment modalities. Clients who report distress concerning their experience of same-sex attraction [*sic*] have the right to choose among various treatment options. This right to choose is grounded not only in the autonomy and self-respect of persons, but also in the multicultural dimension of the work of psychologists" (1998, p. 251).

[27]In the American Psychological Association's *Religion and the Clinical Practice of Psychology*, authors Bergin, Payne and Richards (1996) assert that "religion is now a legitimate part of human diversity and must be afforded the same consideration in therapy as all other forms of diversity" (p. 307).

complete freedom to choose the life *she* wants, including embracing a homosexual identity and homosexual relationship. God gives us all this amazing freedom. What's more, God does not abandon or condemn us when we are unsure, when we change our minds or even when we make harmful decisions. I have found that my unconditional love, acceptance and genuine desire to *understand* a woman's choices with respect to her life is what provides the safety in which *she* can continue to explore, accept or challenge her choices. I want to reflect God's undying faithfulness and enduring presence to these women. I therefore remain committed to a woman regardless of her current decisions as long as she remains committed to a therapeutic process and as long as I remain professionally competent to address her therapeutic needs.

Similarly, in her book *Female Homosexuality: Choice Without Volition*, Elaine Siegel—a former supervising and training analyst at the New York Center for Psychoanalytical Training—discusses her own realization that if she had dogmatically clung to the notion that homosexuality is simply a normal identity and resisted her clients' attempts at understanding and even changing the pattern of their lesbian attractions, she and her clients would have been cemented into a "rigid mode that precluded change of *whatever* [italics added] nature. Thus, I kept on analyzing, always trying to open myself to the often heavy developmental needs of the women" (1988, p. xii). Siegel reports that more than half of the lesbian women with whom she worked became fully heterosexual. As she concludes, "*The patient* [italics added], not the analyst, decides what is 'good' for him or her and what he or she wishes to change, what to retain" (p. xiii).

OFFERING A SAFE PLACE

The initial goal in therapy with any woman with SSA should be to offer "a safe space free from judgment and bias" (Beckstead and Morrow, 2004, p. 687), regardless of the philosophical starting point from which a professional embarks. Nicolosi, Byrd & Potts (2000a) suggest that rather than imposing conversion or gay affirmative therapy on clients, psychologists "should do their best to provide a professionally noncoercive environment that gives clients maximum freedom to express, explore, and clarify their values and beliefs about homosexuality" (p. 1085).

It will probably require a tremendous amount of courage for a woman to make the initial phone call to, let alone actually show up in, a counselor's office. She comes scared, tentative and unsure of her goals for therapy yet possibly unable to continue life on her own without support and outside help. Most women with SSA enter therapy believing they are bad people—dangerous, malformed and even repulsive to God. Shame often shades every aspect of their being. It seems to me that the last thing they need is for their new therapist to focus on perhaps the most shameful issue in their life in an effort to affirm *or* disaffirm. I have observed that as I offer my respect by first getting to know my client and understanding *all* aspects of her life, bolstering her sense of dignity and value, she is then able to expose and explore these deep and perhaps shameful aspects of her life. With every new client, I make it my aim to

- *Communicate that she has value.* I do not offer therapy simply because she is in conflict with her sexual attractions or orientation. I offer her therapy because *she* matters and her life is important.

- *Commit to her as a person, not to a particular therapeutic outcome.* I reassure her, through my words and attitudes, that I will not place any demands or expectations on her with respect to her same-sex struggle that would in any way violate her dignity or condition or impede our ongoing work together. I have discovered that a woman with SSA will often not feel safe enough to trust me unless I am genuinely committed to engage and work with her even if she ultimately decides to embrace lesbian behaviors or identity.

- *Know her as an individual.* I do not want to miss knowing her by attempting to rigidly apply my theoretical models. Rather, I want to genuinely respect her *unique* story, experiences, choices, relationships and goals for therapy.

- *Support growth and development in all aspects of her life, promoting her overall welfare and well-being.* My ultimate goal as a therapist with a woman in conflict with SSA is to provide an environment in which she can apprehend her true identity as a feminine being and develop a stability as she walks through the ebbs and flows of intimacy within her same *and* opposite-sex relationships. I want to help her reach a place of security in her own sense of self and within a broader healing community so she no longer lives out of a desperate grasping for security outside of her self and God. I want to invite her into a radical self-love and self-acceptance that frees her to live an other-centered life rather than a life consumed by desperation. If she operates from a spiritual perspective, I delight in leading her to the Truest

Lover of her soul and supporting her as she recognizes her life's ultimate purpose and meaning. I long to bless her with existence, attachment, love, friendship, fellowship and an enduring and experiential knowledge that she is the beloved, just as she is.

CHAPTER TWO

The Therapist and Professional Competency

Knowing trees, I understand the meaning of patience.
Knowing grass, I can appreciate persistence.

HAL BORLAND

Each time I open my office door to a new client, I expect the unexpected. I prepare myself ahead of time to meet a special woman. I also prepare myself to begin therapy the moment I say hello. There is usually no casual easing-in period with most of my new clients. They are smart and very observant. They are also guarded and on edge, wondering if I will judge or treat them insensitively.

The moment I greet a new client, she may start to scrutinize me: my facial expressions, my body language, my tone of voice and the way I'm dressed. She wants to know who I am as much as I want to know her. And over the years I've come to learn that within this initial encounter, she does not evaluate the content of what I say as much as *how* I say it.[1] My initial words of introduction are extremely important. I want her to immediately begin to experience openness and warmth, not cold, professional detachment.

Within the opening moments and throughout every successive stage, therapy with women with SSA is different. Kristine Falco, Psy.D., a gay affirmative therapist with decades of clinical experience with lesbian women, attributes this therapeutic distinctiveness to the pressures and stresses unique to lesbian women that have affected their "entire life functioning in some way" (1991, p. 26). For instance, many women

---

[1]"One researcher summed it up: 'Because lesbians . . . negotiate their daily lives in environments that range from hostile to friendly, they are *acutely aware of subtleties in language and manner that suggest danger or safety* [italics added]' (Deevey, 1990, p. 37)" (Stevens, 1992, p. 111).

- carry a deep ongoing sense of shame and loneliness
- live in fear of themselves, not fully understanding *why* they struggle with same-sex feelings
- sense more acceptance and love from their openly gay or nonreligious friends than from their religious family or friends, yet are criticized by their openly gay friends for seeking "change" or are pressured to accept and celebrate their homosexuality
- lack freedom to talk about their ongoing struggle with their faith-based community or feel the expectation to "change" over night
- live a double life when they are in an intimate relationship with another woman,[2] because the risk of losing their church, marriage, family, friends or children, is simply too great, and ending the relationship is simply too hard (if not impossible)
- endure heart-wrenching endings to their same-sex relationships

I regularly remind myself that these additional, unusual burdens may compromise a woman's ability, for example, to cope with painful psychological insight or new therapeutic homework assignments at any given point in time. Many of the above dilemmas may also remain as ongoing stressors within my clients' lives. I therefore must balance a woman's need to sort through and grieve past experiences, for example, with her ongoing difficult present circumstances.

Women with SSA have certain traits and styles of relating that also create distinctiveness in the therapeutic setting. They are deep thinkers, dynamic and delightful. They have an endless capacity to give and help others and are extremely creative and passionate. They are also refreshingly honest and direct. If I accomplish nothing else within this book, I hope to communicate my respect and honor for each one of them and to pay tribute by introducing them as the exceptional women they truly are. I have spoken to many counselors who have secretly admitted to me that their favorite client is a woman with SSA.

However these women can also be very challenging. They often display more defiance, defensiveness and open aggression than other clients. They

---

[2]Concealing "a major part of her life from the rest of the world" may result in an extremely negative self-image (Gartrell, 1981, p. 504), leaving a woman questioning whether anyone truly knows or loves her. Long-term duplicity, whether intentional or not, can also eventually lead to the development of habitual lying, deception and manipulation, encasing a woman in falsehood instead of providing open and authentic intimacy.

want to cut to the chase. They will not tolerate what they call "psychobabble" and will immediately recognize inauthenticity on the therapist's part. They have no problem with confronting or challenging their therapist's counsel or underlying attitude. They may be hypersensitive and seemingly resistant to common therapeutic interventions. Work with these women requires more energy, ingenuity and level of commitment than with other clients.

There is also a spiritual intensity that is unmatched with other clients. The battle being waged over the lives of these women far exceeds the normal trials and tribulations of sexual temptation or low self-esteem, for example. It is a battle for their very souls and personhoods. There is a force that seeks to extinguish their spirits and vitality. As their counselor, I must regularly stand in the gap and fight on their behalf. I fight for their voice, their right to live *(be)*, and their inner and outer strengths and beauty. Yet these women exhibit incredible tenacity and commitment to grow and heal in light of this battle. While therapy with women with SSA is often the most rewarding work that a counselor will ever do, it is rarely done casually or comfortably.

THERE IS A DIFFERENCE: CONTRAINDICATED APPROACHES

As I began to experience these distinctions in my work with women with SSA, I had to rethink some commonly accepted therapeutic frameworks, techniques and counseling styles. I have learned, mostly through my mistakes, that the following maxims are usually not effective with my clients. Instead of creating safety and inviting a therapeutic alliance, they often interfere with these processes and, worse, threaten my clients.

A therapist should remain objective and professionally detached. Most women with SSA do not feel safe within a cold professional environment.[3] I therefore strive to remain warm, authentic and engaged. When I unintentionally appear detached due to countertransference, lack of direction or personal distraction, my clients often feel abandoned and are triggered into a deep sense of aloneness. If this occurs at the beginning of therapy, they may not be able to identify or articulate their inner turmoil; they simply terminate counseling.

---

[3]A study identifying effective health care approaches with lesbian patients notes that the paternalistic style of emotional coolness and detached directiveness left the "women feeling emotionally traumatized, and sometimes resonated with the painful estrangement and disapproval that had occurred in their families of origin. . . . The usual outcome of this approach was that the *client discontinued treatment* [italics added]" (Hall, 1994, p. 241).

We can teach our clients about healthy relationship, but should never become emotionally involved. Sometimes I catch myself instructing and coaching a client about relationships, only to watch her eyes glaze over as she dreams of being someplace else. My clients ultimately need an actual *experience* of healthy relationship. I cannot establish a corrective experience of safety, trust and attachment for my clients unless I am emotionally available as a real person[4] and offer them genuine interest and concern. It is through the experience of being loved and nurtured that my clients can solidify as women who in turn can love.

Therapists should only work with patients who are engaged and making progress. As a new therapist, I would frequently hear that a counselor had boldly announced to a disengaged, ambivalent client, "I am here to help. If you want to receive my help, great. If not, you are free to quit or go find someone else."

This matter-of-fact statement angers many women with SSA. It essentially communicates ambivalence on the therapist's part with respect to their own commitment to the client. In spite of a possible legitimate need to be challenged to engage in the therapeutic process, these women need even more to be constantly reassured that their therapist is committed to work with them no matter what. They cannot afford to open their heart and build trust if their counselor might determine at some point that their work together is too exasperating.

> *I have been with therapists who seem to think that female SSA is just like any other discipline issue. "You just have to work and get through it." I sensed a bit of impatience or frustration on their part because I wasn't just "getting through it." That subtle pressure coming from them did not motivate me to work on anything. In some sense, it kept me stuck.*
>
> *Andrea*

Avoidance, defensiveness and lack of cooperation with the goals of therapy, as well as the refusal to articulate needs and goals, are signs of resistance and should be confronted directly. This maxim is not true for most of my clients. In general, women with SSA have been my most faithful and dedicated clients, yet they

---

[4]This does not mean the relationship is mutual in all respects. My emotional energy and investment must always be directed toward the client for the sake of the client, not toward finding or getting my own emotional needs met.

are often the most ostensibly resistant within our sessions.[5] Until a woman can build trust and learn healthier ways to cope with her anxieties and fears, she will *necessarily* continue in her defensive patterns. Until a woman establishes a greater sense of her core self and inner realities, she may be unable to articulate feelings, needs and desires. If a woman continues to show up for therapy, I give her the full benefit of the doubt and assume she is committed to therapy and will engage in the best way she can.

Counselors should never work harder than their clients. Adult women who did not perceive or experience a steady flow of love and support as children may still need a parent figure that can both recognize their feelings *and* lovingly respond. As little girls who did not sense a safe and supportive environment, they may not have learned how to ask for help. Many of my clients still need me to support and guide them even in their attempts to cooperate with the helping process. At times, it feels that I am working harder than they.

Clients should not become dependent on their therapist. In graduate school I was informed that a therapist should never foster dependency within clients. However, within a therapeutic setting, it is not uncommon for a client to experience a regression or transference of primal unmet dependency needs.[6] When this happens, as it often does for women with SSA, the client may *feel* dependent on their therapist. These situations can provide significant therapeutic opportunities for a woman with SSA. First, some of her unmet dependency needs may be met as she simply continues in a boundaried and caring relationship with her therapist. Second, she will have a chance to consciously explore and understand her dependent feelings and behaviors, rather than be unconsciously controlled by them. Third, she will have a chance to move beyond the *dependent* state she might regularly find herself in, especially within her same-sex relationships. Chapter eleven will detail how to work with dependency needs and transferences.

If a woman wants to understand or alter her response to same-sex feelings, she will have to be very motivated to change. I have become very cautious in asserting this proposition. Most women who come to see me believe homosexuality is outside

---

[5]This resistance may be indicative of a dismissive attachment style. Dismissive attachment patterns have been found in 45% out of 317 highly educated, nonclinical, self-identified lesbians (Wells & Hansen, 2003) and 28% of 100 self-identified lesbians in ongoing psychotherapy (Wells, 2003). See also Bartholomew & Horowitz (1991).

[6]Transference of this nature can also occur in a safe nontherapeutic setting. Clergy and lay counselors must be alert to this phenomenon.

of God's plan or are exhausted with the heart wrenching nature of their same-sex relationships. But they still feel torn. They may believe erotic same-sex relationships are wrong or unsatisfying but do not know *how* to have any other type of meaningful relationship. They might fear that "change" will require them to abandon all same-sex relating or their existing community of friends. They may also fear the unknown of such radical change. In the initial stages of therapy, many women are therefore initially ambivalent about "change." They will first need the safety and security of a relationship with their therapist or pastoral counselor before they can even begin to explore such a life-changing commitment. Even then, ambivalence may remain. It is important that they be respected and granted the ongoing freedom to make decisions regarding their own life and the direction of their therapy. Besides being ethically important, full autonomy within a supportive relationship aids in establishing and solidifying a sense of self. This is a primary need for many women with SSA.

Male and female homosexuality are essentially the same. While some broad principles in understanding and working with men struggling with SSA may apply to women, I do not believe that the specific therapeutic processes are necessarily the same. To the extent that female sexuality, in general, diverges from male sexuality, female homosexuality will necessarily embody distinctive nuances and internal structures. Clinicians who seek to work with both genders will need to be thoroughly educated on male and female SSA separately.

HARMFUL THERAPEUTIC EXPERIENCES

Not every individual who receives psychotherapy finds the help he or she was hoping for, nor does everyone conclude therapy with a positive attitude or experience. Some men and women in conflict with SSA have reported negative or unhelpful experiences within therapeutic settings that supported their desire to change.[7] Collectively, they have described such things as an increase in shame and self-loathing, self-contempt, confusion, depression and even suicidal ideation.

The seriousness of these reported negative experiences and the extent of the damage may be arguable, but the allegations are worth reviewing. Therapists entering into this field should always initially assess whether intervention can

---

[7]See Beckstead & Morrow (2004); Garnets, Hancock, Cochran, Goodchilds & Peplau (1991); Shidlo & Schroeder (2002). It should also be noted that many men and women sampled in these studies reported *positive* results and outcomes.

be done without harm, which will obviously require a fundamental knowledge of the women themselves.

Assumptions, judgments and lack of understanding—as outlined below—can indeed be detrimental to the therapeutic process.

The therapist has negative attitudes toward homosexuals or homosexuality. It is not essential (and probably not possible) that mental health or pastoral professionals completely purge themselves of any and all personal bias or prejudice before they can counsel effectively. But it is vital that professionals seeking to work in this field both evaluate the impact that an identified bias toward men and women with SSA may have on the therapeutic process and be willing to seek professional accountability to explore and resolve the source of the bias. James Krajeski, M.D., a gay affirmative therapist, explains that

> many gay patients, because of previous experiences, are quite sensitive to any signs of rejection or bias and will readily note minor indications of discomfort on the part of the therapist. For example, one patient stated that he was sure that his psychiatrist was homophobic because when he discussed issues connected with homosexuality, the psychiatrist changed positions in his chair, his face reddened slightly, and there was some alteration in his voice. (1984, pp. 81-82)

To effectively work with women who have SSA, it is important to continually challenge any psychological bias that homosexuals are mentally ill or any moral bias that homosexuality is a greater wrong than any other human condition, temptation or sin.[8] Over the years homosexual men and women have been referred to as being sick, neurotic, perverted, psychotic, pathological, deviant and inverted, among other things. These terms are categorically offensive. In addition, faith-based women with SSA often hear that they are beyond redemption, contemptible, hated by God and condemnable. A woman can be irreparably damaged by the toxicity of the sentiment of these terms and beliefs. The time needed for a woman to heal, trust and assimilate affirming words about her personhood will depend on the extent to which a woman has been exposed to derogatory words and attitudes and on the authenticity of her therapist's care and unconditional acceptance.

---

[8]In reviewing the progression of human depravity in Romans 1, it appears that the *lowest* step in our downward fall as a human race is *not* homosexual relations but such things as greed, envy, strife, gossip, slander, faithlessness and heartlessness (Rom 1:28-32).

The therapist believes that all of a woman's problems arise out of her SSA. Some women have been misled to believe that their personal or interpersonal problems and difficulties—such as depression, financial stress or conflict with their boss—will be resolved once their same-sex feelings or behaviors are "changed." Not only is this assertion untrue, but it also places an unbearable burden on a woman to "fix" an aspect of her life that is not even directly "fixable."

The therapist is insensitive or dogmatic in their speech about homosexuality. I have learned to be extremely cautious in how I reference the presence of SSA in my client's lives. A woman may initially be vague as she describes the thoughts and feelings that lead her to believe she may have SSA. I listen closely to the words and metaphors she uses to express herself, knowing that she may use the word *lesbian,* for lack of a better descriptive word or in a spirit of confession, while still not actually identifying with it. I prefer to follow her lead in how she speaks about or references her SSA. If I believe it will aid my client to name a struggle in a particular way, I will disclose my reasoning and intent while still exploring options with her. I am always willing to adjust my terminology as a woman finds more fitting words.

I have also learned to be sensitive in my communications about the nature of homosexuality in general. For example, some clients describe deep discouragement after being told by their therapist that they had "chosen" their homosexual feelings. While a discussion regarding self-determination may be appropriate at some future point as a client explores her same-sex behaviors, a blunt statement suggesting that she simply chose homosexuality is neither helpful nor true. Nor is it true that all homosexual relationships are dysfunctional or are never meaningful. It is also overly simplistic to allege that homosexuality is singly caused by poor parenting or sexual abuse, just as it is overly simplistic to assert that homosexuality is solely biologically based or that all homosexual people can be fully self-actualized and satisfied as a homosexual.

After emphasizing the extremely complex nature of human sexuality and the lack of concrete or scientific proof as to the causes or roots of one's sexual orientation, Margo Rivera, a gay affirmative therapist, offers this exhortation to any therapist working with gay, lesbian or transgendered clients:

> It is our responsibility to educate ourselves so that we do not promote or reinforce simplifications, and so that we are able to be a helpful and challenging travelling companion if our clients choose to explore the territory beyond simple answers and soothing rationalizations. (1996, p. 206)

The therapist makes false promises or exaggerated claims about change. When a client with SSA begins therapy in crisis or overwhelming shame, another person's success story or supportive scientific evidence will be of little value to her.

> *To try to encourage me they said, "I know you can change because others have," and "Just think, some day you might even get married!" But these things didn't help. I'm not like everyone else and, besides, if you don't like men or are not attracted to them, the thought of marriage does not sweeten the deal.*[9]
>
> *Rebecca*

Eventually, discussions about the nature or possibility of change will emerge, and when they do, therapists must use wisdom and moderation.

For example, it is not true that *all* lesbian women can completely change their sexual orientation. Nor is it true that radical measures—such as aversive shock therapy, sexual experimentation with men, reading the Bible and praying harder or using lipstick—will alter a woman's SSA. Many behavioral and cognitive methods *are* effective for a variety of issues that my clients address in therapy, but these interventions reflect misinformation about female SSA, are misleading and, at worst, abusive.

It is true that many men and women with SSA have reported substantial shifts in their same-sex arousal patterns, behaviors, fantasies, desires and even overall sexual orientation and identity.[10] But if you listen to them closely, most admit that they still occasionally experience same-sex feelings or temptations. Many of the women with whom I have worked start therapy with a conscious or unconscious hope that eventually (and the sooner the better) they will no longer struggle with *any* residual SSA, fantasy or desire. One to two years into therapy, however, they often discover that their same-sex erotic desires are literally intertwined with their legitimate desires for emotional closeness and friendship with women. They realize that if they attempt to simply extinguish their same-sex desire, they will also inadvertently exterminate their natural,

---

[9]Marriage is a completely separate goal from altering SSA and emotional dependencies. It should never be treated as if it is one in the same.

[10]See Jones & Yarhouse (2007); MacIntosh (1994); Nicolosi, Byrd & Potts (2000a, 2000b); Schaeffer, Hyde, Kroencke, McCormick & Nottebaum (2000); Schaeffer, Nottebaum, Smith, Dech & Krawczyk (1999); Spitzer (2003).

healthy need for female relationship. Committing to nonsexual friendships with women means they must continually confront and challenge the tendency (habit) to eroticize longings for female warmth and closeness. This can become a very discouraging point in therapy.

It is not uncommon for some women to eventually decide to reintegrate and embrace their eroticized same-sex desires, believing that the level of change they originally wanted is simply not possible. They may acquiesce into believing that God made them this way, or they may conclude that the ongoing work and effort required to remain in a life-altering process is simply too destabilizing and no longer justifiable. It is important to stress that although these decisions may seem contrary to a woman's original goals, they are never easily made and may still be subject to future reconsideration. Other women, at this same stage of self-realization, renew their commitment to do whatever it takes to live a life free from the ultimate control of their same-sex struggle.

When I begin therapy with a new client, I have no idea how she might respond to crossroads such as these, so I cannot make any promises or claims in terms of the extent of "change" she may experience. I refrain from saying the trite words, "Yes, you can change if you work hard in therapy" if the *change* will be interpreted as meaning she will no longer be oriented toward the same-sex but will be fully oriented to the opposite-sex. In general, I do not sensationalize the possibility of change. If she asks, I sensitively present what has been experienced by some and explain the various options beyond merely accepting and acting out her same-sex feelings or lesbian identity.[11]

The therapist harbors a negative attitude toward the client's parents, partners and friends. Some men and women report that their relationships with their parents deteriorated during therapy since they were told that their parents were the cause of their SSA. Many children who experience inadequate parenting do not later struggle with SSA. I have had the privilege, over the years, to meet hundreds of parents of daughters struggling with SSA. The great majority of them loved their daughters wholeheartedly and did the best

---

[11]Some of these options might include (1) curtailing same-sex behavioral or relational patterns and reducing the identification with lesbianism, (2) pursuing sexual purity and celibacy in light of ongoing same-sex feelings and temptations, (3) decreasing same-sex desires and behavior while increasing heterosexual desires and relational capacities, (4) integrating religious beliefs and lesbian identity without an intention to pursue lesbian relationships and (5) continuing attempts at radically changing sexual orientation. Beckstead & Morrow (2004); Haldeman (2004); Yarhouse, Tan & Pawlowski (2005).

they could raising them. When it *is* important for my client and I to candidly address the difficulties and imperfections that did exist in her family, I do so with compassion and a spirit of grace toward her family.

Other men and women with SSA also report being forced to cut off same-sex relationships and long-term friendships with homosexual friends. This is unhelpful for a several reasons. First and foremost, unless the client is in danger or is becoming dangerous to others, mandating that he or she terminate any relationship violates the principle of self-determination and client autonomy. Second, it is extremely inadvisable to make such a recommendation during the initial stage of therapy or at least prior to assessing a woman's ability and interest in taking such a drastic step. More often than not, it will launch a woman into overwhelming anxiety, perhaps creating an internal crisis that may require hospitalization. Third, such a recommendation may also impede the therapeutic process, creating a sense of threat rather than trust within the client. And finally, a client must first be in agreement with any recommendation related to shifting or ending relationships.

The therapist forces premature disclosure. Disclosure is a very individual, sensitive topic. It should never be taken for granted or assumed, especially in the opening stages of therapy. More often than not, there will be a time in a woman's process for some disclosure, but it will rarely be to a large number of people. When a woman is stable enough and exhibits adequate ego strength, she might first be encouraged to attend a support or therapy group at which she can be assured that others will empathize with her struggle.

Any additional disclosure to friends or family members should be made intentionally and with as much preparation as possible. It is never wise to assume how certain people (including husbands and pastors) will react. It is also important that she first establish a sense of therapeutic trust so she can access adequate support and care if her disclosures result in negative reactions and rejections. While disclosure for some women may be extremely difficult and problematic, it is always worth exploring since the potential benefit of being known and still loved far outweighs the risk of rejection.

PREPARATION AND PROFESSIONAL COMPETENCY

To responsibly work with this special population, it is important that therapists and pastoral counselors first undergo personal reflection and education on the issue of homosexuality in general, and on the women themselves. In a one-of-a-kind study evaluating the benefit of a variety of counseling practices employed with clients who were requesting reorientation therapy, Dr. Warren Throckmorton and Dr. Gary Welton of Grove City College found that clients preferred counselors who "never made an issue of sexual orientation when it was not relevant" (2005, p. 340), helped them to explore and understand causes of their same-sex attraction, supported the development of opposite-sex relating, and encouraged nonsexual same-sex friendships.[12] They also discovered that clients were helped most by counselors who were *knowledgeable and respectful of gays and lesbians and people in conflict with SSA.*[13]

I recommend that therapists prepare for such work through personal reflection on their

- *psychological and theological beliefs* about homosexuality or homosexual men and women
- *unconscious biases* toward or *negative stereotypes* of men and women with SSA or their families
- *feelings* about or *emotional reactions* to the subject of homosexuality or men and women with SSA
- *political and social viewpoints* on the plethora of issues related to homosexuality, such as same-sex marriage or adoptions
- *own gender, sexual orientation* or *personal struggle with sexual brokenness* and how this may affect a client's experience of therapy

It has been my experience that, over the course of therapy, many of my clients want to discuss my positions and sentiments on the above issues. I have therefore had to regularly revisit my own story, beliefs and feelings—always seeking for compassionate, non-offensive ways to articulate and dialogue about them. And when I am aware of a growing sentiment within myself that may appear counter to my client's current beliefs or feelings, I enter the dia-

---

[12]Schaeffer, Nottebaum, Smith, Dech and Krawczyk (1999) found that men and women seeking to reduce their SSA were also helped by *long-term therapy.*

[13]Reported benefits of reorientation therapy include enhanced self awareness, emotional growth and stability; an increased sense of trust, hope and belonging; renewed belief structures; increased assertiveness and self-confidence; improved coping skills; improved relationships with people of both the same and the opposite sex; a decrease in compulsive behaviors and thoughts; a decrease in same-sex attractions; and a stronger belief in God. See also Beckstead & Morrow (2004); Jones & Yarhouse (2007); Shidlo & Schroeder (2002); Nicolosi, Byrd & Potts (2000a, 2000b); Schaeffer, Hyde, Kroencke, McCormick & Nottebaum (2000); Schaeffer, Nottebaum, Smith, Dech & Krawczyk (1999); Spitzer (2003); Throckmorton (2002).

logue with an even greater sensitivity and sincere desire to learn and be open to my client's positions or beliefs.

I also recommend that therapists familiarize themselves with the pertinent resources on homosexuality, cultural trends related to gender and female sexuality, the postmodern attitudes and beliefs of our youth pertaining to sexuality, and the notable characteristics, common experiences and struggles within the lives of women with SSA.

Pursue education and firsthand knowledge of resources for women in conflict with SSA. Besides reviewing this book and the many other sources referenced herein, attending support groups for people in conflict with SSA (or at least familiarizing yourself with them), participating in lay and professional conferences, following new research and consulting with other skilled professionals are essential for gaining a foundational understanding of women with SSA. Over the years I have also learned—primarily through my clients' feedback and reactions—whether (and when) it is appropriate to *recommend* these resources to women with SSA. Just about every resource available, whether in the form of a book or a conference, has the potential to negatively trigger a woman, sometimes plummeting her into severe anxiety, depression, disillusionment or shame. I therefore do not make recommendations casually. I introduce the resource and openly discuss with my client any possible unexpected reactions. This way, each woman is able to make an informed decision to utilize a resource.

Gain understanding of cultural trends and stories. Many faith-based young women, including adolescent girls, are beginning to enter therapy, bringing with them a new mix of sexual fluidity and bisexuality. They are not necessarily interested in exploring change around their SSA but are seeking support for many other life-consuming difficulties. Most of my younger clients have stressed that they don't label themselves with a particular sexual identity; they want to keep their options open. Being happy or feeling good (or in some cases, surviving the onslaught of adolescent chaos) is what is most important.

In a *Glamour* article, Jennifer Baumgardner notes that her bisexuality began to emerge when she realized that "the people I had sex with (men) weren't the people I effortlessly connected to (women)" (2007, p. 175). After cycling through several opposite- and same-sex relationships, she decided she wasn't straight, but she wasn't a lesbian either. Recognizing the commonality of bisexuality and concluding that it offers the best of both worlds, she declares,

"Gender aside, I want the right *person*—and I'm willing to wait for him. Or her" (p. 175). These are the exact sentiments of many of my young clients.

An increase in media and technology has added to a disconnected and disillusioned sense of reality for this generation of young people. E-mail, text messaging and instant messaging have replaced in-person communication and even telephone usage. The mass media is blurring the lines between the genders, promoting alternative "genders" and, perhaps more than ever, sexually objectifying women. Lifestyles of the young, rich and famous, the slender yet large-breasted female body, the availability of "fluid" partners—these are fast becoming the new objects of fantasy. I suspect that in the next few years, young women will bring to counseling a whole new level of issues related to emotional disconnection, gender discontentment, delusional reality and impulse control.

Legal separations and stepparenting and custody issues will also become more complex as more lesbian women pursue civil unions and adoption. Therapists will need to be able to help women navigate these circumstances and complex relational issues.

Increase personal knowledge of women in conflict with SSA. This may be the most important step of a therapist's preparation. It is imperative that a therapist become familiar with the broader population of women with SSA, not simply with one or two past or present clients: it is important to not only understand their stories, but see life through their eyes and learn their language. Personal knowledge will go a long way in establishing therapeutic rapport.

There are many common characteristics, developmental themes and life experiences in the histories of women with SSA. There are also common relational dynamics within female same-sex relationships. Therefore, the remainder of part one is dedicated to further introducing this special population.

CHAPTER THREE

Missing a "Home"

Attachment and Self

*Students of history continue to ignore the simple facts
that all individuals are borne by mothers; that everybody was once a child;
that people and peoples begin in their nurseries;
and that society consists of individuals in the process of developing.*

ERIK ERIKSON, *IDENTITY AND THE LIFE CYCLE*

Pamela, an attractive, successful 35-year-old businesswoman, came to see me because of the dissonance between her religious beliefs and her sexuality. She came from a middle-class family with no divorce, abuse or alcoholism. Her family was loving and stable, and Pamela knew they cared about her. She was born two years into her parents' marriage. Although her parents were excited about a new baby, the pregnancy was difficult. Though she would have rather worked, her mother quit her semi-professional job to be a stay at home mom.

Pamela remembers her mother rocking her when she was a child, and she enjoyed romping with her father. She felt very close to both her parents. Pamela loved the outdoors and played with the neighborhood boys during most of her childhood. Before she started school, her brother was born. Pamela showed signs of separation anxiety when she started school and had a difficult time relating to the other kids. However, she loved sports and finally met other girls who were also athletic. In high school, Pamela became almost inseparable with her first best female friend. Pamela didn't date much, but she kept busy with school and extracurricular activities, excelling in both.

After college, Pamela moved away to launch what would become a successful business career. In her new location, it was hard for her to find new friends. Her job was stressful and she felt very isolated. She finally met a few women she enjoyed, one of whom was gay. Pamela felt safe with her; they had much in common. They often held each other as they watched television or listened to music. Pamela realized she felt more comfortable being held by her female friend than she ever had felt being held by a man. But she quickly found herself in shock and buried with guilt as the affection turned sexual. She had always believed that homosexuality was outside of God's plan, yet she couldn't give up this new relationship. It made her feel alive. She despaired at the thought of being alone again, but she also didn't want to disappoint God.

"BUT SHE CAME FROM A GOOD FAMILY!"

I have consulted and interviewed many parents of minor and adult daughters with SSA. Like Pamela's parents, most of these parents were, and still are, dedicated and extremely conscientious in caring for their daughters. They loved their daughters from the moment they were born, they provided nice homes and stable enough environments. I've also consulted and interviewed parents who acknowledge that their parenting was not adequate or that theirs was an extremely unstable family history. One mother, having come from a very abusive family, told me story after story of how she was either physically absent from or negligent of her daughter. Her daughter, now in her third lesbian relationship, grew up with deep deprivations, trauma and emotional abandonment. Yet many girls who grow up in horrific families with unspeakable abuses do *not* struggle with same-sex feelings. How do we explain such variations?

A GIRL *INTERACTS* WITH HER WORLD

All that is human, including sexuality, involves a mysterious weaving of our biological blueprint with our experiences, perceptions, cognitions, emotions, reactions and choices. Our genetically or biologically based qualities and traits cast a certain hue on our environments, uniquely shading all of our experiences: *Who we are directly affects how we perceive and process our worlds.* How we perceive and process our worlds in turn affects who we become. The *interactions* or transactions among biological components—including hormonal, neurological, genetic or inborn personality characteristics and traits (nature)—and our surrounding environment and experiences (nurture)[1]—start at the moment of conception and directly influence our ongoing process of physiological development (brain or neurological growth), psychological development (memories and sense of self) and sexual development.[2] All that is human, then, is extremely complex, categorically mysterious and potentially in flux.

To be sure, female homosexuality is a multidimensional infrastructure, intricately linked to a woman's biology, experiences, cognitions, emotionality, relational networks, concept of self and inherent design as a female made for relationship and meaning. In light of this complexity, it is understandable that, as researchers attest, female SSA cannot be explained by a single clinical picture with common underlying dynamics. At best, it is proposed that there are many "different sequences of biopsychosocial interactions, occurring during different life cycle phases" (Friedman & Downey, 2002, p. 145), and therefore "multiple developmental pathways" (Byne & Parsons, 1993, p. 237).[3]

COMMON THEMES: BIOLOGICAL COMPONENTS

Studies exploring the genetic causes of female homosexuality have primarily focused on concordance rates of homosexuality between twins and other siblings. Over the years, as samples have become increasingly larger and more representative, these rates have generally dropped, ranging historically from 40 to 50% to currently 20 to 25%. In one of the most recent studies involving

---

[1]The concept of nurture includes all environmental influences and experiences, such as attachment patterns, social and relational interactions *as well as* an individual's reactions, choices, decisions and adopted beliefs made in response to these experiences. There are a multitude of environmental and social influences within a child's life—including parents, siblings, relatives, childhood friends, parents' friends, neighbors, teachers, pastors, youth leaders, camp counselors, adolescent friends, enemies, television, radio, music, Internet, politics, social milieus and much more. Parents, although important, are by far not the only influence in a child's developing life.

[2]On psychological development, see Schore (1994, 2002); Siegel (1999a).

[3]Byne and Parsons (1993) propose "an interactional model in which genes or hormones do not specify sexual orientation per se, but instead bias particular personality traits and thereby influence the manner in which an individual and his or her environment interact as sexual orientation and other personality characteristics unfold developmentally" (pp. 236-237). Zucker (2001) suggests a "multifactorial model of sexual orientation differentiation, which includes not only diverse biological pathways, but psychosocial pathways as well" (p. 115). See also Bem (1996); Byne (1995, 1997); Friedman & Downey (1993b); Hamer & Copeland (1994); Meyer-Bahlburg, Ehrhardt, Rosen, Gruen, Veridiano, Vann, et al. (1995, pp. 19-20); Pattatucci (1998); Risman & Schwartz (1988); Williams, Green & Goodman (1979).

a large twin registry, Bailey, Dunne and Martin (2000)—pioneers in the research on causal factors of homosexuality—refuted their earlier findings of fairly large concordance rates, stating that they failed to find a *significant* genetic influence on homosexual orientation (Jones & Kwee, 2005). This does not mean that genetics do not play some role in sexual orientation; it means that the exact role is inconclusive, is most likely small, is ill defined in terms of "underlying mechanisms," and is one of many other psychobiological and psychosocial factors (Zucker, 2001, p. 111).

Similarly, studies focused on the effect of prenatal hormonal imbalances that may "masculinize" genitalia or other physiological traits in females—such as finger-length ratios, otoacoustic emissions or handedness (right or left)—also remain inconclusive. Bearman and Bruckner (2002), discussing the literature on hormonal influences on homosexuality, stress that "even if females were 'masculinized' by androgen washing in utero, it is not clear why this would lead them to prefer females as romantic partners. . . . The mechanism linking hormone imbalance to same-sex preference appears extremely weak" (p. 1190). Even if there is a hormonal influence in some women, it still only accounts for one pathway among several that might lead to female homosexuality.[4]

Jeffrey Satinover, M.D., a fellow in psychiatry and child psychiatry at Yale University and lecturer in psychology and religion at Harvard, challenges *all* purist models of origins of homosexuality by suggesting we stop asking simplistic questions such as whether homosexuality is genetic and begin to

ask the much more realistic—but frustratingly complex—question, "To what degree is homosexuality (or any other behavioral trait) genetic and nongenetic, innate and acquired, familial and nonfamilial, intrauterine-influenced and extrauterine-influenced, affected by the environment and independent of the environment, responsive to social cues and unresponsive to these cues, and when and in what sequence do these various influences emerge to generate their effects and how do they *interact* [italics added] with one another; and after we have put these all together, how much is left over to attribute to choice, repetition, and habit?" (1996a, pp. 93-94)

Sadly, this unbiased type of inquiry has been generally curtailed due to the

---

[4]For more information on scientific evidence on the etiology of homosexuality, refer to the book website at www.ivpress.com.

supposed merits of political correctness.[5] Even though current research supports the influence of *both* biological and psychosocial factors, it is generally considered politically incorrect to formally consider and research the latter or the developmental and environmental elements underlying homosexuality. Nevertheless, Satinover's questions are vital for women (and men) with SSA who want to gain a deeper understanding of their own self and ultimately challenge their inner structures, relational patterns, sexual behaviors and even biological constitution.

Over the years, I have observed several common biopsychosocial processes in my clients that I believe could be helpful in gaining a better understanding of the dynamics that *may* create pathways toward same-sex sexuality. The material in the remainder of this and the following chapter is structured around my present opinions and observations; it is not a dogmatic attempt to prove the exact "cause" of female SSA. By presenting the common traits and experiences of women with SSA, I will be suggesting how each factor *may* have an influence within a context of many other factors and processes; I do not believe that any single factor *individually determines* or *directly causes* female SSA.

In addition to the possible underlying indeterminable genetic or hormonal influences, I observe, on a fairly consistent basis, the following exceptional, and quite probable, inherited characteristics and personality traits in the women with whom I have worked:

- They have above average intelligence.[6]

- They are profoundly sensitive and attuned to other people and relational dynamics.

---

[5]In their groundbreaking 2005 book *Destructive Trends in Mental Health: The Well-Intentioned Path to Harm*, Rogers Wright and Nicholas Cummings assert "that political correctness [including the status of homosexuality within the mental health community] is hostile to certain research questions that may be unpopular, and can have a chilling effect on science" (Byrd, 2005, p. 6). They go on to note, sadly, "that there is no empirical data on political correctness because it is 'politically incorrect to question political correctness' (p. 22)" (Byrd, 2005, pp. 5-6, quoting Wright & Cummings, 2005).

[6]Many studies observe that lesbian women are significantly more educated than their heterosexual counterparts (Kenyon, 1968; Laumann, Gagnon, Michael & Michaels, 1994; Rothblum, Balsam & Mickey, 2004; Rothblum & Factor, 2001). It is conjectured that the college experience may have influenced women to consider same-sex sexuality or that women with a propensity toward same-sex sexuality might, on average, boast of greater gender nonconformity or a higher level of resourcefulness and, I would add, a higher level of intelligence. In a literature review of studies contrasting intelligence levels between homosexual and heterosexual men and women, Weinrich (1978) notes that the more representative the sample studied, the more statistically significant was the superiority in intelligence of homosexual groups.

- They are observant and curious (Stevens, 1992), with a propensity to ponder, analyze and reflect.
- They exhibit gender nonconforming abilities and interests[7] (e.g., tomboyishness).
- They have an innate sense of justice.
- They are gifted and talented; their creativity is far reaching.
- They have a high level of energy and are adventurous and often athletic.

The parents of daughters with SSA with whom I have spoken confirm the above traits. It is not uncommon for a mother to say to me, "My daughter is not normal—she is exceptional! She excels in everything." Many of their daughters exhibited special abilities and sensitivities and a passion for humanitarian concerns at a very young age; these are the proverbial champions of the underdog, with a great capacity for advocacy and care. It is also not uncommon to hear that their daughters now hold postgraduate degrees, have received endless honors and awards, and have achieved national recognition in their fields of expertise or athleticism.

Pamela, introduced above, exhibited many of these traits. According to her mother, she was "beyond her years," constantly asking questions and extremely observant. She was sensitive to and cared about everyone else's feelings. However, Pamela admits that she felt burdened as a child. She was almost hyperaware of the painful and difficult aspects of her family environment, including her parents' personal and relational needs, weaknesses and imperfections. She was especially attuned to what she perceived to be an inequity between the men and women in her family. The women appeared to do all the work. Yet because she was gifted in athletics and preferred to play with the boys, she identified more with her dad. Although she didn't fit with the women, she carried a deep resentment toward the men because of the perceived inequity. This created a profound inner conflict surrounding her sense of belonging and gender identity. Even though her family was an above average family in terms of exhibiting affection and love, Pamela grew up with a chronic sense of pain and loneliness. An intelligent, sensitive, curious and reflective girl can be gravely affected by subtleties in parental influence or her broader environment. "The human situation is such that hurt may sometimes occur without it being a

---

[7]In a study involving 4,900 Australian twins, Bailey, Dunne and Martin (2000) report that childhood gender nonconformity was significantly heritable for both men and women.

matter for blaming anyone" (Moberly, 1983, p. 3). And so it may be for these women and their families.

COMMON THEMES: ENVIRONMENTAL FACTORS

Many of the influences and experiences that I discuss below are not necessarily unique to women with SSA, yet they seem significant in that they consistently arise as these women tell their stories and in that they appear to be dynamically connected to the other underlying themes. I cannot emphasize enough that it is more important to consider *how* an individual woman (with a certain biological blueprint) perceives and *processes* the effects of her environment or relational experiences than the actual qualities of the environment or relationships themselves.[8] This is not to dismiss the significant impact that abusive or traumatic experiences may have on a little girl's development but rather to gain an understanding of a girl's *internalized subjective experience*. It is this inner perspective that may offer clues as to why some girls struggle with SSA and some do not.

In the end, a full understanding or explanation of the presence and unique nature of SSA in a woman's life can only come from her. I believe female same-sex relationships are, at their core, a reflection of our God-given need as human beings for identity and attachment, albeit often confusedly sexualized or misappropriately directed. It is only when I can see a woman's confusion *within* the context of her dignity or natural human longings for connection and meaning that I can offer compassionate and affirming care.

In general, I see one or all of the following four developmental categories as being extremely conflicted in women with SSA:

- attachment
- formation of self
- gender identity
- socialization

Again, the conflict is not necessarily due solely to a poor environment or

---

[8]When any child interacts with her environment, many (often unconscious) inner formational processes are activated; these include but are not limited to the following: (1) creating mental representations of self and other, (2) formulating impressions or perceptions and judgments of any given event or relational dynamic, (3) responding emotionally to these perceptions, (4) developing core beliefs about self and other, (5) making unconscious vows and promises (choices) about what she will or will not *do* or will or will not *become*, (6) experimenting with styles of relating for needs fulfillment and (7) creating defenses.

abusive experience but is more fully understood in the context of the unique biological and neurological structures that influenced the way these women processed certain environmental and experiential material.

The remainder of this chapter will address the issues related to attachment and self. The following chapter will unpack the gender and socialization difficulties.

ATTACHMENT: A WOMAN'S FIRST HOME

Attachment is defined as an "*emotional* [italics added] relationship that develops gradually, after weeks and months of daily contact, conversation, care giving, and cuddling" (Brodzinsky, Schecter & Henig, 1992, p. 32). It is the "enduring affectional relationship between child and caregiver, the purpose of which is to provide protection and nurturance for the child" (Batgos & Leadbeater, 1994, p. 161). Secure attachment does not occur during a single bonding moment; it requires ongoing maintenance and repair across a girl's developmental lifespan.

Typical in the history of women with SSA are interferences, stressors or failures in their most primal attachment, often arising at birth and continuing throughout childhood.[9] These perceived or actual disruptions are usually rooted in

- prenatal, birth and postnatal difficulties or complications[10]
- accidental or uncontrollable separations from the mother due to maternal death,[11] adoption,[12] major illness, divorce[13] or other extenuating circumstances

---

[9]Historically this is also observed by Gundlach & Riess (1973); Siegel (1988); Socarides (1963).

[10]At least two studies have directly evaluated the relationship between prenatal stress and gender role development and sexual orientation in female offspring, respectively (Bailey, Willerman & Parks, 1991; Hines, Johnston, Golombok, Rust, Stevens, Golding & the ALSPAC Study Teams, 2002). The former found no significant correlation between prenatal stress and gender role development. The latter found that women who experienced greater levels of same-sex preferences had mothers who experienced greater numbers of stress events during their pregnancy.

[11]I have worked with several women who lost their mothers in early childhood, often initiating a string of traumatic events. In a recent cohort study involving a sample of 2 million Danes, Frisch and Hviid (2006) report that women who lost their mothers between ages 12 and 17 "opted for homosexual marriage almost twice as often as women who did not experience the loss of a parent" (p. 540). According to another, older comprehensive study by Saghir and Robins (1973) comparing 146 homosexual and 131 heterosexual men and women, 39% of women with SSA—as compared to 5% of heterosexual women—had lost one or both parents by death or divorce prior to the age of 10 (p. 398).

[12]In his study comparing 123 lesbians with 123 nonlesbian women, Kenyon (1968) found a much higher percentage of adoption among homosexual women (6.5%) than among nonhomosexual women (0.8%).

[13]It has been found that both men and women whose parents divorced after less than six years of marriage are more apt to enter into a homosexual marriage, 36% and 26% respectively, than are their peers whose parents remained married throughout their adolescence (Frisch & Hviid, 2006).

- maternal deficits or weakness arising out of the mother's own personal attachment history and developmental difficulties[14]
- actual maternal abuse or abandonment
- defensive detachment on the daughter's part due to the daughter's perceptions, sensitivities or negative conclusions and beliefs about her mother and the nature of their relationship

Most of these attachment difficulties *cannot* be attributed to a mother's intentional failure or shortcomings. Nor can we assume that a mother had ill intent even if she was categorically abusive. She may simply have been repeating what she experienced in her own childhood. Every woman with SSA who is seeking to understand her life will have to, at some point, grapple with the realities of her mother's own life, her circumstances and possibly her emotional poverty.

> *When my daughter was two, she would grab hold of my leg and not let go, so I would walk around the house with her clinging to my leg. I was working and had recently been in the hospital several times. I couldn't even tell you who took care of her and the other kids. I realize that sounds terrible, but at the time, we didn't think anything about it.*
>
> *a mother*

PRENATAL, BIRTH AND POSTNATAL COMPLICATIONS

Women with SSA tell me that their mothers' lives were often extremely difficult during their pregnancies or that the pregnancies themselves were unexpected or difficult. I hear that their mothers often faced family deaths, disruptive moves, financial crises or a general lack of support during the pregnancy. In the best of situations, pregnancy is a very fragile time for both mother and unborn child. Babies in the womb are alert, sensitive, responsive and capable of learning and remembering at least on a cellular level.[15] Research has shown that anything which upsets the mother can also upset the fetus; prenates feel what their mothers feel (Emerson, 1996) on a physiological and sensate level (Lipton, 1995). It is highly probable, then, that these women sensed their mothers' heightened levels of anxiety, depression or exhaustion prenatally.

---

[14]Siegel (1988).
[15]See Chamberlain (1999); Emerson (1996); and McCarty (n.d.).

And because these sensations and "memories" were among their first, they may have been extremely influential in my clients' primal formation.[16]

> *I was conceived only three months after my brother was born. My mother was hospitalized the last couple of months that she was pregnant with me. She was very sick with toxemia. There were horrible, stressful situations at home. . . . My father's first wife was suing him for child support. There was not enough money and my mother was angry.*
>
> *Diane*

In addition, a fetus can sense when it is wanted or unwanted (Chamberlain, 1999, p. 37; Lipton, 1995) and "sense and react to love and hate, as well as ambivalence and ambiguity" (Levy & Orlans, 1998, p. 29). Some of my clients' mothers, based on how they were carrying the pregnancy, were sure they were having a boy. While there is no clear evidence of whether a parent's belief or wish for an opposite sex child directly influences the development of their child's sense of value or gender—let alone sexual orientation—specialists in gender identity development admit that a *parent's reaction* to the infant of the nonpreferred sex after birth may indeed be influential (Zucker & Bradley, 1995, p. 213). Siegel (1988) notes that if "a female child is regarded with displeasure or depression, the baby will assume from birth that something is not right with her" (pp. 21-22); she believes this is the case with many of her female clients with SSA.[17] Many women with SSA are aware of having felt wrong or different for as long as they can remember. This primal sense of difference has no direct relationship to the presence of homosexuality as often believed by some people—sexual development occurs at a later stage in life—but

---

[16]Emerson (1996); Schore (2002). These early memories are encoded or processed on a preverbal or unconscious level, but they will nevertheless "form a rudimentary template from which all other experiences will be appraised" (Thomson, 2004, p. 11; referring to Fogel, 2002). Further, these events are imprinted in and become a part of the infant's developing biological and neurological (brain) structures (Schore, 2002). Prenatal experiences can have a lifelong impact on the fetus, especially if they are followed by further *interactional traumas*, that is, traumas that interact with each other in producing additional effects (Emerson, 1996, p. 126). The following discussion addresses the interactional nature of the various experiences or traumas in many of my clients' lives.

[17]If a mother is not pleased or secure with her own femininity, she may also *unknowingly* transmit disappointment and her own discontent (or fear) to her little girl. "Those qualities that the mother values and devalues in herself as a 'mother' [or woman] are [unfortunately] transmitted in a powerful, unconscious manner" to her child (Surrey, 1991a, p. 41). See also Jacobs (1990) and McDougall (1989).

it may be associated with these early impressions and attachment difficulties.

Researchers have also discovered that a pregnant mother's experience of stress or negative emotions can predispose her to a negative emotional state prior to delivery, thereby adversely affecting her "sensitivity to and ability to participate in the attachment process" (Ward 1991, p. 109).[18] If there were birth complications or hospitalizations (separations)—as was often the case with my clients—these women, as neonates, may have also experienced a physiological dulling of their minds and bodies to defend against the shock of trauma, further inhibiting the bonding process.

> *I was born two months early. I was a breech baby and got stuck. Once I was born, I was given blood transfusions and was in an incubator for over a month. My mom still tears up when she talks about it. She wanted to be at the hospital every minute she could, but she had to be at home to take care of the other kids. She had no one to help except my dad, who was always at work. Even when she did come to the hospital, I wouldn't eat. She would leave crying.*
>
> *Nicole*

The primal separations, negative feeling states and possible bonding difficulties commonly reported may have also disrupted the rhythmic dance between these mothers and their baby girls—the mother's preparedness to give and the baby's preparedness to receive. Erik Erikson describes the success of this harmonious dance as the *mutuality of relaxation*. He emphasizes that this dance is, in fact, a baby's first encounter with "friendly otherness," an important element in establishing a deep center of trust. Most of my clients seem extremely conflicted in the basic realm of trust. Restful relaxation by themselves or with others seems only a pipedream. Many live with a gnawing sense of personal and relational insecurity.

Attachment specialists Levy and Orlans (1998) note that an infant's experience of maternal inconsistency or loss of an attachment figure can cause "pathological mourning, resulting in disturbed development, emotional detachment, inability to love and trust" (p. 14); and this "may give a depressive undertone to the whole remainder of life" (Erikson, 1980, p. 62). Depression

---

[18]See also Emerson (1996); Levy & Orlans (1998).

and anxiety are also common in the lives of women with SSA.

In summary, many women with SSA may have had multiple traumatic experiences by the time they were 6 months old. If we were to conceptualize their lives in terms of building blocks, the first layer of blocks is missing several pieces. Trust is compromised, attachment is threatened, and their fledgling foundational self may be fracturing.

INTERGENERATIONAL ATTACHMENT ISSUES

It is not uncommon to find that *both* parents of a woman with SSA grew up in environments fraught with insecure attachment, relational deprivations or actual abandonment. Bowlby (1988) notes that parents' affections and attachment behaviors directed toward their children are deeply influenced by their previous personal experiences, especially those they had or are still having with their own parents (p. 15).[19] That many parents grew up in unhealthy or unsatisfactory environments does not make them categorically bad parents, yet they may be unaware of possible ineffective attachment patterns in relation to their own children (and spouses). Sadly, it is these relational and emotional weaknesses on which my clients seem to focus. My clients are often not able to see their parents' underlying care and loving sentiment because of their felt sense of relational deprivation.

> *My mother was an orphan and didn't know her parents, let alone her grandparents. My dad's father died when my dad was a young boy. His mother remarried and eventually she and her new husband sent him off to boarding school. He only came home at Christmas and during the summer. There were no parenting models for either my mother or my father to follow.*
>
> *Monica*

MATERNAL PATTERNS

In general, women with SSA describe the *relational dynamic* with their mothers on the *extreme* ends of a continuum from connectedness to separateness. There seems to be no middle ground. Those who experienced excessive *closeness* or connectedness with their moms often describe the mother-daughter

---

[19]See also Levy & Orlans (1998); Schore (2002).

bond as more of a mutual absorption than a healthy attachment. They were undifferentiated from and emotionally enmeshed with their moms, often feeling what their mother felt.[20] They worried about mom's sadness or difficulty in her marriage. At times, it was hard for them to distinguish between their mother's feelings and their own. Many women, unbeknownst to their mothers, assumed the role of mother's caretaker.[21] They came to believe if Mom is OK, I am OK. In severe cases, in order to maintain a sense of connection with their mother, these daughters had to deny or dismiss their own needs or feelings in lieu of mom's concerns or feelings.

Within these enmeshed dynamics, many daughters perceived their mothers as dependent, weak, needy or childlike.[22] Ironically, mothers who were more than competent—and therefore able to "do it all" with little obvious support from their husbands—were also viewed as weak. According to their alert and justice-oriented daughters, they were unable to stand up for their rights within the marriage or to adequately address their personal needs.

Women who experienced excessive *distance* or separateness in their relationships with their mothers often speak in terms of a *total* absence of warm emotional connection (McDougall, 1970). They perceived their mothers as being dutiful but detached, stoic and empty: they explain that their mothers fixed meals, cleaned the house, joined carpools and regularly attended sporting events, but were never truly "present." The daughters didn't *feel* connected, and questioned whether their mothers were *ever* engaged with their inner thoughts or feelings. Some women claim that reaching out to mom was like grasping at thin air; mom was a "shell of a woman." Mother, these women believed, lacked any identifiable substance of her own and therefore could not nurture or support her daughter's own process of self-formation and identification.[23] One of my clients said her mother's apparent insubstantiality and emotional unavail-

---

[20]An enmeshed family system is one in which healthy boundaries of individual personhood or autonomy are weak or nonexistent. "In enmeshment, the family members are over involved with one another and over responsive. Interpersonal boundaries are diffuse, with the family members intruding on each other's thoughts, feelings, and communications" (Minuchin, 1974, p. 242).

[21]This caretaking role also often ignited a growing resentment toward their dad. They wondered why they, instead of he, were the ones to take care of their mom (McDougall, 1980).

[22]In some cases, the mothers may have been "emotionally fragile" (Siegel, 1988, p. 218). It was as if "motherhood was too much for them" (p. 220) and they still wanted (or needed) to be nurtured themselves.

[23]Siegel (1988) suggests that many of these mothers may have felt unworthy and possibly lacked the important virtue of self-love. "Indeed, they loved their daughters as much as, and with the same *lack of regard* [italics added] as, they loved themselves" (p. 216).

ability left her feeling like she didn't even exist. For most of her life her heart's cry has been directed toward other women, asking, *Do you see me? Do you care?*

Many women also report that their mothers were emotionally unavailable because of maternal depression.[24] Being depressed does not mean a mother doesn't care; however, her emotions and reactions are often numbed and delayed, restricting her ability to emotionally connect with her daughter. This failure in attunement can weaken a mother-daughter attachment and create a sense of relational distance. In many cases, my client's mothers were so chronically depressed that they explicitly relied on their daughters for physical and emotional support.[25]

In the saddest cases, my clients came to believe that they were a burden to their mothers—unwanted, unloved and "in the way." They lived with what felt like an abortive energy directed toward their very demise. One woman felt so unsafe with her mom that she believed her mother was intentionally causing, or at least refusing to protect her from, all the pain in her life.

MISSING A "HOME"

Regardless of how or why a girl's attachment with mom is threatened or malformed, her future development *will* be affected.[26] Carol Gilligan (1982), a leading theorist in female development, explains the significance of a girl's solid attachment with her mother by comparing and contrasting the developmental differences between boys and girls. The following illustration can help to understand her points.

As illustrated by the lower set of arrows in the figure, mom is the first person with whom both a baby girl and baby boy attach. In contrast to a boy's critical developmental process of differentiating from mother and moving out of mother's world into the world of father (the masculine), a girl is to remain securely attached to mom and grow as a unique individual *within* the world of mother (the feminine). Her father is to move into her world, protecting the

---

[24]Of interest, Zucker and Bradley (1995) note that depression is the most common psychopathology of mothers with girls who struggle with gender identity disorder (p. 252), the symptoms of which were often present in the childhoods of women with SSA.

[25]"Research has found that children of depressed mothers have a heightened sensitivity to and sense of responsibility for others' distress" (Levy & Orlans, 1998, p. 58; see also Tronick, 1989, p. 117).

[26]All future relationships will be seen through the lens of a daughter's primal relationship with mother. However, negative developmental effects can be ameliorated if the daughter warmly attaches to an alternative adult female who is consistently available for needs fulfillment.

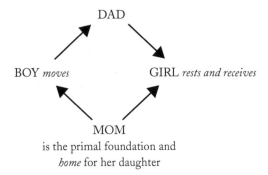

Figure 3.1.

special mother-daughter relationship and blessing her unique self and feminine identity.

A mother, then, is a little girl's primal and enduring home. It is through this warm, secure, ongoing attachment with mother (with the help of father, as discussed below) that a girl will form her basic sense of self;[27] mirror, model and identify with mother; understand herself as a female;[28] differentiate and discover her unique and individual identity; and learn how to *do* relationship. A girl's primal attachment with her mother will act as a model for all future emotional relationships (Chodorow, 1978).

Because of the inherent insecurities (also arising out of the perceived emotional absence of their fathers) and anxieties within this relationship, women with SSA regularly report feeling deeply deprived of maternal nurturing and affection. They speak as if their very personhood (and developing autonomy) was felt to be under constant attack or threat of annihilation. These women did not symbolize or internalize a sense of mother as the home base from which they could develop an autonomous self. Instead they felt unsafe and depleted as they were continuously attuned to their mother's stressors and

[27]Female developmental theorists react against an objective definition of "a static and lone self" but suggest that the female "self" is inextricably linked to the social or relational interactions with others, primarily mother as her first caretaker (Miller, 1991, p. 14; Surrey, 1991b, p. 52; see also Chodorow, 1978; Gilligan, 1982). "Women stay with, build on, and develop in a context of attachment and affiliation with others. Indeed, women's *sense of self* [italics added] becomes very much organized around being able to make and then to maintain affiliations and relationships" (Miller, 1976, p. 83).
[28]A core definition and basic sense of personhood must be formed before a girl can fully appropriate a healthy feminine gender identity.

needs.[29] Essentially, these women experienced a burgeoning weight of negative affect, a foundational sense of mistrust or abandonment, and, as some are heartbroken to admit, disrespect for their mothers.[30]

DEFENSIVE DETACHMENT AND DISIDENTIFICATION: A MEANS TO SURVIVE

In an effort to survive the overwhelming insecurity and negative feelings associated with their attachment with mother, these women, as young girls, often instigated an unconscious process of self-preservation by developing defenses, distancing tactics and detachment behaviors that contribute unfortunately to further attachment difficulties. Historically, two of the most common defensive postures for women with SSA include maternal defensive detachment and disidentification.

Elizabeth Moberly, a research psychologist and pioneer in the study of homosexuality, describes *defensive detachment,* as observed in men and women with SSA, as not only childhood withdrawal or disinclination to emotionally connect with the same-sex parent, but also the decisive refusal to *ever* reconnect (Moberly, 1983). Many of my clients can recall the very moments when they began to disavow or reject their mother—cutting off or blocking all emotional connection with her.

> *I remember when I was 5 or so my parents had gotten into a fight. My mother got into the car and just drove off. I was crying, asking, "Where is she going? What's going on?" My dad seemed helpless. I think that was when I checked out with mom. I was devastated and remember the feeling was just unbearable. So I checked out. . . . I had this deep feeling of pain, realizing I can't control this. Mom would leave and I don't matter. It doesn't matter. She will leave me. So it was sort of my way of making a*

---

[29]According to a large study comparing 979 homosexual and 477 heterosexual men and women, Bell, Weinberg and Hammersmith (1981) note that, in general, women with SSA describe their relationships with and opinions of their mothers in more negative terms than do heterosexual women (pp. 119, 121). A similar finding was made by Saghir and Robins (1973, p. 301). Because of the era in which these studies were conducted, the results may not be representative of younger women with SSA.

[30]For a secure attachment to endure between a mother and daughter, the daughter must have a sense of ongoing trust, respect for and desire to be close to mom. In general, if a daughter senses that mom is consistently available and responsive to her needs, she will have a "strong and pervasive feeling of security" and will be encouraged "to value and continue the relationship" (Bowlby, 1988, p. 27).

*resolve, Yes, mother will leave—she's gone, she didn't want you—now get
over it. I had to detach to stop that feeling of abandonment.*

Sam

Like attachment, defensive detachment does not occur in a single isolated
moment; it is a progressive, patterned response within a girl to her ongoing
dissatisfaction in her relationship with her mom. My clients detached not necessarily for fear of abuse or physical harm from mom, but rather because they
feared being engulfed or being met with nothingness or casual disinterest.
These girls could no longer endure this painful disappointment. A daughter's
detachment from mother, and possibly from other members of the same sex,
may take on an overtly hostile flavor, as seen in antagonistic behaviors, fault
finding, resentment, coldness or defiance; or it may be more latent, as seen in
a girl who remains ostensibly close to mom because she is mom's caretaker or
is helplessly enmeshed.

But sadly, when a daughter begins to cut herself off from her mother, she
effectively shuts out any of the good that her mother *was* offering. In my conversations with the mothers of adult daughters, many remarked that no matter
how hard they tried to love or connect with their girls when they were little,
they couldn't get through. They felt like their daughters had shut them out.
The doorway into their hearts seemed closed.

*I was so disconnected from my mom. By kindergarten I was completely cut
off from her. There wasn't anything. I didn't like my mom. I believed she
had little to give me by way of nurture, attention or love.*

Andrea

In order to sustain an attitude of defensive detachment, these young girls
also had to actively fight against or detach from their *natural longing and
need* for connection to and intimacy with mother (and others), further curtailing any opportunity for a loving or warm exchange.[31] Many women with
SSA eventually come to experience profound deficits in their own relational
capacities.

---

[31]This may also be the starting point of an avoidant or dismissive attachment style, which is common
among women with SSA (Wells & Hansen, 2003; Wells, 2003).

Clinicians operating from a psychoanalytical framework have historically reported the frequency with which women with SSA, as girls, disidentified, rather than identified, with their mothers.[32] In general, these
women recall feeling more dissimilar to and had far less desire to be like
their mothers than do other women (Bell, Weinberg & Hammersmith,
1981, p. 124). *Disidentification,* like defensive detachment, is not merely
the result of a breakdown in a girl's identification process, but is also an
ongoing dynamic or reaction against identification with mother (Moberly,
1983, p. 12).

For example, because of Pamela's lack of respect for or admiration of her
mother (explained earlier in this chapter), she disowned and disavowed many
behaviors, physical appearances or fashion styles similar to her mother's. She
vowed to *never* appear weak or needy or to become dependent on a man.
Women with SSA often react with disgust toward *anything* even closely re-
sembling femininity or female roles. Joyce McDougall, a psychoanalyst specializing in female homosexuality, notes that many of her clients held the belief that their mothers were not enhanced as wives but instead were in an
unhappy or dangerous role: "To be a woman meant to be nothing, to have
nothing, to create nothing" (1970, p. 179). As girls, they may have also disidentified with other women and rejected aspects of their own personhood associated with femaleness, including their female body parts and their tender
and sensitive attributes (McDougall, 1980).

PATERNAL PATTERNS

As illustrated in the above diagram, a loving and engaged father is also essential for a girl's healthy growth and development. Her father is to move into her
world (and the world of mother), protecting their special mother-daughter relationship by supporting his wife and affirming and calling forth his daughter's
unique self and feminine identity. Sadly, many women with SSA do not recall
this type of supportive involvement by their fathers.

---

[32]Loney (1973); Siegel (1988); Socarides (1968); Wilbur (1965). Siegel (1988) believes that many
women with SSA received an unconscious message from their mother that it was "unacceptable, even
dangerous," to become like them or to be female (p. 22). Gender specialists speculate a girl who
struggles with gender identity disorder may have also "failed to identify with her mother or deiden-
tified from her mother because she perceived her mother as weak, incompetent, or helpless. In fact,
many of the mothers devalued their own efficacy and regarded the female gender role with disdain"
(Zucker & Bradley, 1995, p. 252).

Women with SSA also describe the relational dynamic with their fathers in terms of *extreme* closeness or distance. Many a client reflects on her dad's warm, kind and fun presence. As a child, she often considered herself as dad's favorite or his "special pal."[33] But this sense of *closeness* only occurred when these girls stepped into their fathers' world, engaging in *his* interests and activities. Granted, many of these girls genuinely enjoyed fishing—and perhaps mechanics—but the fun or the nature of their interactions during these activities was often more about dad than daughter. Rarely did one of these women experience her dad's devoted attunement to her inner thoughts and feelings or her special interests that fell outside his world. In extreme cases, many of these women knowingly shifted aspects of their identity or became like their dads in order to maintain a sense of connection.

Sometimes the daughters perceived that their dads had an unconscious energy to make them more masculine, grooming them to be tough and self-sufficient. Because many of these women showed superior athletic abilities and scholastic excellence, their dads often assumed the roles of coach, chief critic or academic advisor. They felt pressure to try to meet his often-unreachable standards or follow his academic goals for their lives. This put these daughters into a double bind. They believed that to remain in relationship with dad, they had to let go of their own thoughts, desires and goals. When they tried to voice their opinions or needs, they were often met with their father's anger and accusation that they were ungrateful for his involvement or help. They could not win. They either had to give up their relationship with dad or their own self. As girls, many had the sense that their dads were vicariously living some sort of childhood dream through them—leaving them feeling used rather than valued and nurtured.

So even though many of my clients refer to their fathers as their lifeline and closest ally, the majority (if not all) of them struggle with an equally strong sense that their fathers were *emotionally absent*[34] or unpredictably *angry*.[35] It is not necessarily true that their dads were more absent or angry than other dads. It is true, however, that these relational traits, as perceived by their daughters,

---

[33]This playful or platonic connection may have excluded mom, creating jealousy and possibly causing an even greater rift between her and her daughter (not to mention between her and her husband).

[34]In Paulk's (2003) survey of 265 women with SSA, 46% described their father as detached (p. 244).

[35]Bell, Weinberg and Hammersmith (1981) note that more homosexual women than nonhomosexual women rate their fathers as relatively high on a "detached-hostile" measure (p. 129).

left an indelible impact. Perhaps because of their sensitivity, these women report severe reactions whenever they encountered their fathers' anger, cold controlling personality or authoritarian, nonnegotiating attitudes. They cultivated a deep fear, which often developed into the belief that men are not safe. Again, as a means to regain a sense of connection, many unconsciously aligned themselves with their fathers (aggressor) in an attempt to identify and associate with his apparent power and strength.[36]

> *Once my dad became really angry with my youngest sister. His face was bright red. I know at that moment I made a vow that I was never going to be like my sister. I was going to be strong like him. And I would never do anything that would make him that mad at me.*
>
> Connie

An overarching *sense* of their fathers' absence or unavailability may have affected these girls in multiple ways. First, because their mother was often not supported physically or emotionally within the marriage, her energy and availability to meet her daughter's emotional needs were often diminished. Second, these daughters were denied the significant experience of emotionally connecting or interacting with a man. Instead, Dad (a man) was viewed as unknown or undesirable. He was often depersonalized; perceived as weak, irrelevant and useless; and consequently ignored (Whitehead, 1996, pp. 352-53). Third, these daughters developed the belief that they, as females in relationship to a man, didn't matter. But perhaps even more important, their very process of differentiation was curtailed.

LACKING IN AFFIRMATION, STUCK IN DEPENDENCY

As previously mentioned, a daughter's core sense of self will gradually emerge as she continues in a warm and empathic relationship with mom. However, her emerging self needs to *differentiate* and become a unique, *individuated* self, not a mere appendage of mother. To gain this sense of autonomy or differentiation (within an ongoing attachment with mom), a girl is utterly dependent on the involvement of an attuned father who will notice, validate, affirm and

---

[36]Little girls who identify with a male aggressor and become preoccupied with power, aggression and protection fantasies often struggle with gender identity disorders (Zucker & Bradley, 1995).

support the delineation of her personhood and healthy individuation.[37]

If a girl's basic sense of trust or attachment to either parent is disrupted, her individuation process can breakdown. In instances where a daughter is not securely or affectionately attached to *mom* or disengaged from the identification or mirroring process, a father's affirmation will be limited. A daughter's active detachment and disidentification with mom creates more of a *submerging* or vanishing self than a vital and unique personhood.[38] There may simply be a lack of an emerging or developing self to affirm (Jordan & Surrey, 1989). In instances where a daughter is not securely or affectionately attached to dad or disengaged from the affirmation and differentiation process, a mother's loving influence will be limited. Those parts of the daughter's self that *are* being found or identified within her mother may become inextricably merged, so to speak, or lost within her mother's personhood and identity instead of being recognized as her own distinctive characteristics and traits.[39]

Indeed, many women with SSA suffer from having never completed this psychological and emotional differentiation process (Jacobs, 1990). Their ongoing existence is *unconsciously* felt to be still *dependent* on their mothers (from whom they are possibly consciously or unconsciously detaching and disidentifying due to core anxiety within the "insecure attachment") and to be utterly *independent* of their fathers, who are not available, appropriately affectionate or truly known. They remain arrested within the developmental stages of dependency and differentiation, and are therefore simply not able to secure their own self or unique identity.

Returning to the above diagram, their lives could be graphically illustrated by placing an "X" through the lines of attachment that should have existed between both of their parents and themselves. As children, women with SSA often felt untethered or fundamentally "homeless," exposed to the dangers of life and des-

---

[37]See Masterson (1988, p. 33); Wakerman (1984, p. 22). It should also be noted *I am not mom* is the voice of a girl experiencing healthy differentiation. *I don't want to be like mom* is an assertive detachment and disidentification implying there has not been healthy separation or a secure base or attachment from which to start.

[38]In her book *Homosexuality: A Symbolic Confusion*, Ruth Tiffany Barnhouse (1977), an Episcopal priest and professor of psychiatry, also claims that "women who have never adequately relinquished their infantile attachment to their mothers [due to unmet dependency needs] find it more difficult to take the subsequent steps in psychosexual development which are required for the establishment of a satisfactory heterosexual adjustment" (p. 89). They remain unable to fully sexually differentiate with father if they have not already fully identified with mother.

[39]Because of the innate differences between dad (male) and daughter (female), a daughter's close relationship with dad will, in and of itself, create an energy of differentiation.

perate for someone to care. Their fledgling existence was precarious at best.

FAMILY PATTERNS

These sensitive, smart, reflective little girls are further affected by additional subtleties in family dynamics and roles. Women raised in the 1960s and 1970s often emphasize the repressed nature of their family systems, including a lack of physical or verbal affection,[40] an inhibited expression of feelings other than anger, a "buck up" philosophy,[41] unresolved marital troubles,[42] and traditional or rigid gender roles. (The vast majority of my clients in this age group had stay-at-home moms.) The younger generation of faith-based women with SSA, raised in the 1980s and 1990s do not report these familial traits as often as the older women (other than their mother's status as a stay-at-home mom). However, another pattern commonly emerges in my conversations with them and their mothers. Their families are often characterized by extreme conservatism and religious scrupulosity. The parents have been led to believe that their first and foremost responsibility is to shield their daughter from outside negative influences. As adolescents, these girls felt (feel) scrutinized and under constant surveillance. They did not feel free to develop certain friendships nor were they allowed to engage in "normal" adolescent functions or socialization. As a result, they often felt "missed" as their parents continuously reacted in fear to the culture or environments in which the daughters had to function and live. The girls were regularly exhorted to work harder, do better and, above all else, *be good*. But try as they might, they never felt as if they measured up. They concluded that their parents cared more about external dangers than their thoughts, feelings and emerging uniqueness. In the end, they felt detached and like strangers within their own families.

---

[40] According to Bell, Weinberg and Hammersmith (1981), in general, homosexual women did not observe as much meaningful affection *between* their parents (pp. 136-37) as did nonhomosexual women.

[41] Siegel (1988) speaks of how belittling and disapproving some her client's fathers were of the fact that their daughters were in counseling. The fathers accused "them of being too weak to help themselves. Their daughters were to stop being homosexual at once—by an act of will" (p. 217).

[42] In a Danish national cohort study on childhood family correlates and heterosexual and homosexual marriage, Frisch and Hviid (2006) found that girls who experienced parental divorce during childhood were more likely to enter a homosexual marriage (which is legal in Denmark) as adults. Historically, it has been shown that women with SSA are "more likely to recall a 'a great deal' of friction or bad feeling between their parents while they were growing up" (Bell, Weinberg & Hammersmith, 1981, p. 137; see also Loney, 1973) than women without SSA (Saghir & Robins, 1973, p. 300) and to experience parental divorce (Kenyon, 1968).

Many women with SSA, whether young or old, never experienced what it was like to have their deepest feelings and concerns regularly pursued, let alone understood or honored. In their efforts to please, they learned to keep everything inside. They ruminated and internalized beliefs such as *Feelings are not good. It's not safe to feel. No one can handle my feelings or thoughts.* If a woman's family was founded upon strong ethics of self-sufficiency and hard work, she may have also internalized the message, *It doesn't matter how you feel, just do it.* Many of my clients believe it is a virtue to live independent of all supportive resources and to never admit vulnerability or need. To some, vulnerability and need are the ultimate signs of female weakness.

YET THEIR HEARTS MUST GO ON

So even though Pamela comes from a good family, she still grew up with a deep sense of homelessness and loneliness. Despite her flight from mom, her confusion about dad and her departure from her own true and feminine self, a deep rumbling was heard. She can still hear a cry from deep within. She knows she must survive. She knows she is meant to live. Her desperate heart cannot stop reaching out for the home and love for which she was made.

> *Even though I got to the point of hating my mom and vowing to never let her hurt me again, I knew there was still a longing in me: "Love me. Just love me."*
>
> *Abby*

CHAPTER FOUR

Lost in Confusion

Gender Nonconformity and Socialization

It is far from easy to enter into the painful experience of loneliness.
You like to stay away from it.
Still it is an experience that enters into everyone's life at some point.

HENRI NOUWEN, *REACHING OUT*

Abby is the second child in her family, born four years after her older brother and just thirteen months before her younger brother. Abby's mother told her that when she was little she used to sit on her father's lap and watch baseball games, but when she was four or five that stopped. Abby recalls that that was about the same time her older brother started sexually abusing her. From then on, she remembers thinking that men were not safe. When Abby was older she played football with the boys in her neighborhood, which was one way she was able to get back at her brother for the abuse. Abby says her younger brother played with dolls; she played with tanks that blew up the dolls because it was more fun. She learned to be one of the boys and was even introduced as a boy by her family. She also remembers becoming her younger sister's "protector." Abby says that during those early years, her family moved a lot, which made it difficult for her and her siblings to establish friendships with other kids.

She became the peacemaker in her family. Outside of the house, she became a people pleaser. She didn't want to create waves, so she learned to be quiet and never express her own desires; she attempted to figure out what everyone else wanted or needed. On reflection, she feels like she "lost her self," essentially becoming who and what everyone else wanted her to be.

After many years of never having a best friend, Abby met Suzie in high school. They hit it off. For the first time, Abby did some of the things that best friends do, like listen to loud music and uninhibitedly sing along. With Suzie, Abby laughed, something she hadn't done in a long time. Abby also gladly took care of Suzie, proudly proclaiming, "No guy could even come close to giving her what I did." In reflection, Abby admits that they were so emotionally enmeshed that she had no identity outside of Suzie. They eventually became physically involved, but Abby explains that even to this day, her temptation is not so much to have sex with another woman but to help or care for her.

Abby has had one long-term same-sex relationship, lasting 17 years. Because of her spiritual beliefs and values, she is now committed to sexual chastity. She is pursuing ordination and works in the field of electrical engineering.

SETTLING FOR A RE-CREATED SELF

When women like Abby come to see me, they often describe their souls as dead or vacant. As girls and young women, they developed physically, intellectually and professionally and they appeared independent and emotionally self-sufficient; but they were often emotionally and psychologically disconnected and underdeveloped, unaware of neglecting their own feelings, opinions, likes and dislikes, not to mention their femininity.

Yet my clients, like any other child or adolescent girl, could not survive within this internal vacuum. In lieu of having an affirmed and loved core self, they often latched onto an imaginary self or role from which to draw even the most meager sense of identity. They may have become the peacemaker like Abby or the "strong one." At age six, one of my clients entertained fantasies of her parents dying. She methodically mapped out a way to single handedly care for her younger siblings. The fantasy provided her with a sense of power and security.

Besides providing a sense of grounding for their existence, their "created selves" also often provided a sense of relief from inner pain. For instance, some of my clients identified themselves as the "unlovable one" or the "bad one." This allowed them to believe that *they* were the cause of their existential loneliness and emptiness, which was preferable to facing the reality that mom or dad had failed or were less than god-like. Many of their false selves or self-assumed roles also provided them with a sense of attachment (e.g., if I am the helper, I will be loved) or supplied the methods of self-protection (e.g., if I am tough, I will be safe).

By age 10 I just kind of lived in a fantasy world. I used to listen to all those
heroes on the radio, like the Lone Ranger and the Shadow. I used to think
I was the hero and I would rescue everybody. I took care of my brother and
my mom, who was sick a lot. I never felt fear though. I didn't really feel
anything. I just went along with whatever was happening.

Margaret

Living with a false or created self, however, means these girls had to exert
most of their formational energy on external behaviors, attitudes and expressions that furthered their aim of survival *to the exclusion* of their internal structures and the development of an authentic self. Unconsciously, they were still
dependent on the signals and reactions of parents and others around them to
stabilize their wavering inner definition. As adolescents and adults, they often
became unhealthily dependent on the affirmation of their partners or friends
to verify that they are attached, acceptable or safe.

GENDER NONCONFORMITY

Many of my clients faced an additional dimension to their mounting relational
and identity issues. As children, they often displayed what are stereotypically
defined as masculine or gender nonconforming behaviors and interests—running, romping, exploring, riding bikes, building forts and playing sports,
among other things (Bell, Weinberg & Hammersmith, 1981). They enjoyed
being outside and often demonstrated a downright fearlessness and aggression
in their outdoor endeavors, completely oblivious to dirt, scrapes or bruises.
They did not typically enjoy playing house, cuddling dolls, having tea parties
or dressing up. They had little interest in kitchen or household chores. It was
difficult for many of them to sit quietly[1] or "properly." They were quintessential tomboys.[2]

I asked my mom why she never sat down and read to me. All I remember
is playing outside with the neighborhood kids. And she said, "Nicole, I

---

[1] It would be interesting to conduct a study on the correlation between childhood attention deficit disorder or attention deficit and hyperactivity disorder and adult female SSA.

[2] Historical literature on female homosexuality commonly notes that many more homosexual than heterosexual women report being tomboys. See Bell, Weinberg & Hammersmith (1981); Friedman &
Downey (1993b); Gundlach & Riess (1973); Paulk (2003); Saghir & Robins, (1971, 1973).

tried. But you did not want to sit still." My earliest memories are of being
with the kids, climbing trees and playing.
Nicole

Since these women, as girls, demonstrated a natural interest and enjoyment of these cross-gender interests and behaviors *combined* with superior performance, acumen and skill, I suggest that their gender nonconforming traits most likely represent a genetic or biological component of their innate personhood or nature.[3] Shari, for example, reported that she played all-star softball, was nationally ranked in swimming and held high school cross-country and track records. Gender nonconforming traits would also include those innate giftings that lead some women into hobbies and careers more culturally identified as masculine. Indeed, based on their 2000 study involving approximately 1,891 twin pairs, researchers Bailey, Dunne and Martin (2000) found that gender nonconformity is significantly heritable for both men and women.

Research has shown that "a substantial proportion of homosexual men and women recall greater rates of childhood cross-gender behavior than those of their heterosexual counterparts" (Zucker & Bradley, 1995, p. 27).[4] In fact, gender nonconformity in childhood is considered to be one of the strongest *correlating* factors with later adult homosexuality.[5] This does not mean that gender nonconformity directly *causes* homosexuality, but it may still have a substantial developmental influence.[6] As Hilary Mullins writes in *Evolution of a Tomboy,*

> In the beginning, it had nothing to do with liking girls. In fact, in the beginning, being a tomboy was not about whom I liked at all; it was about

---

[3]Gender atypical behavior in girls has been associated with prenatal neurohormonal influences such as an increased exposure to androgen (Hines, Brook & Conway, 2004). In one large study involving a sample size of over 14,000 children, birth order was seen to be significant in later gender role behavior and development. Girls showed more masculine-typical behavior if they had older brothers (Hines, Johnston, Golombok, Rust, Stevens, Golding & the ALSPAC Study Teams, 2002).

[4]See also Bailey & Zucker (1995); Bell, Weinberg & Hammersmith (1981); Dunne, Bailey, Kirk & Martin (2000); Green (1980); Gundlach & Riess (1973); Lippa (2000); Phillips, Psych & Over (1995); Saghir & Robins (1973).

[5]See Bailey, Dunne & Martin (2000); Bailey & Zucker (1995); Bell, Weinberg & Hammersmith (1981); Bem (1996); Dunne, Bailey, Kirk & Martin (2000); Gundlach & Riess (1968); Hamer & Copeland (1994); Phillips, Psych & Over (1995); Saghir & Robins (1971); Thompson, Schwartz, McCandless & Edwards (1973).

[6]Not all women with SSA recall atypical sex-typed behaviors. Likewise, many gender nonconforming girls do not struggle with cross-gender identification or homosexuality.

what I liked: climbing trees, building forts, playing any kind of game that involved throwing or hitting a ball. (1995, p. 40)

THE ROOTS OF GENDER IDENTITY CONFUSION

Gender identification is a heavily affect-laden process wherein a girl develops, integrates and accepts her femaleness (Zucker & Bradley, 1995). Gender identity formation arises out of a twofold question: Who am I as a girl, and is it a good thing? This process of identification, while framed as a normative process for all boys and girls, is far from easy for many children.

Women with SSA are typically born as biological females; they knew this as children and appropriately applied sex labels to others and themselves.[7] This is the first step in a girl's gender identity development. The next step requires her to become aware of and distinguish between the cultural sex roles that discriminate between girls and boys. A girl can become cognitively aware of these stereotypes (e.g., girls play with dolls, boys play with cars) as early as 26 months old. In fact, one researcher notes that the higher a girl's intelligence—as I suspect is the case with my clients—the more she is attuned to these gender-based stereotypes (Weinraub, Clemens, Sockloff, Ethridge, Gracely & Myers, 1984).

The difficulty at this stage was not in my clients' recognition of these sex-role stereotypes, but in their lack of interest or preference for the discriminating characteristics and social roles unique to females as portrayed within their families, schools, churches or broader culture. This disinterest or even disgust may have been partially due to (1) their gender nonconforming strengths and interests, (2) the perceived restrictive and oppressive nature of the female characteristics and roles presented to them, or (3) the preexisting pattern of disidentifying from females and female roles in general. Nevertheless, to become ultimately secure in their girlhood or feminine identity, these girls at least needed to discover and identify with *some* desirable and respectable characteristics and traits within *some* women or social images of females. If a gender nonconforming girl finds other females who enjoy the same things she enjoys and if she receives ongoing acceptance, respect and affirmation as a girl, all may be well. A girl can still proceed to develop a healthy sense of femaleness and femininity.

---

[7]This is not always the case. Some lesbian women may have qualified for the formal diagnosis of Gender Identity Disorder in childhood.

Sadly, many of my clients did not find other girls who shared their interests. Instead, they noticed the boys and came to the conclusion that boys, compared to their tea-party sisters, definitely have more fun! Watching their parents, many women, as girls, also came to the conclusion that compared to subservient women, men have more freedom and power. In addition, many were in environments that insisted they mold themselves into a rigid definition of femaleness or were shamed into believing that their interests and abilities made them less of a girl or unacceptably different.

> *In sixth grade I went to the music teacher and told him I wanted to play the drums. He just laughed at me and said girls don't play the drums. I didn't understand why girls couldn't do the same things boys could. I was very innocent. It wasn't like I was this feminist at 12 years old.*
> *Ellen*

This type of humiliation and implicit rejection of a girl's unique interests can place a looming question mark inside her inquiring mind. She wonders whether it a good thing to be a girl, especially if she already carries a negative view of female sex roles. She may also wonder whether she is "normal," since she has no interest in traditional female roles. She might then ask herself, *Do I want to be a girl? Do I want to be like the other females in my life?* These questions and doubts around whether she is *acceptable and valuable* as a female—not the nonconforming interests in and of themselves—are what may create difficulty in her gender identity formation (Aardweg, 1997). It is important to stress that a girl's nonstereotypical gender characteristics and associated tomboyishness (such as preferring functional clothes and short hair) in no way directly diminishes her femaleness and can usually be viewed as normative variations of individual diversity,

"I WISH I WERE A BOY"

When a young girl answers the above questions in the negative, an overarching dissatisfaction with her femaleness lodges into her vulnerable self-image. Instead of being content with being a girl who plays soccer better than most boys, she begins to reject the notion of girlhood altogether. And if she has concluded that being a boy is just better all around, then the thought *I wish I were a boy* naturally follows.

When a young girl regularly dwells on a fantasy wish to be a boy, she may find it evolves into an obsessive desire. At this point, all is not well. Beyond simply preferring and therefore naturally pursuing stereotypical masculine interests because of her inborn gifting, she may intentionally develop or strengthen masculine attitudes and behaviors to escape from her dreaded girlhood or anxiety-laden female roles.[8]

So while other tomboyish girls are casually dressing in masculinized clothing, these girls begin to forcefully insist on boys' clothing (and mannerisms and behaviors such as urinating while standing) with a simultaneous *intense aversion* to looking or acting like a girl. Many may unequivocally identify with a male aggressor, becoming preoccupied with power, aggression and protection fantasies. At this point they are most likely experiencing deep-seated gender identity confusion. Indeed, many women with SSA report a failure to integrate a solid gender identity. Like girls with Gender Identity Disorder (*DSM-IV-TR*, 302.6),[9] these girls found safety or possible relief from anxiety by identifying with and fully assuming male roles. Nicole remembers modeling her brother by going outside, taking her shirt off and spitting: "My brother was cool, and people liked him, so I wanted to be like him." Connie remembers being the big bad cowboy, or being the brother or father when playing house. At Halloween, Cathy once dressed as Peter Best, the drummer. Another time she was a football player. She says it was just more comfortable to be in that mode.

A girl may also receive social reinforcement for her masculinized appearance and roles. And to the extent that her attachments with others are based on a male role, her gender identity confusion becomes an integral part of her attachment system and, therefore, means of survival.[10]

In a book written about lesbian women who were tomboys as girls, the editors of *Tomboys: Tales of Dyke Derring-do* note that for many women, being a

---

[8]Lillian Faderman (1991), in offering a literal historical look at lesbianism, reports that in the 1960s, many lesbians were uncomfortable with the weak, passive, powerless traditional female role and did indeed form an underlying masculine gender identity, which often preceded lesbian sexuality.

[9]It has been found that "gender identity disorder in childhood is strongly associated with subsequent homosexuality" (Zucker & Bradley, 1995, p. 25).

[10]In comparing tomboys with nontomboy girls, researchers Williams, Goodman and Green (1985) discovered that tomboys experienced significantly less physical contact with their mothers during the first year of life, were less likely to model their mothers, preferred their fathers over their mothers, and had mothers who were rated as less feminine than mothers of nontomboys and who were primarily responsible for discipline and family social planning, possibly pointing to an absent or passive father.

tomboy was more than simply acting or looking a bit boyish; it was "a source of strength that enabled them to survive . . . sexual abuse, prejudice, social disapprobation, familial dysfunction, and other assaults on selfhood" (Yamaguchi & Barber, 1995, p. 13). One self-acclaimed lesbian says that the tomboy "was the piece of me . . . who kept me alive and later nudged all of me—not just my head, but my heart and body too—into that leap of faith called lesbianism" (Mullins, 1995, pp. 48-49). Rejecting a purely genetic explanation of lesbianism, she suggests that her lesbianism resulted from a complex process that unfolded beneath the level of her consciousness, somehow intricately built on her extreme tomboy self (p. 48).

Many of my clients, after assuming an extreme tomboyish appearance and masculinized identity (often including a boy's nickname), were mistaken as boys or heard derogatory comments about their appearance, further confounding their gender identification process. Lynn, a client of mine, said that although she always wanted to be a boy, it bothered her when people *thought* she was a boy. And Mary, another of my clients, said that her mother's efforts to domesticate her by criticizing her masculinized appearance only strengthened her inner resolve to become even more like a boy.

DEFAULT IDENTIFICATION WITH THE MASCULINE AND LACK OF PSYCHOSEXUAL DIFFERENTIATION

So with whom did these women truly identify? Historical and current literature and research on female homosexuality commonly suggest that many women with SSA identified with their fathers as opposed to their mothers.[11] While these women certainly modeled themselves after boys and men, I question to what extent they actually *emotionally* identified with them. The mirroring process of identification builds on a foundation of secure attachment, admiration and mutual respect. As mentioned above, even those girls who were admittedly close to their dads rarely subjectively experienced their dads' warm engagement or respect based on their true unique self. I would also suggest that in the instances where a girl reportedly identified with rather than differ-

---

[11] See Jacobs (1990); Saghir & Robins (1973); Socarides (1968, 1978); van Eeden-Moorefield & Lindsey (2005). Dissenting reports suggest that women with SSA were not close to either parent (Thompson, Schwartz, McCandless & Edwards, 1973, p. 125) and therefore did not want to be like or identify with either of them (MacIntosh, 2002). In fact, some studies show that women with SSA identified with their fathers less often than even heterosexual women (Bell, Weinberg & Hammersmith, 1981, p. 133).

entiated from her father, she did so out of necessity—perhaps looking for a sense of power (safety) in an effort to overcome the felt helplessness or anxiety within the relational dynamic with her mother.[12] These types of *default* identification are defensive maneuvers, a desperate attempt to survive, and cannot be interpreted as a nourishing or genuine identification.

If a girl defensively identifies with her father (or the masculine) as a means of surviving her fragile sense of self, her sexual differentiation process will be further confounded. It is well-established that fathers have a pivotal influence on both boys' and girls' developing notions of maleness and femaleness and gender identity: a boy's secure attachment with dad provides the support for his sexual differentiation with mom; a girl's secure attachment with dad provides the support for her sexual differentiation with him. Whether or not a girl is also actively disidentifying or detaching from her femaleness, this lack of sexual differentiation with her dad may disallow her from accepting her body or gender identity as distinctly female.

Many women with SSA had a deep sense of inferiority and a belief that something was intrinsically wrong with them in terms of their femaleness possibly as early as age 3 or 4. Profound confusions and even cross-gendered thoughts about their body parts were often formational. Lynn says that she thought she would be cute as a boy, but as a girl she was not. Jordan says that in her dreams she had a penis and was a man.[13]

Although not all women with SSA struggle with such profound gender confusion, they usually have an underlying discomfort, insecurity or distorted perception of femininity.[14] In the current cultural milieu, there is a trend to mini-

---

[12]Quinodoz (1989) suggests that a daughter unable to healthily separate or identify with her mother will preserve "the father by way of a melancholic type of identification with the aim of upholding the cohesion of the ego" (p. 57). "She uses this identification [with father] to achieve a certain detachment from the maternal imago in its more dangerous and forbidding aspects," helping her to still sustain a sense of *subjective identity* (McDougall, 1980, p. 87).

[13]Based on their retrospective reports, some of my clients may have met most of the criteria for the official diagnosis of childhood Gender Identity Disorder (GID). Zucker and Bradley (1995), leading specialists in childhood GID, note several common factors within the lives and families of girls with GID that parallel those in the lives and families of many women with SSA: e.g., insecure attachment patterns, parental difficulty with affect regulation, maternal depression or lack of availability, rigid gender roles and parental conflict. Innate characteristics of the girls include acute sensitivities to parental affect and need for help; difficulty in forming emotional connection with mother; gender non-conforming interests; and identification with the "aggressor," usually dad (see pp. 253-64).

[14]Paulk (2003) reports that 90% of the 265 women she surveyed "felt somewhere from ambivalent to greatly disliking being a girl" (p. 248). Lesbian women report significantly more often than heterosexual women that they "felt like a man or boy" (Phillips, Psych & Over, 1995, p. 13).

mize or ignore the reality of gender, as if we were truly androgynous or nongendered beings. Images of male and female are becoming clouded with mixed or cross-gender images and personas, which means that young women—some of whom are already struggling to identify with mother and differentiate from father—are encouraged to view this assortment of gendered images as a legitimate and viable option for modeling and drawing forth meaning for their own ultimate identity. Sadly, this cultural ambiguity will likely further confuse the next generation of young women as they develop sexually.

TRAUMA AND SEXUAL ABUSE

Trauma and sexual abuse do not directly cause female SSA, contrary to common assertions. Some women with SSA have a history of childhood sexual abuse (CSA), such as Abby; some do not, such as Pamela.[15] Yet many women like Pamela still struggle with trust, low self-esteem, shame, mood disorders, and identity and intimacy issues—all common symptoms of sexual abuse. Emotional enmeshment can produce some of these same confusions and symptoms,[16] but many of my clients with these symptoms also lack enmeshment within their history. I have also never felt comfortable going on a witch hunt, so to speak, to uncover repressed memories or potentially denied or minimized experiences, for I believe there is yet another explanation.

Dr. Colin Ross (2000), a trauma specialist, remarks that it is possible for a person to grow up in an average family with neither physical neglect nor physical or sexual abuse and yet still bear the symptom profile of trauma (p. 76), such as depression, anxiety, post-traumatic stress disorder, somatic symptoms or relationship difficulties and disturbances of self (Gold & Seifer, 2002, p. 61). Challenging the prevailing definition of trauma in the *Diagnostic and Statistical Manual of Mental Disorders*, Ross (2000) explains that

> trauma can be *subtle* [italics added], or it can stretch the boundaries of the term. Harsh criticism, emotional absence, punitive perfectionism, borderline double binds, and other parental pressures are not usually thought of as "trauma," but they can certainly have a traumatic impact on development. (pp. 212-13)

---

[15]It is, however, acknowledged that most females growing up in modern or postmodern cultures do experience some level of indirect sexual abuse due to the sexualized nature of mainstream media and culture.

[16]See *The Emotional Incest Syndrome* by Love & Robinson (1990).

He notes that for many patients who present with multiple clinical diagnoses,[17] most fundamental are "the errors of omission by the parents, not the errors of commission. . . . The deeper trauma is the absence of normal love, affection, attention, care, and protection. The trauma is not being special to mom and dad" (p. 71). He concludes that *the truest kind of trauma is the disruption of a child's attachment systems*.[18] In light of my clients' subjective *experience* of insecure attachments and assumed dysfunctional familial roles, it is understandable why so many of them may suffer the effects of severe trauma.

Of course many women with SSA do recall and report classical childhood trauma and sexual abuse. Several studies have shown that the prevalence rates of CSA[19] are higher among lesbian populations (30-56%)[20] when compared to women in the general population (15-32%).[21] Lechner, Vogel, Garcia-Shelton, Leichter and Steibel (1993), and Wise, Zierler, Krieger and Harlow (2001) discovered that women with CSA are more likely to have adult homosexual experiences than women without CSA.

Women with SSA who are victims of sexual abuse report a variety of experiences,[22] ranging from rape, paternal or maternal incest, and abuse by another family member (male or female) to one or two abusive memories involving boys close to their same age. Perhaps because of their deep sensitivity and insecure gender identity, even a single violation often

---

[17]Several studies confirm a high comorbidity rate among gay and lesbian people: Cochran, Sullivan & Mays (2003); Sandfort, de Graaf, Bijl & Schnabel (2001); Warner, McKeown, Griffin, Johnson, Ramsay, Cort, et al. (2004). See "Psychopathology and Homosexuality" on book website at www .ivpress.com for more information.

[18]Attachment theorists agree: actual or perceived emotional neglect (such as that arising from detached and unresponsive mothers) is more harmful to children than physical neglect or other forms of abuse (Levy & Orlans, 1998).

[19]Note that the studies referenced below used various definitions of CSA as well as various age spans when defining "childhood."

[20]See Balsam, Rothblum & Beauchaine (2005); Hall (1996); Hughes, Haas, Razzano, Cassidy & Matthews (2000); Hughes, Johnson & Wilsnack (2001); Matthews, Hughes, Johnson, Razzano & Cassidy (2002); Roberts & Sorensen (1999); Tjaden, Thoennes & Allison (1999); Welch, Collings & Howden-Chapman (2000).

[21]See Anderson, Martin, Mullen, Romans & Herbison (1993); Fergusson, Lynskey, Horwood (1996); Lechner, Vogel, Garcia-Shelton, Leichter & Steibel (1993); Vogeltanz, Wilsnack, Harris, Wilsnack, Wonderlich & Kristjanson (1999). For more information on the prevalence and nature of sexual abuse among lesbian women, see the book website at www.ivpress.com.

[22]Balsam, Rothblum & Beauchaine (2005); Bradford, Ryan & Rothblum (1994); Cameron & Cameron (1995); Peters & Cantrell (1991); Tjaden, Thoennes & Allison (1999); Tomeo, Templer, Anderson & Kotler (2001).

clenched their self-hatred as a girl and secured their conviction that all boys (and men) are "pigs." It was the *context of the abuse,* how the trauma was processed and the presence (or lack) of any mediating factors (such as a supportive parent) that seemed to determine the nature and intensity of the abuse's negative effects on my clients.[23]

The girls who regularly played with boys often became targets for their male friends' childish curiosities and not-so-innocent overt sexual experimentation. Some girls were not allowed to lock bedroom or bathroom doors, were regularly confronted with male nudity within the home, or were required to hug and give backrubs to parents even if they expressed resistance. Many of my clients have openly admitted to *knowing* they prefer women to men because they have had their fill of "male slobbering" sexuality.

Many women with SSA also suffer the direct impact of what *is* classically defined as trauma and verbal, emotional or physical abuse.[24]

> When my mother died, I was 5, and I was immediately separated from my only sister. She was quite a bit older than me and had to go live somewhere else. Whenever I saw her and showed her affection, my stepmother would yell, "Quit acting stupid!" My sister got married at 17 and my stepmother would angrily whine, "Why doesn't she just take you? I wonder why she doesn't take you in?"
>
> Alaina

These girls took in a deep sense of shame and badness. In families characterized by chaos and violence, my clients were often the only ones trying to stop the insanity.

But regardless of the nature of the abuse, a girl's life and reality, as she knows it, will never be the same once she is sexually abused or traumatized. Her "home" now looks to her as if it has been hit by a hurricane. The walls are still standing (sometimes barely), but the roof is gone, as are the windows and

---

[23]The long-term effects of such trauma and abuse are further intensified within families that have insecure attachment patterns or lack family cohesion (Alexander, 1992, p. 185).

[24]Generally, women with SSA report far more maltreatment by their parents (Corliss, Cochran & Mays, 2002, pp. 1172-73) and greater levels of childhood abuse (Balsam, Rothblum & Beauchaine, 2005; Ross & Durkin, 2005; Tjaden, Thoennes & Allison, 1999) than women without SSA.

doors—leaving her desolate and exposed. Typical of many children facing abuse or trauma, these girls dealt with the physical, emotional and psychological wreckage of their lives *all alone*, fueling their independent persona. And finally, many of them eventually questioned God, growing in mistrust and misperceptions of his character and care. But there is still more that assails many of my client's ongoing effort to survive.

FEW CHILDHOOD GIRL FRIENDS

Because her mother worked, Margaret was taken care of by her grandmother. At times, Margaret also lived with her aunt. At six-and-a-half, her parents divorced, so she moved to another town with her mother. A year later they moved to California and within a year moved again to Wyoming, where they stayed with her grandparents until they found a home of their own. But only two or three months after they found their own place, they moved again. At age 9, Margaret moved to Idaho, living with a relative until they found a permanent place. That "permanent" place lasted another year or so before they moved again.[25] In reflection, Margaret admits that as a child she was very unsettled and never had any friends.

Women with SSA report lower levels of social involvement and fewer close girlfriends during grade-school years than other women.[26]

> *I remember noticing Suzie and Monica. They were best friends. So I asked myself, Why don't I have a best friend like that? Here are Debbie and Martha, Linda and Gabrielle. But I was hanging out with Tom and Benny and Ricky and all these other boys. I didn't have a best girl friend and I didn't understand why. I wanted that.*
> Connie

Many of my clients knew they did not fit in with the other girls. Some say that was fine—they "didn't want to do stupid girl stuff anyway." But their defensiveness betrays deep loss and pain. They often felt helpless because they couldn't figure out why they felt so different or why they couldn't make or keep

---

[25]Multiple family moves are common in many of my clients' childhoods.

[26]Bell et al. (1981, p. 15); Gundlach & Riess (1968, 1973); Van Wyk & Geist (1984). Nontraditional or gender nonconforming girls typically relate best to boys, tend to be loners, and do not mix socially as easily as traditional girls do (Green, Williams & Goodman, 1982).

friends.[27] Many can recount multiple instances where they were intentionally ostracized, betrayed or teased by the other girls.

Terri Apter and Ruthellen Josselson, in their book about female friendships, capture the tragedy of this type of isolation: "When we come to fear that we have no friend who can understand the muddled or unsightly aspects of our character, we imprison ourselves with psychological symptoms or lapse into depression" (1998, p. 110). In general, besides feeling depressed, my clients felt unknown, insecure and entirely ineffective in terms of finding and sustaining relationships. This fed their negative self-image and growing lack of self-esteem, especially given how significantly a sense of relational competence contributes to positive self-esteem in developing females. What little self-esteem my clients had as girls likely came from external achievement and performance rather than from relational success.

> *I became friends with this really cool girl. I couldn't even believe she would want me for a friend. One night I had her over for a sleepover. I had this urge to touch her and felt very ashamed and embarrassed. So I cut off the friendship, for no reason. Well, actually I knew the reason: I was a bad person. She tried to reconnect but I just gave her the cold shoulder, kind of like an "I don't really care how you feel" attitude. But truthfully, I was devastated for over two years!*
>
> *Sam*

Even though they were bored by what girls typically did or talked about, they still felt the loss of never belonging. A sense of inclusion is extremely important to a girl's ability to receive and integrate her feminine identity.[28] Similarly, in adolescence many were not privy to wearing makeup, high-heeled shoes or nylons, nor did they necessarily want to be. Yet they still had a sense of being on the outside looking in,[29] missing out on the important stage of

---

[27]Yarhouse, Brooke, Pisano and Tan (2005) found that "feeling different" was a significant theme among a small sample of young men and women struggling with SSA, often beginning as early as 7 years old. Yarhouse, Tan and Pawlowski (2005) made a similar finding.

[28]For girls to become themselves, they need other girls "to serve as models, to nurture them, to dare them to scale the walls of convention. And to become fully themselves, they need to set limits with and define themselves independently of those friends" (Sheehy, 2000, p. 167).

[29]In her bestseller *Reviving Ophelia: Saving the Selves of Adolescent Girls*, Mary Pipher (1994) remarks that girls who are plain in their appearance are often left out of social life (p. 56).

gender socialization or learning *how* girls "played" or conversed.[30]

Their growing need for a childhood or adolescent female friend, not to mention their lingering need for the "home" of mother and "home" of self, often launched these girls into a relational desperation, which meant they would be friends with just about anybody who was available. Later in adolescence, many of their friendships began to show signs of possessiveness and growing dependency.

SAME-SEX ADMIRATIONS

If a developing girl experiences underlying depression and anxiety, unconsciously missing her primal "home" with mother (and father), deprived of female friendship and confused about her own femaleness (possibly combined with a growing fear of males)—it seems normal that she would grow restless and long deeply for that which she intuits she needs.

> *By fourth or fifth grade I had a crush on one of my teachers. I wanted so much to just be loved and appreciated. I wanted to feel worthy by someone I looked up to—not just anyone. I wanted affirmation from someone I thought was important. I have always been drawn to very attractive and intelligent women, women I admire.*
>
> *Shari*

Older women, school teachers, pretty and popular girls at school, mothers of girls her age—all become the object of a young girl's affection. They appear to her larger than life and take on iconic meaning as females who can fill or resolve her inner and relational deficits and confusions. Many women with SSA admit that, often as early as 4 or 5 years old, they admired or daydreamed about a special woman or girl. They wanted to spend time with them and be noticed, liked or loved. These fantasized relationships were certainly unconscious attempts at mirroring and identification.

---

[30]Sandy Sheehy (2000), in her book *Connecting: The Enduring Power of Female Friendship*, explains that it is through female childhood friendships that girls gain opportunities to experience mutuality, practice empathy and develop socially; in fact, she claims that female friendships, in general, provide the *most* fertile ground for female development. "It is probable that, for women at all life stages, relational needs are primary and that healthy, dynamic relationships are the motivating force that propels psychological growth" (Surrey, 1991a, p. 37).

A girl may also begin to rely on her masculinized identity to win the affections of another girl with whom she longs to be close (McDougall, 1980, p. 137). By age 11 or 12, Joyce would imagine herself as the heroic man whenever she watched romantic movies. She identified with him because he always "got the woman." Lauren says that when she was in junior high, she would imagine fighting off the enemies of her special, admired female friend; she would be the hero and maybe even be rewarded with a kiss.[31] One of my adolescent clients admitted that she knows that many of her girlfriends (i.e., romantic partners) do not feel loved by their dads, so she becomes the "best" dad or man that they ever had. She proudly announced to me, "They can't resist me."

GLANCING BACKWARD TOWARD "HOME"

Many researchers note that it is still common for an adolescent girl to consider her mother to be the most important person in her life. In fact, the desire to have even more connection often grows throughout later adolescence (Batgos & Leadbeater, 1994, p. 159). Fathering is also indispensable throughout a daughter's developmental stages. Having a continuing close relationship with father is a significant contributor to an adolescent daughter's sense of well-being (Popenoe, 1996, p. 149).[32] Sadly, many of my clients continued to experience emotional distance in their relationships with their parents.[33] This does not necessarily mean that a mother (or father) was not loving or available; it may be instead that the girl's own defensive maneuvers and unconscious disidentifications prevent her from opening up to her parents' love. I have spoken with many parents who are currently attempting to repair a healthy connection with an adolescent daughter with SSA. They are often quickly discouraged, however, as

---

[31]Friedman and Downey (1993a) assert that "sexual behavior in humans is greatly influenced by gender identity" (p. 1174). A girl who doesn't feel like a girl or identify with femaleness—but feels more like a boy and identifies easier with maleness—may naturally begin to view emotional connection or closeness with other girls from a romanticized or sexualized lens.

[32]Female developmental theorists note that even for college-age women, a healthy relationship with their parents "remains the core out of which a positive sense of relational self-esteem emerges" (Kaplan, Gleason & Klein, 1991, p. 127) and "a healthy capacity for relationships with her peers" (p. 127).

[33]Girls who experience emotional distance in their relationship with their parents "are, by and large, the most inhibited and constricted in their movement toward evolving new and intimate relationships with their peers and are most uncertain of their own capacities as relational being" (Kaplan, Gleason & Klein, 1991, p. 127). In a comparative study of 524 lesbian, 143 bisexual and 637 heterosexual women, Koh and Ross (2006) found that lesbian women "were 97% more likely to have experienced teenage stress than heterosexual women" (p. 43).

they encounter what seems to be insatiable neediness (endless demands for their time or money) or an extreme hypersensitivity to the slightest mistake, such as the incorrect use of a term (according to their daughter). One minute the daughter might call her mother "mommy" and want to cuddle, but the next minute she is yelling and accusing her mother of not caring. Many parents say they aren't merely "walking on eggshells," they are gingerly tiptoeing on eggshells so volatile or unpredictable is their relationship with their daughters.

THE SHOCK OF PUBERTY

By the time they reach puberty, these girls are neither expecting nor prepared for the advent of womanhood. They may still be modeling and hanging with the boys, mirroring dad and completely disinterested in anything related to the female realm. If they subconsciously fear dad or men in general, they may also fear sexuality and their own sexual development.

Many of my clients were shocked and devastated when they started their periods or noticed their growing breasts.[34] Some of their mothers tried to prepare their active, disinterested daughters; others did not. I suspect that this latter group of mothers had not been adequately prepared by their own mothers.

> *I remember when I started my period. I came out of the bathroom, looked out into the living room at my family sitting there watching TV and asked myself, Who's going to handle this? I put on my coat and walked to the store and shoplifted sanitary napkins. It wasn't until a few months later that a friend of mine, fearing I'd be arrested for shoplifting, called and told my mother I had started my period.*
>
> *Diane*

Some women report that well into adolescence and sometimes adulthood, they were grossed out or turned off by the thought of kissing boys or dating and were generally embarrassed by sexual talk or overt sexualized behavior.[35] Many

---

[34]In comparing the feelings about menstruation among 226 lesbian women and 234 nonlesbian women, Gundlach and Riess (1968) discovered that "fewer of those who became Lesbians in later life welcomed this compelling mark of femaleness as a sign of maturation into womanhood" (p. 223).

[35]Gundlach and Riess (1973) mention that many women with SSA "are burdened with feelings of little self-worth, compounded with fright or suspicion of any kind of intimacy, especially sexual" (p. 167).

were more interested in sports and academics than any type of romance. Their apprehensions and focused interests stood in contrast to most of their female peers, who were beginning to explore the opposite sex and even pair up with boys. My clients were left believing that "normal" girls talk about boys and primp for their attention and so concluded that they must not be "normal."

I do not believe that these hesitations or fears were indicators of an inborn same-sex sexual orientation. I believe that these girls were simply delayed in their sexual development. They were still occupied with negotiating friend-ships with girls and perhaps "finding" themselves as one of the girls. Because they had not yet established a firm foundation for their own identity and a sense of belonging within the world of females, they were not ready to engage or focus their natural adolescent curiosity and surging sexual drives on the opposite sex. Keep in mind that up until now, these young women may have seen boys as platonic pals and baseball teammates. Kissing boys would have been like kissing their brothers.

> *I dated one guy early in high school. He went to kiss me and I gave him my cheek. Later, in my senior year, another guy tried to kiss me and he did. It freaked me out, so I pushed him away and exclaimed, "What are you do-ing? This is freaky! Don't do that!" I was so naive and scared. In my mind, if you kiss, then you will have sex and then babies start popping out. I wasn't interested in kissing girls at this point either. I wasn't sexually in-terested in anyone.*
>
> *Connie*

DISPARAGING SELF AND BODY IMAGE

If these girls hadn't felt different already, they most certainly did at this stage.[36] Bombarded by the culturally ideal female image—thin, heftily breasted, blond haired, blue eyed and scantily clad—they felt even more de-fective and defeated. Not only do many of these women lack the body type and genetic traits to mimic this image (as do most women), but they are also far too self-conscious and ashamed about their bodies to even consider cloth-

---

[36]As already noted, far more women with SSA report feeling different (including feeling sexually dif-ferent) while they were growing up than non-SSA women (Bell, Weinberg & Hammersmith, 1981, p. 157). Paulk (2003) observes a significant positive correlation between when these women "felt dif-ferent" and when they first experienced a same-sex attraction.

ing styles that would be revealing. They may continue with an extreme tomboyish look or select androgynous clothing in adolescence, often choosing outfits that hide their developing female form. In addition, because these intelligent young women value human dignity, justice and equality, they understand that the sexual objectification of women damages not only women, but our larger culture as well. They are apt to view women who cooperate with these trends with disdain, even as they believe something is intrinsically wrong with themselves.

Most of the women who were able to integrate an external feminine style in their youth still disqualified themselves, believing that they were ugly, that they could never look or act like a real girl or that a nice guy would never find them attractive. They often carry this sense of disqualification well into adulthood.

> *One day on campus, I saw a guy whom I had dated a few times. He looked fabulous, so I remarked, "You sure are looking nice today. Why are you so dressed up?" He flirtatiously answered, "Well, I'm looking for a girlfriend. Do you know anybody that's available?" His comment went right over my head. I thought, Nobody that good looking is going to be interested in me. At that moment, all my desire for a relationship with him faded away.*
>
> *Linda*

Besides feeling ugly, my clients navigated their social network with a multitude of hidden beliefs that they were an embarrassment, an outcast, a peculiar misfit, stupid, worthless or even "bad," for example. Gundlach and Riess (1973) speak of one lesbian woman who felt so flawed and worthless that she wished she could have died in the place of her father (who had passed away when she was a child) if only then her mother would have loved her. In their case study, they report that this woman was literally

> preoccupied with dislike for herself as being dumb, athletic (and a girl!) and ugly. She has no sense of self, no feeling that she can express her will. She always goes along with what others say and never did a thing on her own until college. (pp. 166-67)

As young adults, many of these women merely floated through life, completing (usually quite successfully) the next task or stage of school, career development or even marriage, without knowing why or who they truly were.

DISAPPOINTING OR NEGATIVE EXPERIENCES WITH YOUNG MEN

Most of the women with whom I have worked eventually have, as adolescents or young adults, *some* desire to be noticed and genuinely liked and appreciated by a male. But these women were not interested in just any male. They saw most of their girl friends chasing after guys who appeared to be self-centered immature boys only interested in sex. My clients wanted to find an intelligent, caring, respectful young man, and they wanted to build an emotional relationship with him before becoming physically involved. But their dreams were often met with severe disappointment,[37] betrayal and even violation.

> *I was the tomboy, never the pretty one. My friends were the pretty ones. So when we'd be out, the guys would look at them and ask them out, and there I would be left, sitting at the table. So I finally quit going to places like dance clubs. I had lots of crushes but they never turned into anything.*
>
> *Nicole*

> *I hung out with the guys until they started liking the girls. One of my best male friends asked a girl to go steady with him. It crushed me. Its not that I wanted to go steady, but it just seemed strange that out of the blue he would ask someone else.*
>
> *Joyce*

Many women with SSA were shocked and horrified by their first innocent kiss, perhaps due to a delay in their sexual development. They felt such a deep sense of violation that they now process the experience as if it were a violent assault. Others just became increasingly confused about men and how to "do" relationship with them.

---

[37]Bell, Weinberg and Hammersmith (1981) found that fewer women with SSA, compared with non-SSA women, enjoyed their dating experiences with men; Jay and Young (1979) report that 55% of 250 lesbians found their past experiences with men to be negative; another 21% found them neutral. Nichols (1982, 1987) suggests that these negative reactions may be due to the initial lack of authentic sexual interest on the part of the women. Brannock and Chapman (1990) found no significant difference between heterosexual or homosexual women in terms of negative experiences with men.

> *After about the fifth kiss over the course of the night, I finally pulled away
> and said, "Bill, I don't understand. I barely know you, and if this is what
> you do on the first date, I don't want to find out about the second!" He
> scared me to death!*
>
> *Linda*

Many of the younger women with whom I work describe extremely negative experiences with or disparaging attitudes toward young men. Some have
had their hearts broken by their first love. Their mothers report that they were
inconsolable, often becoming depressed and hopeless about life itself. Some of
my clients have been date raped by their lifelong best male friend or are privy
to the male abuses waylaid on most of their girlfriends. Many of them have
been the only support for a friend having a secret abortion. They are acutely
aware that the majority of the boys their age are addicted to pornography and
lack the social graces typically attributed to gentlemen. My adolescent clients
often announce, "I just can't deal with the guy thing right now." They pour
themselves into female friendships, academics or extracurricular activities. Yet
they harbor a growing ambivalence toward young men.

SATISFYING RELATIONSHIP WITH A YOUNG WOMAN

During late adolescence or young adulthood,[38] my clients often met another
female with whom they felt an immediate connection. Typically, both women
had similar histories and outlooks on life. Both were strong intellectually or
athletically and confident in their achievements and performance, yet they still
doubted their own value; neither had a solid sense of self. But when they met,
there was often an instantaneous and shocking moment of recognition. They
saw themselves in each other's eyes! And as they mirrored each other, they felt
known and understood in ways that they had never formerly experienced.[39]

---

[38]Historically, women with SSA report having their first same-sex relationship much later in life than
do men with SSA (Van Wyk & Geist, 1984, p. 527). They are usually 18 years or older (Jay & Young,
1979; Michael, Gagnon, Laumann & Kolata, 1994, p. 176; Saghir & Robins, 1973, p. 222) or in college (Diamond, 1998, p. 14). This age however, seems to be statistically decreasing over time.
Warner, McKeown, Griffin, Johnson, Ramsay, Cort, et al. (2004) report that almost 45% of 430 predominantly homosexual women were aware of their homosexuality by 16 years old.

[39]Apter and Josselson (1998) note that "the soul-filling pleasures of being understood by someone who
feels, in some important ways, like our twin are so intense that for those lucky enough to find such a
friend, the illusion of sameness can become highly seductive" (p. 83).

Almost immediately and simultaneously, they loved and felt loved. They accepted and felt accepted—perhaps for the first time in their life. Something released and relaxed within each young woman as she realized, *She is like me, so I must be OK.* These young women finally found what they describe as "home."

Not all female same-sex relationships form in such an immediate or explosive fashion, but most are still established on a *sensed* basis of trust (she feels safe), respect (she is admirable) and affirmation (I feel special). This deeply affectionate connection between two lonely young women can stir one's human desire for closeness, including physical closeness. Twenty years ago, two women may have paused before they took the next step into physical intimacy, but in our current culture, children and young adults are encouraged to explore all forms of physical affection and sexual intimacy. Sensualized or sexualized touch between friends of either the same or opposite sex no longer carries any stigma, although it may still carry psychological and emotional implications.

> *I had been emotionally involved with many women, but when I became physically involved with Suzie, something kind of cemented in me. It was the touch. It felt addictive.*
>
> *Jordan*

Affectionate touch, even apart from sexual arousal, serves as a vital medium for increasing a sense of attachment *and* providing affirmation of one's self and body. Between two women who share many of the experiences discussed above, it typically results in a powerful (and natural) feeling of well-being. Having felt such pleasure and comfort, they may think it foolish to deny themselves the closeness for which they hunger.

> *We had been friends for quite a while. When a physical relationship started, I was really scared. I thought, This isn't right. I'm not supposed to do this. But it was comfortable and natural. But what made it even more powerful was that we were both exploring sexuality for the first time. It felt very safe. The word lesbian never even crossed my mind.*
>
> *Connie*

If a woman experiences the electricity of a female-to-female connection during the same time period that she experiences distress or difficulty in her male relationships, she may begin to symbolize relational or sexual pleasure with women rather than men. But of even greater force in establishing a pattern of same-sex preference—or ultimately *orientation*—is the repeated pleasurable experience of same-sex closeness and sensuality. Researchers Van Wyk and Geist (1984) explain:

> Once arousal to a particular type of stimulus occurs, it tends quite rapidly to form a pattern. . . . To the extent that the repeated experience . . . is arousing, stimulating, and pleasing, it tends to continue to be repeated and elaborated on and thus gains values [*sic*] as an erotic stimulus. More by neglect than anything else, other types of experiences and fantasies soon begin to pale by comparison, and unless a person becomes involved in another type of sexual experience that for whatever reason is particularly exciting, he or she tends to continue to fantasize about and participate in the first type of satisfying or arousing activity to the exclusion of others. (p. 536)

A woman's initial same-sex experience can therefore be understood as one of the factors that might eventuate a same-sex orientation or identity within an adolescent or young woman.[40] In fact, it may only take one such same-sex experience for a young woman to fully embrace and even publicly own a lesbian identity, especially given the popularity of bisexuality and the acceptance of homosexuality amongst the younger generation.[41] Further, for a young woman who is seeking differentiation or separateness from her parents or their values or who is looking for a consolidated core identity, "becoming a lesbian" might unconsciously appear to meet all goals.

However, for many other young women, especially those rooted in a faith tradition, these early experiences are not so welcome; they often create turbulence during an already confusing time of sexual development and identity consolidation.[42] They are shocked by their behavior and feel deeply disturbed

---

[40]Laumann, Gagnon, Michael and Michaels (1994) report that women who have sex between puberty and age 18 with a female partner almost always have sex with a woman after age 18 (p. 296).

[41]A *Time* article on gay teens points out how kids can now observe openly gay teens, real and fictional, in a myriad of prime-time television shows, books, magazines and websites, and can participate in gay chat rooms and campus clubs. Not surprisingly, the article also reports that "kids are disclosing their homosexuality with unprecedented regularity—and they are doing so much younger" (Cloud, 2005, p. 44).

[42]Yarhouse, Brooke, Pisano & Tan (2005); Yarhouse, Tan & Pawlowski (2005).

and ashamed of themselves. Because they fear judgment or rejection, many young women hide their same-sex experience and possible burgeoning same-sex feelings, increasing their sense of isolation.[43]

Yet as shocking or shaming as it might be, their first experience may be so compelling that they will do whatever it takes to hold on to the relationship, even if it means they must lie, deny basic needs or compromise moral values.

THE HEART OF FEMALE SAME-SEX ATTRACTION: A "HOME" AWAY FROM HOME

Women with SSA are not sexually attracted to *all* women.[44] While I cannot claim that every woman's same-sex attractions are based on subconscious material, most of the women with whom I work are selectively drawn and attracted to women who possess certain individual characteristics or relational traits that ostensibly, albeit unconsciously, promise to reduce or eliminate some internal deficit or conflict.

At the heart of female SSA is often an unconscious or symbolic search for mother, secure attachment, a sense of self, specialness, femininity, safety and fun. For example, one self-identified lesbian woman interviewed by Hope Edelman in her book *Motherless Daughters* admits that she sometimes wants to say to her lovers, "'Oh, I'm sorry. I was just thinking you were my mother. I hope you don't mind'" (1994, p. 169). Another lesbian woman confesses that she has avoided dating women because she's "hyperconscious of trying to reunite with her mother": "When I'm with a woman, there's always a transference going on" (p. 173).

A woman with SSA is often drawn to another women whom she admires for her beauty, strength, sense of purpose or other positive attributes. By becoming close and identifying with this special woman, she vicariously gains a sense of her own specialness and femininity. Abby reports that she falls in love with women who make her feel safe. "They were always physically bigger than

---

[43]Contrary to many gay affirmative points of view, I do not believe that the source of my client's internal conflict begins when they realize or integrate their same-sex feelings and orientation in the midst of a heterosexist or stigmatizing environment. As indicated above, most of their difficulties have much more longevity.

[44]In fact, female SSA can be conceptualized as a same-sex ambivalence, a simultaneous urge to draw close to some women and to distance or detach from others (Moberly, 1983). I believe that most women also struggle with opposite-sex ambivalence. For definitions and discussions, see "Confused About Both Sexes" on the book website at www.ivpress.com.

me. Yet I was always the protector. I was not going to let anyone hurt them. If they weren't hurt then I wouldn't hurt." A female-to-female relationship can also provide a symbolic means to avoid the perceived threat of men. Margaret Nichols (1990), a counselor and openly gay woman, writes that "lesbian relationships represent, above all, the interactions of women with each other in the absence of a male influence, or at least in a setting that is as free of male influence as one can get" (p. 356). More than once, a client has said, "I just want to have some fun." When they finally encounter a woman who is fun and adventurous and with whom they feel safe, they no longer feel like strangers in a foreign land; they have found "home."

A woman's drive to be close and intimate with other females, setting aside religious beliefs, appears to me as an innocent yet creative and adaptive strategy to further her own growth and development, to resolve deep inner conflicts and to fill legitimate unmet needs.[45] Unfortunately, these legitimate needs and developmental concerns are now confusedly intertwined with her natural romantic and sexual longings. For a woman to substantially alter her same-sex behaviors or relating, she will need to painstakingly disentangle these legitimate longings, fears and developmental issues from her adult sexual desire. Sexual desire is still a wonderful and legitimate force in her life, but it is misdirected if the underlying drive arises out of a primal need for mom or self.

Part two of this book offers guidance for therapists to help a woman gently unravel the cords that have previously defined her existence, cords that were woven into place years ago, perhaps even while she was in her mother's womb. She will need our patient and compassionate help and support as she navigates through the deep recesses of her own story and heart.

---

[45]A chronology of the developmental progression of female SSA can be found on the book website.

CHAPTER FIVE

Looking for Home
Depending on You for Me

To live as a child of God is to live with love and hope and growth,
but it is also to live with longing, with aching
for a fullness of love that is never quite within our grasp.

GERALD MAY, *ADDICTION AND GRACE*

Emmy is a young woman who lives with chronic depression and a persistent sense of emptiness. She sometimes questions whether life is even worth living. Although she has a good job and owns her own condo, she has few close friends. No one at her church has ever spoken about the kind of loneliness and emptiness she feels; most of the parishioners are married and appear happy. One day a new woman showed up at Emmy's work and smiled at her from across the office. To Emmy, the smile was like a morsel of food to her starving soul. She could hardly believe that someone noticed her, let alone bothered to smile at her. The following week, the new woman asked Emmy to join her for lunch. Emmy hesitated but finally said yes. Emmy felt awkward and unsure of herself at first, but she managed to get through lunch. That evening, something like hope began to stir within her. She felt warm and excited as she thought of this woman's kindheartedness. She couldn't sleep that night. All she could think about the next day was seeing her new friend. They bumped into each other and agreed to have dinner after work. Emmy discovered they had a lot in common. They talked well into the morning hours. Emmy's longing for intimacy, her hopes for companionship and her dreams of a fulfilling life were eagerly awakened.

HER RELATIONSHIPS ARE REAL

Before discussing the most common emotional dynamic of female same-sex relationships, I want to clarify that I am not suggesting these relationships lack any genuine or authentic meaning to these women. Many women with SSA have been harmed by the attitudes of some professionals and lay counselors who assume nothing good can come out of a homosexual relationship. While not negating the inherent difficulties in many of these relationships, I suggest that these women often experience elements of authentic friendship, genuine affection and even a sense of family. Such relationships may be providing the closest thing to intimacy, acceptance, tenderness and love that they have *ever* experienced. Within a relationship, a woman may

- have discovered her first best friend
- be genuinely liked, enjoyed, known and accepted for who she truly is
- be taken care of physically and financially for the first time in her life
- learn about feminine things from her friend
- grow and develop relationally and in self-understanding
- experience a genuine bolstering in her self-esteem
- gain a sense of family for the first time, especially if she is "adopted" into her partner's family
- build meaningful relationships with her partner's children or have children of their own
- build a community of mutual friends
- lead the other woman into a new or deeper relationship with God

To effectively support and understand my clients, I must spend time to understand both the depth of meaning provided by a relationship and the possible stabilizing force that a same-sex relationship may be playing in their lives (even if the relationship itself is unstable). When I do eventually address the real problems that may exist within the relationship, such as idealization or dependency, for example, I do so with respect and sensitivity. Further, the genuine relational experiences described above are likely to present as genuine losses or points of grief should the relationship end.

I can remember Lynn coming home and our being so excited to see each other. We would just hold each other. I wanted to make dinner. I wanted to clean the house. I wanted to do all of these things just because I loved her and wanted to do them for her—or we would do them together.

Nicole

In the opening stage of therapy, I do not attempt to analyze my client's relationship, minimize its realness or sleuth out the unhealthy or dysfunctional parts until my client expresses a desire for me to do so. Instead, I listen and empathize with whatever sentiments she shares as she talks about her relationship and friend. I trust that my client is on a journey of self-discovery. I know that, in time, she will take honest inventories of her self, others and her relationships.

EMOTIONAL DEPENDENCY

Within weeks of meeting, Emmy and her new friend began a same-sex relationship that, although stormy, lasted for four years—an endless cycle of pursuing closeness yet simultaneously engaging in distancing behaviors, even to the point of overt hostile and aggressive behavior. Both women knew the relationship needed to end, but Emmy was overwhelmed by old feelings of isolation and loneliness. She had poured what little self she had into her partner, thinking it would secure her partner's ongoing affection. She had nothing left and no safe place to go when it all ended. Fearing she could not survive alone, she made a renewed effort to please her partner. When her partner finally moved out, Emmy lost her will to live—her life as she knew it was gone. After months of living with agonizing depression and sorrow, Emmy mustered up the strength to call me.

Even though there may have been genuine elements to Emmy's relationship, Emmy had unconsciously viewed her friend as a magical character: she thought her partner could meet some of her deepest and most primal needs. Unfortunately, when a woman like Emmy looks to another woman (or her connection with another woman) to survive or adapt to unresolved childhood deficits and traumas, she can inadvertently become extremely emotionally dependent on her friend and block or negate her own *autonomous* growth and healing process.

Lori Rentzel, in her excellent pamphlet titled *Emotional Dependency*, states that *"emotional dependency occurs when the ongoing presence and nurturing of another is believed to be necessary for personal security.* This nurturing might come in many different forms, such as attentiveness, listening, admiration, counsel, affirmation and time spent together" (1990, p. 7, italics in original). Dr. Carol Ahrens takes this discussion a step deeper, defining emotional dependency as "*a state* [italics added] in which a woman feels totally reliant on another woman for safety and functioning. . . . When a woman is emotionally dependent, she feels as though she literally cannot exist without the object of her dependency" (1991, p. 204).[1]

Dependency is a healthy construct in relationships to the extent that each party can mutually *rely* on the other when one's own resources are not adequate to face a besetting need or circumstance. In healthy relationships, a woman is not consciously or unconsciously consumed with her own developmental needs but is established and secure; she can tend and be tended to in a satisfying, mutual association. Emotional dependency, on the other hand, takes on the flavor of a childhood attachment. Attachment has been defined as "a state of emotional connection where the presence of the 'object' becomes related to a sense of well-being, security, and need gratification" (Surrey, 1991b, p. 61). While we all need a sense of secure attachment throughout our lives, securely attached adults are not chiefly driven by their primal attachment needs.

Many women with SSA are not able to exert healthy adult mutuality and *reliance;* they remain subject to the simultaneous pressures and influences of their unresolved attachment and dependency needs and differentiation processes. As one might imagine, these two forces—a need to attach and the seemingly opposing need to separate and differentiate—create incredible relational confusion and chaos, not to mention deep inherent relational instability.

Before reviewing the characteristics of emotional dependency, I want to further highlight the nature of a woman's vulnerability to dependent relationships.

---

[1]Theologically speaking, emotional dependency is often categorized as a spiritual bentness or a form of idolatry. This is based on the belief that anything or anyone we look to for a sense of life or identity can be considered a false god or idol since only the true God can give us these things. Mario Bergner, an Episcopal priest who ministers to women struggling with SSA, comments that

emotional dependency is an unmet need gone awry. The anxious clinging to women characterizing emotional dependency is a substitute for the real comfort of mother's arms, which is neither anxious nor clingy. For some women, the real aching need for maternal connection emerges only after emotional dependency is disengaged and named as the idolatry of women. (2004, p. 3)

SURVIVAL OF THE FITTEST

One of the conundrums I have faced in working with my clients over the years is the striking contrast between their well-developed, strong and competent external or public self and their fairly fragile and needy inner or private self. It is as if they have two selves: The *outer self* is competent, composed, strong, self-sufficient, intelligent, gifted, productive and achievement oriented. The *inner personal self* is insecure, needy, ashamed, lonely, weak and dependent and feels inadequate, worthless, afraid and desperately needy.

This apparent split has been documented in the literature on female homosexuality. In a case study of a woman with advanced degrees who was in gay affirmative therapy and diagnosed with social phobia, the therapist noted that her client's "domain of work somehow seemed different from other social contact." The client, Martha, "was more confident about her work identity than her personal, social identity. It was as if she were able to play the role of professional more easily" (Eckleberry-Hunt & Dohrenwend, 2005, p. 107). Similarly, Smalley, a therapist who works primarily with lesbian women, observes that many of her clients appear to be "integrated in their work and public identity. They are able to be their own person, to explore, to succeed, to achieve. In contrast, in their relationships there is hesitancy, bewilderment, and confusion" (1987, p. 130).

My clients' lives are so compartmentalized that their professional associates would be shocked if they knew that, at times, these women crumble emotionally because of their deep inner insecurity and loneliness. When confronted with a situation—outside of their professional realm—that requires heartfelt or personally vulnerable communication, many might experience tremendous inner anxiety and self-doubt. My clients attest to this apparent split, explaining that as long as they can avoid or sidestep uncomfortable "interpersonal" moments and primarily operate out of their intellectual or achieving (or over-achieving) side, they have some sense of an intact identity and avenue through which to relate.

> *I kept getting promotion after promotion because I kept giving and giving and giving. I knew how to perform and I knew how to please. Everyone in the company knew my name. So I sort of had an identity—but it wasn't my real identity.*
>
> *Abby*

Beverly Burch offers some explanation to the origin of this phenomenon. She describes a self-identified lesbian woman who, as a child,

> developed a rigid stance of self-sufficiency. There had really been no alternative for her, no possibility of getting her needs met because her mother was unavailable and too needy herself. Rather than being helped into a secure autonomy, she had had to be falsely independent at an early age and to identify with her father in some respects. Beneath this self-sufficiency, she felt incredibly weak and vulnerable, *although she was unaware of this until she'd been in therapy almost two years.* (1987, p. 137, italics added)

Once my clients recognize this weak, needy or tender inner part, they often want to rid themselves of it as soon as possible. However, the more a woman hides this shameful side, the more she may struggle with a sense of being unknown, unlovable and lost.

A VULNERABLE LITTLE GIRL WHO WANTS TO BE FOUND

This split creates a severe vulnerability in most women. Unconsciously, a woman's inner self—which is like a small, weak, fragile little girl—is screaming to be known and loved. It is often another woman, one who also exhibits external strengths while housing a hidden fragile side, that will recognize and appreciate the vulnerable tenderness within her. When she finally feels seen and known in her *entirety*, she may begin to feel whole, floating pleasurably within the river of her friends' attuned sensitivities and affirmations. Her previously negative self-images and disparaging feelings may begin to dissolve. As she opens herself to another who cares, she is pervaded with a sense of well-being and filled with glimpses of her own self-worth. She feels integrated but only through the loving gaze of another.

Unfortunately, she is neither permanently resolving her former negative feelings or self-images nor healthily integrating with her previously hidden, weak, frightened or vulnerable self. *It is only through her connection with her partner and the attention her partner provides that she feels such relief and subjective sense of value and change.* Without this other woman, she would literally be back to her "old" hated self.

Once a woman experiences these feelings of relief and a subjective sense of wholeness and self-worth, she may forget the fears and defenses that have fortified her tough external self. Instead, she begins to naturally and easily relate to her new friend out of her innocent, small and tender little-girl or internal self. Within her same-sex relationship, the strong, independent, competent woman begins to disappear. Her well-developed logic, analysis and superior ability to read people now become part of what is hidden and separated—so much so that even when she needs to gain objectivity in order to stabilize her overwhelming desires and emotions for this other woman, she is unable to do so. She is now, for all intents and purposes, cut off from the competent, adult self. Lost to her *true* strength and autonomy, a woman can easily slide into a consuming, enmeshed and desperately dependent relationship with her partner. It is this collapsed oneness and merger of two little-girl selves that characterizes many emotionally dependent female same-sex relationships.

> *Whenever I am in a relationship, I always feel like I am two separate people. I'm this 40-year-old intelligent, competent woman. Everyone thinks I have my life together. But then inside there's this 18-month-old child that is desperate. To continue to live in this split, I have to numb out. I have to live with a certain level of deception because the competent part of me knows that the 18-month-old is not going to get all of her needs met in this relationship.*
>
> *Ellen*

THE CHARACTERISTICS OF EMOTIONAL DEPENDENCY OR FUSION

Many writers and researchers refer to this common phenomenon of extreme closeness within lesbian relationships as "fusion," or "merger," or as a higher level of dyadic attachment or commitment (Renzetti, 1992) than that observed within relationships of gay men or heterosexual couples.[2] Nichols (1982) describes this closeness and dependency as being akin to "twinning" or to the "over-identification of monozygotic twins" (p. 60) and stresses that it is characterized by two female partners losing sight of their separate ego boundaries. So common is the presence of fusion in lesbian relationships that some therapists have simply concluded that it is a normative, albeit unique, factor (McCandlish, 1982).[3]

---

[2]See Falco (1991); Kaufman, Harrison & Hyde (1984); Nichols (1982; 1990); Pearlman (1989); and Roth (1984).

[3]Emotional dependency is common, but this is not to say that *all* lesbian relationships are emotionally dependent.

The following are the twelve most common characteristics of emotionally dependent same-sex relationships:

The relationship's rapid or extremely intense formation is often based on idealization. Dr. Bronwyn Anthony, a gay affirmative lesbian psychologist, discusses the tendency for lesbian women to "bond" almost overnight.[4] She claims that "it is a standing joke that 'two lesbians meet and next week they move in together' precisely because it is such a common occurrence" (1982, p. 51).[5] Sometimes all it takes to start a relationship is a mutual glance of recognition. Unfortunately, this mutual recognition is not so much a recognition of the other woman's unique identity, but a recognition of one's own heart's cry and identity struggles as mirrored in the other woman.[6] Nevertheless, a woman will experience this as finding her true self.

I know I was drawn to her because she was full of life. She was alive. Then I realized she liked me. Me! And then she always took care of me. Those are huge things for me. She was fun and I could completely be who I was. I could be silly. I could be—whatever I was that moment, I could be.

Teresa

This is not to discredit the genuine affirmation that a woman may be receiving from her new friend, but the intensity with which she responds to this affirmation exposes a deeper dynamic. Leanne Payne, a popular author of books on sexual brokenness and healing, discusses the idealization and associated passionate desire for closeness akin to the feeling of wanting to metaphorically eat or devour another. She refers to this dynamic as the "cannibal compulsion" (1984, p. 2). The myth of cannibalism is that the cannibal will acquire all admirable traits of the person being consumed: if you "eat" somebody,

---

[4]Nichols (1990) emphasizes how many gay women interpret sexual attraction as love and move very rapidly into a live-in commitment within weeks or even days. She admits that "the high dissolution rate of gay women's partnerships probably reflects to an extent the initial inappropriateness of partner choice" (p. 360).

[5]However, many same-sex relationships can arise slowly out of a woman's first "best" or close friendship.

[6]Jean-Michel Quinodoz, a practitioner and theorist on female homosexuality, notes that many women with SSA are really much more driven to identify with their partners than to "love" them (1989, p. 59). McDougall (1980) believes that "something which is missing in the inner object world" of many women with SSA "is thus sought in the partner: through identification with her, instinctual satisfactions and lost parts of the self are recovered" (p. 131).

you will become like them. Empty selves are the ones that hunger to consume another so that they can finally find a self. Sadly, if a woman unconsciously chooses to "devour" another to fill her empty self, she is essentially covering or resisting her own unique identity.

The relationship is about connection, not sex. Rarely do I find these women focusing on or becoming addicted to sexual behavior. Some researchers note that lesbian women report the lowest level of sexual exchange and desire of any pair-bonded relationship (Blumstein & Schwartz, 1983; Nichols, 1982, 1988a). In terms of physical behavior, my clients express much more of a desire to be *held* than to reach orgasm. Indeed, one might expect that a woman who is experiencing primal little-girl feelings or needs would have low or even absent sexual desire. Nevertheless, touch is a powerfully bonding behavior and, when introduced, will not just strengthen but often cement an attachment or emotionally dependent relationship between two women.

> *It was more important to have her in my life than it was to be physically affectionate. When she told me she no longer wanted sex, I said, "No problem. Whatever it takes to keep you close."*
> *Abby*

The relationship demands constant connection. It often appears that the highest goal of women within emotionally dependent relationships is to be with or be in constant contact with their partner. Attachment theorists stress that while "the goal of the attachment system is maintenance of proximity with the attachment figure, *from the perspective of the attached individual* [italics added], the goal is the regulation of a sense of *felt security* [italics in original]" (Bartholomew, Kwong & Hart, 2001, p. 197). The quintessential focus within an emotionally dependent relationship is not necessarily time with the other woman but rather the *felt sense of an ongoing and secure connection.* A woman unconsciously says to her partner, "My well-being and very life depends on my connection with you. If our connection is threatened in any way, I am in crisis. I am not OK." This obsession on the quality and continuity of their connection may reflect the primal stage of an infant's absolute dependency on her attachment to mother.

Without an established internal sense of self, a woman may come to depend on her partner's continual mirroring to maintain any sense of existence or valuable self. In other words, as long her partner is emotionally engaged and connected, she knows she exists and has value. But if that connection is broken, she may spiral into a separation anxiety that exposes her inner nothingness and worthlessness. Many women actually fear extinction or even death.[7]

To sustain this sense of primal security, a woman may behave uncharacteristically, such as calling her friend five times a day, secretly driving by her friend's house or workplace, casually showing up at her church, stalking her on the Internet or not letting her hang up the phone even though they have already talked for two hours.[8]

> *The women I have been with show me so much attention. They say they are not idolizing me but want to talk to me on the phone for three hours. I know it's not right, but it feels so good to have someone be that interested.*
>
> *Rhonda*

In addition to being conduits for a sense of primal security, emotionally dependent relationships are reflective of the intensity in adolescent female friendships. Adolescent girls commonly spend hours "connecting" with friends. They might sit at the computer sending multiple instant messages, chatting in a chatroom while talking on the phone (with call waiting) to another. This constant connection—a theme in both adolescent friendships and female SSA—provides a sense of belonging to a group of friends or at least to one significant other.

The relationship fosters enmeshment and loss of self. Sadly, an ironic dynamic begins to emerge within the same-sex bond. A woman looks to another in order to gain a sense of self or a sense of well-being, but in so doing, she actually loses the very thing she hopes to gain.[9] Nichols (1988a) asserts that

---

[7]The characteristics of "love addiction," as discussed by Mellody, Miller and Miller (2003) are strikingly similar to those of same-sex emotional dependency. I strongly recommend their book, *Facing Love Addiction*, as an additional resource on this issue. (For more information, see "Emotional Dependency and Love Addiction" on the book website at www.ivpress.com.)

[8]Pearlman (1989) notes, however, that the consequences of these distance-reducing behaviors include "individual restriction and limitation and an increasingly isolated and stagnant relationship system" (p. 82).

[9]Gilligan (1982) emphasizes that the balance between closeness and autonomous separateness or between maintaining one's identity while entering into deep intimacy, may be more difficult to achieve for women than men. For "we know ourselves as separate only insofar as we live in connection with others, and that we experience relationship only insofar as we differentiate other from self" (p. 63).

the closeness achieved in fused lesbian relationships is gained only through a sacrifice of individuality. Individual differences, dislikes, likes, and interests are suppressed in favor of the dyad; indeed, closeness comes to be defined as sameness. It is questionable, in fact, whether this type of closeness, paid for with the price of negating individuality, can even be defined as true intimacy. (p. 398)

In reflecting on her same-sex relationships, author Jeannette Howard asked herself, "I wonder how much of myself I have traded in order to feel fully loved" (2005, p. 80).

Ellen told me that she realized she changes her preference on eggs solely based on the preference of the woman she was with at the time. If her partner likes scrambled eggs, scrambled it is. But if her next partner likes over-easy eggs, over-easy become her favored choice as well. As another woman described, she became a chameleon.[10]

> I wonder how many years of my life I have given up to live out another woman's identity.
>
> Diane

The more a woman essentially ignores or betrays her own self, the more her *self* will become inaccessible to her. One client told me that she eventually came to feel hollow, like a void. She could no longer "find" her self so she became even more dependent on her friend to complete her and tell her she is OK.[11]

> I'd set aside my homework that was due the next day to help her with her projects. I once had a torn muscle in my shoulder but I knew she wanted me to make dinner. So I did, even though I could barely move. As far as losing myself, I didn't even know myself. I had become my mom, who had to look at my dad to make sure she was OK. And my mom would do any-

---

[10]Joyce Lindenbaum (1985) observes that a crisis often emerges in lesbian relationships when one of the women "begins to feel that she has become lost in her partner. She no longer has a sense of who she is. She feels invisible, unacknowledged, 'less than'" (p. 86). This may also cause her to feel panic and despair.

[11]Siegel (1988) notes that her clients with SSA "needed fuel from the outside [another woman] to bolster their self-esteem. Failure to obtain such mostly eroticized refueling left gaping wounds and led to desperate defensive maneuvers" (p. 16).

thing to not lose my dad. It was like my need now defined me. There was no self left.

Karen

The relationship requires exclusivity. A relationship is not balanced or healthy if it is the only relationship a woman has. Healthy friendship occurs within the context of a broader nurturing community. In *The Four Loves*, C. S. Lewis asserts that the hallmark of a true friendship is the fact that the *two* "delight to be joined by a third, and three by a fourth, if only the newcomer is qualified to become a real friend" (1960, p. 92) and share in some common interest. Exclusivity, no matter how romantic it may seem, increases the relational deprivation within a woman with SSA.

Kaufman, Harrison and Hyde (1984) list several clinical indicators of enmeshed and exclusive female same-sex relationships:

- sharing all recreational and social activities, professional services, living space, finances and possessions
- being isolated from individual personal friends unless mutually shared
- working together or remaining in constant contact through phone (or electronic means)
- expecting partner to "mind read" or intuitively know the other partner's needs or wants (Adapted from p. 531)

The relationship is caretaking. Taking care of a needy woman can be highly sexually charged for many women who have historically assumed the role of caretaker.

I was always getting involved with women who were needy. I wanted to help them—rescue them. If I became important to them, or if they really needed me, I felt loved and cared for. That is how I ended up in my first same-sex relationship. My friend was having a tough time, so I was more or less taking care of her. And then it turned into more than that. I wasn't even wanting that or aware of anything happening. It just did.

Nicole

In working with one lesbian couple, Roth (1984) observed how the common "caretaking" role can usurp the good of authentic intimacy. "Curiously, although one of them was always in the position of attending carefully, neither one experienced the other as close. Differences were never openly stated, nor were strong statements made about what each needed for herself" (p. 95). Roth concludes that to the extent either woman persisted in this caretaking stance, she was effectively disrespecting the other woman's "ability to protect and care for herself" and, therefore, was fundamentally demonstrating an actual lack of caring.

The relationship is ambivalent. At some point a woman may sense that the merged quality of her relationship is a threat to her core existence or individuality. Kaufman et al. (1984) assert that as each woman ignores "her own needs for space as well as those of her partner," ambivalence toward and irritation with one another will naturally arise (p. 530). They go on to note that many lesbian women describe a sense of "feeling choked by one another, smothered and suffocated, and too 'locked in together'" (p. 530), suggesting that this tendency toward fusion within lesbian relationships is "a kind of narcissistic failure to allow for separateness or a defense against difference" (p. 530).[12] Some women are relationally ambivalent even prior to entering the relationship. Their desire for closeness is in constant battle with their fear of abandonment.[13] Many women do not have an internal representation of a stable secure relationship, let alone one of a stable secure unique identity in the midst of closeness.

It is not uncommon for a woman, even in the early stages of a new and desirable same-sex relationship, to operate *as if* the relationship is (or will be) unstable, unpredictable or rejecting. She may unknowingly rely on some of her old survival patterns of detachment and defendedness. McCandlish (1982) notes how one lesbian woman, struggling with anger and mistrust, placed con-

---

[12]Dr. Cornelia Wilbur also observes that "female homosexual relationships are characterized by great ambivalence, by great longing for love, by intense elements of hostility, and by the presence of chronic anxiety. These relationships are unstable and often transient. They do not contribute to the individual's need for stability and love" (1965, pp. 280-81). Roth (1984) asserts that the " 'intense anxiety over any desire for separateness or autonomy within the relationship'" is "an *invariant* [italics added] feature of lesbian couples in treatment" (p. 91, quoting Krestan & Bepko, 1980, p. 277). Indeed, most emotionally dependent female same-sex relationships can be characterized as anxious (insecure) or ambivalent attachments, as defined by Hindy & Schwarz (1994, p. 179).

[13]Mothers of daughters with SSA describe a similar ambivalent dynamic in their relationship with their daughters. In one conversation, the daughter may call the mother "Mommy" and talk on the phone for over an hour. In the next interaction, the daughter may be angry, openly verbalizing her complaints and accusing mom of never caring. Mothers will also benefit from following the techniques described in chapters 6 and 7.

tinual demands on her female partner but realized that these demands arose out of her belief (directed at her partner) that "you will fail to love me if you haven't already" (p. 73).

The relationship leads to feelings of jealousy and possessiveness. As the anxiety increases, often reaching "panic proportions" (Pearlman, 1989, p. 82), a woman may insist on knowing where her partner is at all times, even to the extent of timing her partner's drive to and from the grocery store or checking the odometer to make sure she didn't stop anywhere on the way home. Being the object of such scrutiny can be absolutely draining.

> *I've been with over 13 women, some longer than others. I always dreaded it when they would go out by themselves or with other friends. I feared they would start liking someone else. I was very insecure, possessive and smothering. Many of them ended our relationship because of my constant insecurity.*
>
> *Billie*

These women want to "own" one another as their own. Perhaps this sense of ownership is a normal aspect when it is between a little girl and her mother. Mothers are supposed to communicate the message, *You are mine. I treasure you and would do anything for you.* Little children often emphatically exclaim, "She's *my* mommy," as they attempt to eke out their territories, possessions and unique identities. Unfortunately, it is this primal possessiveness and severe jealousy that often launch an emotionally dependent relationship into its eventual demise.

The relationship is dramatic. If a woman is the object of her partner's scrutiny and possessive measures, she too will start implementing distancing tactics, if she hasn't already. She simply needs "room to breathe." But as *she* breathes, her partner may enter into an escalated state of panic or separation anxiety. The sense of secure attachment begins to break down, even driving the woman who has a felt need for space back into a desperate groping for oneness.

Frantic that the relationship is deteriorating, but also frantic that she is suffocating and losing her self, a woman may resort to extremely desperate measures to both hold on and push away. She may activate a range of defensive efforts—such as seduction, manipulation, deceit, coercion, over-attunement or suspicion—to ward off anxiety and fear. She may repeatedly insist that her partner explain in detail why she is unavailable or unwilling to offer the care and love that she originally promised.

The relationship may become pathologically controlling, threatening, verbally abusive and physically violent.[14] A woman may verbalize that she wants closeness yet still rage at her friend, trapped in a state of terror, or she may threaten suicide, since physical death seems preferable to the emotional abandonment that will come with the relationship's termination.[15]

From the perspective of many of my clients, there is an upside to all of this: These relationships are *never* boring. Unfortunately, many also admit that they are "addicted to drama." They despair of conducting friendships slowly and cautiously; it sounds empty and boring. Smalley (1987) notes that when the relationship is "dramatic, fast-moving, and attention-getting," (p. 128) a woman can unconsciously avoid facing the demands of healthy adult intimacy or resist focusing on her own needs for autonomy and individual growth. These dramatic and intense dynamics then create even deeper internal deficits and relational insecurities.

The relationship is resistant to breakups. Even when both women feel abused and used by the other, they may still be unable to end the relationship because they may have projected their own fears of abandonment and inner frailty onto their partners.[16] No longer connecting to fears within themselves, they become consumed with caretaking—making sure their partner doesn't feel abandoned or hurt and doesn't fall apart. So they renew their vow to the relationship, promising to take care of their partner, but in reality, they are vicariously taking care of themselves.

The relationship has a tragic ending. Regardless of how an ending is finally declared,[17] it is possible that both women may feel deep death pangs. Gun-

---

[14] For further research and discussions on violence in female same-sex relationships, please refer to www.ivpress.com.

[15] "Deprived of their love object, homosexual women very often become suicidal. They interpret this loss as a threat to survival and a total abandonment; they fear total extinction" (Jones, 1927, quoted by Socarides, 1978, p. 133).

[16] "Anxious lovers, who often bond with partners quickly and approach adult relationships with a child's expectations, have enormous difficulty withdrawing emotionally when a romance comes to an end. Letting go of a lover is an especially heartbreaking process for the woman who experiences the event as the loss of her mother again and perceives even temporary separations as deep, personal rejections" (Edelman, 1994, p. 161).

[17] Often a relationship ends because of a woman's religious convictions far before the relationship deteriorates into this state of extreme insecurity and volatility.

dlach and Riess (1968) conjecture that it feels "like the wrenching apart of Siamese twins" (p. 226).

> *The separation was harder than I could ever even imagine. I described it at one point like she was my lifeline. I had an umbilical cord going to her, and if that were broken, I would die. She was, it seemed like, every breath in me. I couldn't live without her.*
>
> *Nicole*

During this time, a woman's sleeping and eating cycles may become severely disrupted. Some will experience panic attacks, a major depressive episode, suicide ideation, uncontrollable vomiting or flu-like symptoms. Having lost what she thought was home, she must now return to what feels like homelessness.

The relationship is part of an endless cycle. Every time one of her relationships ends, a woman may perceive the loss as being her fault and internalize the belief that she is relationally incompetent or unlovable. Her fledgling sense of trust, in herself and others, shatters. Most women cannot bear up under the weight of shame and disappointment. And since many of them have few inner resources to recover from such devastation, they may merge with yet another woman—looking for love, support and security out of which to face another day.

Margaret Nichols (1990) admits that "many gay women spend little of their adult lives as single women, moving directly from one love relationship into another" (p. 360).[18] It is not uncommon for a woman to find another girlfriend prior to ending her current same-sex relationship. Instead of grieving and healing, she enters a cycle of dependent relationships. As a result, her fragile sense of self becomes even more susceptible to future emotional dependencies.

Many of my clients come to me after they have lived through three or four of these cycles and feel they cannot survive another.

> *Even though I have my bad days and struggle sometimes with being married to a man and being a stay-at-home mom, I think back to the years of*

---

[18]For more discussion on the longevity of female same-sex relationships, refer to the website www.ivpress.com.

emotionally dependent same-sex relationships and realize I don't really have it that bad after all. To be trapped in all of my former obsessions and emotional dependencies was a living hell. I am nowhere near that any-more. . . . Emotional dependency was just—a living hell for me.

Shari

THERE IS HOPE

As I walk with a woman who is attempting to end or redefine a same-sex relationship (see chapter 10), I must be sensitive to both the difficulty of this decision and the woman's ability to follow through. She will need me to be patient and compassionate. She will also need to be reassured that God is present and working on her behalf. Rare is the woman who can end an emotionally dependent relationship overnight. Rather, this will be a lengthy process in which she reclaims, piece by piece, her heart and her soul, which have been housed or deposited in the other woman. She must salvage the threads of her true self and reknit them around new perceptions, impressions and beliefs that arise out of a corrective *experience* of love, support and acceptance.

> Listen to me, O little girl, my daughter, O woman of God,
> You whom I have upheld since you were conceived,
> And have carried since your birth.
> Even to your old age and gray hairs,
> I am God, I am the one who will sustain you.
> I have made you and I will carry you;
> I will sustain you and I will rescue you.
> (Isaiah 46:3-4, author's paraphrase)

PART TWO

The Work of Restoration
Leading Them Home

I compare therapy to a consultation with an architect. The client brings in hopes, dreams, a life and a vision, and money to pay the professional fee, but cannot design and build a house by herself. The architect contributes technical skill and creativity so that the house can actually be built, not just dreamed of and hoped for. But it is the client's house. Only the client can turn it into a home.

COLIN ROSS, *THE TRAUMA MODEL*

CHAPTER SIX

Securing the Foundation

Acceptance and Attunement

Those who have never been loved

seldom have a sense of real worth or value,

of security or permanence,

for it is only when we are loved

that we can begin to treat ourselves as human.

MORTON KELSEY, *SET YOUR HEARTS ON THE GREATEST GIFT*

Therapy with women with SSA can be broken down into four stages:

1. formation (chapters 6-8)
2. transformation (chapters 9-10)
3. integration (chapters 11-12)
4. consolidation and maturity (chapter 13)

These stages generally follow a female's natural stages of growth and development, as sequenced in chapters three and four, beginning with an infant's need for attachment and security and concluding with a girl's full development into an autonomous, mature adult.

The therapeutic considerations I present in this and the following chapters are comprehensive and are framed to guide therapists through the most complex cases. Not every client will require every intervention, nor will every woman move through the above stages sequentially. Therapy with women with SSA is far from linear. Most women will process the themes in two or more stages simultaneously. The stages, therefore, should be viewed not as a rigid ordering but as fluid categories descriptive of the most common issues faced by the majority of women. A woman's psychological profile, as addressed in chapter eight, will also influence the immediate direction and speed of therapy, necessarily dictating or limiting therapeutic goals and techniques.

Therapeutic goals such as recovery from sexual abuse or trauma, bolstering self-esteem, learning anger management techniques or improving coping skills will naturally arise as a woman works through the various stages. I have not attempted to review the therapeutic strategies for these common processes since information about them is readily available elsewhere. I have limited my discussion to the unique therapeutic needs and nuances of working with this special population.

FIRST STAGE OF THERAPY: FORMATION

One of the most striking common denominators of women with SSA is an unstable, underdeveloped or negative core sense of self. This means that at their core these women commonly experience profound insecurity, emptiness or shame. Because a positive foundational self was never fully established and integrated, their evolving concepts of a separate, valuable, unique, emotional, relational and female self are also usually extremely fragile (McDougall, 1970), vague or unknown, or associated with negative images and affect. When asked who they are, what they feel—or even what they enjoy doing—they might stare at you with a blank face and exclaim, "I don't know!"[1]

Many of my clients can barely endure the thought of being alone, even for five minutes of silent reflection. Just considering such an undertaking can trigger overwhelming dread or what has been called annihilation anxiety (Jacobs, 1990). They lack a solid core or firm foundation on which to stand. As they are swept through life, they have no means to stabilize or control their vessel.

This unsettledness is physically apparent as my clients move from one apartment or condo to another, sometimes several times a year. Living out of boxes is not unusual for them, nor is the premonition that they will be moving again soon. Even if a woman stays in one place for a considerable length of time, it is not uncommon for her dwelling to be bereft of personal decorations and nurturing touches. Empty refrigerators and bare cupboards characterize

---

[1] In a survey exploring the attitudes, opinions and sexual development of 205 homosexual women, researchers Hogan, Fox and Kirchner (1977) were struck by the number of women who demonstrated a "lack of insight into self and the inability to perceive self" based on their neutral selections or complete absence of opinion on questions directly pertaining to personality traits. They admit that this seemed to be an important but unexpected finding in their study (p. 133).

her living space. She is not established and her "home" is not special.

Some openly admit to this sense of core emptiness, especially when they re-alize the power that touch has to connect them with their inner self. Jane Mara, a gay affirmative psychotherapist, speaks of one woman's experience with same-sex touch. The woman reported that as she touched her female lover, "it was as if I was touching my own body and *I became real to myself* [italics added] for the first time in my life" (1983, p. 147). Women with SSA long to be touched or warmly embraced by another woman, a longing that may reflect their basic need to gain a sense of self or a validated existence.

Perhaps because of this core emptiness, near the beginning of therapy I often feel as if my client is being elusive or inauthentic. Her personhood, or identity, seems to drift, untethered to her reported experiences or relationships. My clarity often wanes as I struggle to establish a clear treatment direction. I have come to believe that this common reaction, or countertransference, is rooted in the woman's projected belief that there is no inner "personality" for another to know. And as long as she holds on to this belief, she will mostly likely remain *experientially* unknown. This may translate into the additional be-lief that no one cares enough to fully know her. Her inner self is like a broken flower vase, originally designed to sustain beauty and hold life-giving water. It is now only a channel through which the water drains. I must resolve my initial countertransference of lostness so that I can metaphorically hold her vase in a way that will allow her to form and ultimately contain her beauty.

THE FUNDAMENTAL GOAL

A woman with SSA often faces this dilemma: without a stable and defined self, she cannot connect or relate in ways we expect a healthy adult woman could. Without a secure attachment or healthy connection, she cannot estab-lish a stable core self.

Short of resolving this dilemma, she will merely survive in an empty world and empty self; or seeking to find self and home in another, she will be driven into relationships that may—almost beyond her will or power—become emo-tionally dependent. Her most fundamental need, therefore, is to healthily at-tach and, simultaneously, to discover, accept and solidify her self within this attachment.

My *fundamental goal in therapy*, then, is to offer her an *experience* of consis-tent emotional attunement, unconditional acceptance, genuine care and regulating containment, all within an enduring secure attachment, so that she can begin to grow, heal and complete the work of inner formation.[2] It has been my experience that through our heart-to-heart relationship, she will begin to internalize, perhaps for the first time in her life, a basic sense of trust, belovedness and unique personhood. This powerful corrective relationship also affords her an opportunity to learn new ways of living and relating, allowing her to integrate healthier inner constructs, beliefs, emotional patterns and styles of relating. As in childhood, she needs an external home in which she feels safe enough to become.

The energy and time spent during this opening stage often result in the most meaningful and enduring work accomplished throughout the course of therapy. This therapeutic attachment will become the foundation on which she and I accomplish the overt work of change or growth as directed by her stated goals and immediate needs. Our authentic relationship is the soil in which she will be nourished and sustained.

> *My relationship with my therapist was the closest and most important relationship that I had ever had. In truth, it still is. I am amazed at how I continued to risk and share with her. It felt like she stayed right there with me through it all. I am eternally grateful.*
>
> *Alaina*

THE FUNDAMENTAL THERAPEUTIC TASKS

In order to establish such a powerful and life-changing heart-to-heart relationship, I must reassure my client that she is safe with me and that I am trustworthy. Therefore, the first stage of therapy can be broken down into three separate therapeutic tasks:

Therapist's first task: Create safety, the *heart of the helping environment*
   Fundamental therapeutic processes: Acceptance and attunement
   Client's task: Rest

Therapist's second task: Build trust, the *heart of the helper*

---

[2]Child psychiatrist Dr. Daniel Siegel, an associate clinical professor of psychiatry at UCLA and author of the internationally acclaimed book *The Developing Mind*, proposes that new attachment experiences, such as that provided by the patient-psychotherapist relationship, *can promote* patient growth and development, foster change and "enhance the regulation of emotion throughout the lifespan" (1999a, p. 285).

Fundamental therapeutic processes: Caring, constancy and commitment
Client's task: Receive

Therapist's third task: Establish a secure attachment, the *heart of the relationship*
Fundamental therapeutic processes: Empathy and the here-and-now
Client's task: Become

The first and second tasks should not be viewed as mere means to reach the end goal of a therapeutic attachment since they are, on an ongoing basis, therapeutically curative.[3] All of the therapeutic processes mentioned above are not only initiatory; they should be sustained and revisited throughout the duration of therapy.

Since successful navigation of this opening stage is so crucial to a therapist's ongoing effectiveness and to a woman's ultimate growth and healing, I will take the remainder of this and the following chapter to unpack the processes of creating safety, building trust and establishing a secure attachment. As mentioned in chapter two, undertaking these processes with women with SSA is categorically different from working with other clients.[4]

THERAPIST'S FIRST TASK: CREATE SAFETY

Over the years, my clients have helped me understand what they need in order to feel safe. They want an environment that promotes respect, authenticity, acceptance and protection. They want consistency, warmth and a sense of fullness; they certainly do not want surprises. My declaring that I am safe will not help them feel safe. They are perceptive and intelligent, and they have, unfortunately, learned that words can be cheap. They will determine whether I am safe based on my prevailing character qualities, actions and attitudes.

At the beginning of therapy, I do not attempt to work with abuse material, challenge core beliefs or directly confront a woman's defense mechanisms. I

---

[3]Therapy for women who have experienced emotional deprivation in childhood because of breaches in attunement or insecure attachments "must be directed first of all at an optimal restoration of those conditions which make it possible for the emotional life to resume its natural growth" (Baars & Terruwe, 2002, pp. 73-74).

[4]Parents of women with SSA who desire to repair or strengthen their relationship with their daughters can and should be trained in all the techniques pertinent to this first stage of therapy. A story of a mother who applied these relational techniques in her relationship with her daughter can be found on the website. Parents can also be helped by Richard Cohen's excellent book *Gay Children, Straight Parents* (2007).

have come to recognize that I must earn the right to speak into her life, so I am extremely cautious in offering interpretation or analysis. This does not mean that abuse issues or core beliefs are never addressed in opening sessions; but it does mean that I do not initiate or cultivate their discussions. I conduct a complete psychological assessment[5] as we explore her immediate circumstances, goals for therapy, current crises, nature of existing relationships and support systems, or history—if she is comfortable sharing those things. But foremost, I express a desire to learn more about her life and to know her as a unique individual.

> *I struggled saying things. I was often embarrassed and shy. I was very uncomfortable—but it was safe. The room was safe, soothing. My counselor ended up being safe. She never pushed me too far. She seemed to know what I could handle.*
>
> *Karen*

At this stage, I must be sensitive to how a woman may negatively interpret my actions or suggestions. My friend Kathleen, who had been in lesbian relationships for many years, shared with me that when she was still in the opening stages of therapy, her new therapist suggested that she attend a day program because of her ongoing struggle with depression. Kathleen felt rebuffed, believing that her therapist was trying to push her off onto this program, that her stuff was too big for her therapist to handle. She concluded that her therapist didn't really want to be in relationship with her but just wanted to fix her. Kathleen remained in therapy, but she later admitted to her therapist that she felt unsafe from that point on.

Because these misinterpretations can and do occur with my clients, I take time to qualify many of my ideas or suggestions. For example, in the above situation I might have said, "Kathleen, I am going to suggest something that might help you with your depression, but I want you to know that in making this suggestion, I am *not* trying to terminate or reduce our time together. I am committed to work with you for the long haul. But I do think that there are some additional services that may be beneficial to you right now."

My clients feel safe when they become convinced that they are the true ben-

---

[5]For more information on making an initial assessment, see the book website at www.ivpress.com.

eficiaries of my time, emotional energies and focus. They want to know that I can extend myself, even to a point of sacrifice, for their sake. This is not about manipulation or control on their part; it is a legitimate need to be cared for unconditionally. They somehow know intuitively that this genuine care is crucial for their future growth and healing. Since many women with SSA have spent a lifetime curtailing their own individuation and exploration in order to determine what other people want or like, I've learned to be continually aware of situations where I unconsciously need a client to cooperate with *my* treatment agenda for *my* ease or sense of security. Safety is breached if I use my clients toward *my* end. When a woman assumes the role of caretaker or people pleaser—for whatever reason—she is (unknowingly) abdicating the opportunity for personal growth and formation. If I promote or encourage this caretaking role in any way, I affirm her abandonment of self.

SAFETY IN UNCONDITIONAL ACCEPTANCE

As mentioned in chapter two, a woman with SSA will not feel safe until she knows that she can be fully honest about her life without fear of moralizing or judgment.[6] To lay a foundation of safety for my client, I have learned that I must *unconditionally accept*

- her same-sex feelings and behaviors
- her sexual identity
- her same-sex partner
- her specific (or decidedly vague) goals for therapy
- her attitudes toward men *and* women
- her parents and her current relationship with them
- her spiritual beliefs
- her sin

I allow her to *be* where she *is*. I acknowledge her current circumstances and inner realities and do not initiate a conversation that can be interpreted as invasive or as prematurely challenging. Again, my aim is to provide an en-

---

[6]In observing lesbian women within the health care system, it was discovered that a maternalistic style—"characterized by emotional warmth, *unconditional acceptance* [italics added], and meeting basic subsistence needs"—was effective in maintaining an ongoing working relationship with the women and served as a necessary prelude for a woman's eventual exploration of such things as alcohol abuse (Hall, 1994, pp. 242-43).

vironment in which my client can discover, accept and solidify a self so *she* will have the power to decide whether *she* wants to challenge or change any of these aspects. Before a woman can determine her next step forward, she must first be able to acknowledge, understand and accept her present starting point. My unconditional acceptance helps her to do so.

When a woman is not able to radically accept all of her reality, hiddenness and stagnation can hinder her healing process. This is described by Jeanette Howard in her recent book *Into the Promised Land*:

> I have spent most of my Christian life despising my homosexual tendencies and seeing them as a real problem. Having done all that I could to rid myself of them, I then subconsciously withheld all desires, longings and temptations from God and no longer "bothered" him with that aspect of my life. Ashamed of my failure to "progress" to the next stage of healing (becoming attracted to men in a romantic way), I chose to ignore my sexuality altogether. In effect, I closed down and became asexual in outlook; I disowned and excluded the unchanged and partially changed aspects of my life, and concentrated on the positive attributes that, in my mind, would be useful to the kingdom. I offered God my strengths and gifts in service. Not surprisingly, suppressing such a large part of me helped to plunge my life into the darkness of depression. (2005, p. 69)

By offering unconditional acceptance, I provide the essential support most of my clients need to be able to practice radical self-acceptance.

I have also found that I need to be accepting of a woman's physical appearance and attire, her career or type of work, and even the car or truck she prefers to drive. As mentioned in chapter 4, many women with SSA gravitate toward what are considered stereotypically masculine styles in terms of appearance and occupational preferences. These styles or preferences can be genuinely grounded and centered in her true identity as a sporty, athletic or mechanically inclined woman. On the other hand, her ostensive masculinization may indicate a severe disconnection from her femininity or a means to protect herself from further pain or devaluation as a female. Regardless of the origin of her preferences, however, the early stage of therapy is not the time to address these social externals.[7]

My clients have told me how grateful they are that I am willing to accept

---

[7]Chapter 13 offers guidance on helping a woman integrate with her femininity.

and enter their world *as it is*. They feel honored by my effort to "get into their shoes" for the sake of understanding and connection. They come to learn my camaraderie is not an endorsement of every aspect of their life but is a willingness and commitment to know, love and journey with them just as they are.

ACCEPTANCE DISMANTLES SHAME

I once asked a therapist specializing in female sexual abuse if she saw any differences between sexual abuse survivors who did not have SSA and women who did. She thought for a moment and then said, "The shame." Women with SSA frequently live with the most extreme versions of all aspects of shame.[8] They experience shame as an *emotion* (a feeling of guilt or deep embarrassment), as an *identity* (an inner belief and sense of dread of *being* bad, defective or reprehensible), as an ongoing *dynamic process* (ridiculing or debasing one's self) and as a *defense* (regulating the degree of personal exposure and contact). Although most debilitating in the first stage of therapy, shame must be sensitively addressed throughout all of the stages of therapy.

The type of shame that arises specifically out of an empty core or undeveloped self is the pervasive *identification* as a deformed, lost or nonexistent soul. A sense of shameful nonexistence fills the vacuum created by the absence of a positive sense of self. A woman with SSA often believes that she does not *deserve* to exist or to take up space or someone else's time. She may also internalize a profound sense of shame that results from the belief that she caused her relational losses and, if she is part of a faith tradition, the added shame of feeling that she is a perversion, outside of God's grace and love. Consequently, I have found that the bulk of therapeutic intervention with women with SSA involves providing shame-reducing experiences and supportive and cognitive therapies to help them confront and deal with the overarching and defining presence of shame.

In the beginning stage of therapy, I hold to the therapeutic attitude that my

---

[8]Wells and Hansen (2003), relying on a sample of highly educated lesbians ($n = 317$), discovered that in comparison with heterosexual women involved in an earlier project by Wells in 1996, the lesbian women reported significantly more shame, even though they had reached the highest stage of lesbian identity integration and were occupationally successful. It was formerly thought that as identity integration increased, shame would decrease. Additionally, the higher levels of shame reported by the self-identified lesbian women were associated with insecure attachment patterns, the most common of which was dismissive. In Wells (2003), the reported levels of shame were somewhat lower for a group of self-identified lesbians ($n = 100$) who had been in ongoing psychotherapy versus the nonclinical sample in Wells & Hansen (2003).

client is *always* doing the best she can in her process, her therapy and her walk with God. I try to avoid making any comment that may be interpreted as critical, judgmental or disapproving. As a woman experiences my genuine effort to help her reduce the shame instead of insensitively triggering it, she will begin to feel safe in my presence.

Again, it is important that a client gather up her whole self, both the agreeable and the disagreeable parts, for the journey ahead. Fragmenting or disowning any reality of her life, due to shame, is counterproductive to her formation and healing, not to mention counterproductive to true intimacy with others.

ACCEPTANCE THROUGH REFRAMING

I especially enjoy assailing shame indirectly by *reframing* a woman's struggle with SSA or other issues. There are logical reasons why a woman desperately longs for same-sex closeness and intimacy. I do not have to be afraid of normalizing her struggle within the context of what she needed and didn't receive as a little girl.

I may say things like, "Of course you long for hugs and touch. Your mom didn't even know how to hug. She never got hugged as a little girl either. You must feel like you are starving!" or "Of course you want special uninterrupted attention from your friend. I remember how you sensed your parents were too busy to play with you. You never even remember getting special time alone with them. Your little girl is still looking for that special time and attention."

> *As I told her the story of my life and what I was wanting from other women, my counselor helped me to understand where my same-sex feelings came from and why. She validated them. I came to realize that there wasn't something terribly wrong with me as an individual. It was my circumstances, losses, and some of my reactions to those losses that were wrong—not me.*
>
> *Margaret*

THE SYMPTOMS OF A MISSING "HOME"

Because of the difficulties and disruptions in her primal attachments with mother and father, as outlined in part one, a woman with SSA may have *lacked consistent moments of caring attunement* as an infant or young child.[9] Daniel Siegel, emphasizing the fundamental significance of emotional communication or attunement, notes, "attachment relationships are about the sharing and amplification of positive emotional states (such as joy and elation) and the sharing and reduction of negative states (such as fear or sadness). These emotional transactions allow a child to 'feel felt' " (1999b, p. 49). And as a child "feels felt," they begin to gain a primitive sense of their own core or self.[10] However, if a mother (or father) is unable to provide consistent emotional attunement to her baby (perhaps because of depression, distraction or her own deprivation of this basic human connection), or if she fails to repair breaches in attunement and regulating support, her infant girl may experience some level of

- helplessness and powerlessness in terms of engaging another's *caring* attention (developing a core sense of relational incompetency)
- overwhelming negative feeling states, such as aloneness, shame or emptiness
- an inability to regulate these potentially severe and overwhelming negative feelings (developing a core sense of emotional incompetency)
- negative internal representations (basic beliefs) of herself and her caregiver(s)

Collectively, these negative affective experiences can create an unstable, negative or empty *core* within the girl (Orcutt, 1995; Walant, 1995), not to mention an insecure attachment with their caregiver.[11] Additionally, repeated experiences of misattunement can create such a pervasive sense of shame

---

[9]In her work with women with SSA, Siegel (1988) concludes that because their mothers failed to repair moments of misattunement or exercise empathy, "patients had no way to delineate a stable self" (p. 20; see also Gundlach & Reiss, 1973). Dr. Elizabeth Moberly also discusses the common presence of attachment difficulties in the histories of many homosexual men and women, agreeing that "to the very young child, the parent is his or her source of being, and so one's very *being* [italics added] is felt to be endangered if the attachment to the parent is disrupted" (1983, p. 45).

[10]See Chodorow (1978); Masterson (1985); Schore (1994, 2002); Schwartz & Southern (1999); Siegel (1999); Walant (1995) and Winnicott (1965). Indeed, it is an infant's experience of her mother's (or caretaker's) consistent emotional attunement, reparation of misattunement, affectual regulation (such as reassuring and calming her child when she is agitated), as well as the infant's own associated positive feeling states that arise from her caregiver's attuned attention, that form the primitive core of the self.

[11]It might also be argued—based on research supporting the idea that female infants are more centered and focused on people (especially the face and eyes) and on emotional interactions than are male infants (Benenson, Morash & Petrakos, 1998; Cahill, 2005; Connellan, Baron-Cohen, Wheelwright, Batki & Ahluwalia, 2000)—that this deprivation of attention and affectual attunement may affect a female infant's development more severely than it might a male.

within a child that her whole self is essentially engulfed by it. I believe that many of my clients were deprived of the relational environment in which to develop relational competency, experience positive feeling states, regulate negative feelings or form a positive foundational core.[12] These little girls, now adults, remain unaffirmed as persons and still need the mirror of a mother's face to tell them they *are* and that they *are okay*. Fortunately, attachment specialists note that as a woman continues to interact with her environment, she can indeed change her "emotional, behavioral, and social traits and outcomes" (p. 20). They continue by saying, *"therapeutic interventions* [italics added], can go along way towards attenuating early difficulties" (Levy & Orlans, 1998, p. 20).[13]

SAFETY IN EMOTIONAL ATTUNEMENT

I have therefore learned that my clients find a sense of safety and an opportunity for growth as I provide an environment of consistent emotional connection. To do this, I must be open and allow myself to be influenced by them (Siegel, 1999a, p. 69). My goal is to feel what they feel or to align my inner state so that I can experience, as close as possible, what my client is experiencing within her subjective or inner world in any given moment. Because many women with SSA may unconsciously minimize or negate another's warm social cueing and attuned attention, attunement cannot be presumed; it requires an active effort and intense focus on the part of the therapist.[14] So when I reflect my attuned state through gestures or expression, such as nodding my head in affirmation, I *really* nod my head. I regularly lean forward to demonstrate my active listening and engagement when they are sharing difficult emotions. I smile big and frown hard as my client cues me through her affect or words.

---

[12]For more information on the effects of attunement and misattunement, please see the book website at www.ivpress.com.

[13]See also Bartholomew, Kwong & Hart (2001, p. 209) and Ross (2000).

[14]Attuned emotional connection can be communicated through body language, such as solid eye contact, caring facial expressions and voice modulations, engaged gestures and the sensitive timing of all of the above. Because trained therapists are not available in many areas, telephone therapy is a viable media, but it is *not* the best option for women with SSA. Without face-to-face eye contact and the availability of metacommunication exhibited in body language, the process of building trust (and gaining intimate knowledge of the client) can be painstakingly slow and may never reach the needed depth. Touch is another powerful medium for attunement and empathy, but it should *never* be a presumed part of therapy with women with SSA. Please refer to chapter 11 for further discussion. However, parents can certainly incorporate healthy touch into their warm moments with their daughters, assuming their daughters are comfortable with physical closeness.

When I am attuned to my client, she and I are in harmony, experiencing something together. My hope is that she will see that I am with her for her sake and will say to herself, *Finally, here is someone who gets me and is with me. I am not alone.*

> *I was shocked the first time I visited my new counselor. She was so caring and compassionate. While she listened to me, tears came to her eyes. I knew she was right there with me. I knew I had someone who cared. This was huge for me! I cannot tell you the healing I experienced. I so needed somebody to just listen and care for me. It was a safe haven.*
>
> *Joyce*

Therapeutic attunement is a powerfully healing, curative technique for women with SSA. Attunement sends significant nonverbal messages of affirmation, namely, that my client exists and matters. Through attunement, I see her; she is real. I experience her emotion; her emotion is real. I take the time to be with her; she is important. She is being affirmed and validated in the most basic and deepest sense. Her internalization of these moments of connection and realness will begin to solidify her inner sense of self. She *is* and can therefore *become*.

STAYING ATTUNED TO THE EMERGING SELF

James Masterson (1985) emphasizes that in early childhood, most important to a child's development of a core is the parents' capacity to perceive the unique characteristics of the child's emerging self. As therapists, we must attune ourselves to this "emerging self"—a woman's inner music. Brennan Manning, in his book *Ruthless Trust*, reminds us that "without active listening you cannot hear a thing; if you attend to something only superficially, you will not hear the music of what is happening" (2000, p. 159). I do not want to miss the music playing, albeit ever so quietly, within my client's heart and life. In some cases, I may be the first to hear it. A woman with SSA usually does not realize that she has an inner melody or anything so beautiful as a song. My goal is to learn her song (her true self) so that as I hum it, I can draw her into listening and hopefully recognizing it as her own.

When I begin working with a new client, I am attuned and listening with the intent of discovering at least one aspect of her true self that I can genuinely affirm and enjoy, such as her dogged determination to survive or her honesty and straightforwardness. There will be days when she will attempt to convince me that there is nothing substantial or likable within her, so I must firmly hold onto the melody I've already heard.

> *I would laugh and challenge my therapist, "But I'm paying you to listen!" Yet I knew there was something more. There was a sincere and genuine connection between us. I know God listens, but I'm like, Hey, could you send somebody with skin on? I didn't have any other friends at the time— nobody. But my counselor gave me that: God with skin.*
>
> *Joyce*

I also attune myself to and listen to the parts of my client's true self that have been split off in her effort to avoid painful and overwhelming feelings. When attunement is broken in a developing child's experience, as it most likely was for many women with SSA, it is not uncommon for the child to then disavow her feelings (Alexander, 1992, p. 188). But if disavowal becomes a regular pattern in a child's life, then as an adult, she may be not only severely disconnected from all emotions, a common feature of many women with SSA, but also split off from the valid aspect of self that was associated with the disavowed feeling. For instance, a woman may detach from her gender or femininity, believing that it was the cause for her sexual abuse and her deep inner shame and pain. These splits and disconnections add to her feelings of emptiness and lostness. Attunement and reflective listening are powerful techniques that can directly aid her in reconnecting with the repressed emotions and integrating with the split-off aspects of her authentic self.

STAYING ATTUNED SO YOU CAN GO WHERE SHE GOES

Therapy in this initial stage must be thoroughly centered on the client. Irvin Yalom (2002) unpacks client-centered therapy by saying, "Above all, the therapist must be prepared *to go wherever the patient goes* [italics added], do all that is necessary to continue building trust and safety in the relationship" (pp. 34-35). If I sense that a client is lethargic or ambivalent toward a particular line of questioning or discussion, I may stop and ask, "What are *you* needing right now—in this moment?" Seen metaphorically, I am getting up out of my comfortable chair (my preferred direction and style of therapy) to follow my client's lead.[15] A woman with SSA needs to know she is valuable and important enough to be honored and followed. She longs for a connection that doesn't require her to do all the work.

> *I worked so hard to keep you engaged. I did my homework. I intensely pursued my issues. I wanted to please you. And I figured if I ever stopped working so hard you would leave or terminate our relationship. What I realize now is that you were always engaged and it wasn't dependent on my performance or intensity. You always reflected back to me commitment and stability. When I finally realized you were committed to me, not just my process or work, I knew I was experiencing something completely new. It was absolutely pivotal! I can now say I shifted from a state of performance and intensity to warm and settled intimacy for the first time in my life.*
>
> *A woman speaking to her counselor*

In the beginning stages of therapy, if a woman would rather tell me about an incident at work than continue talking about her childhood story, I will stay wholeheartedly engaged and follow her lead. I want her ultimately to feel safe. It is also the case that, as she shares, I focus more on her affect than on the content of her stories. I remain fully attuned while she shares yet another aspect of who she is. Truth be known, she probably doesn't care that much about addressing childhood issues, at least at this point in time. She is much more concerned about my ongoing emotional connection and ability to stay with her wherever she goes.

STAYING ATTUNED IN THE MIDST OF OUR REACTIONS

The idea of "going wherever a client goes" might be put to the test with a client like Danielle, a 45-year-old woman who had embraced a lesbian identity for more than eleven years. Danielle was in the second or third session with her previous therapist when, at one point, she felt so agitated that she got up out

---

[15]Masterson (1985) says that part of the emerging self is the "unique style or manner in which the child's individuation is expressed in his *exploring, experimenting, self-assertive adventures with reality* [italics added]." It is important that a parent or primary caregiver "respond to these in a positive, supportive manner, to identify, acknowledge and treat with respect" the child's unique temperament (p. 29).

of her chair and began to pace as she and her therapist continued to talk.[16] Danielle's therapist eventually asked her to sit down because her walking was distracting. Evidently, the therapist was unable to stay emotionally attuned to Danielle's agitation as manifested by her getting up and walking. Danielle never returned.

Dr. Daniel Hughes, a leading expert in childhood attachment therapies, claims that if a client's (or child's) "disordered" behaviors habitually annoy parents and therapists, those behaviors will resist change. However, "if we truly accept these behaviors, they are much more likely to change" (2004, p. 10). Danielle's therapist missed an incredible opportunity to enter into Danielle's "disordered" world and simply be with her in her agitation and restlessness.

I have learned how important it is to allow my client to experience and express her visceral feelings in the best way she knows how, even if that expression is somewhat childlike or uncomfortable for me. If she is corrected, restricted or shamed when she attempts to assert what is true for herself in the moment, her sense of safety will be shattered and the process of inner formation may be altogether derailed. I must be patient and remain calm as she sorts through, connects and even displays certain behaviors related to her inner turmoil.

Following is an example of how I interacted with a client after she had started pacing in my office. My eyes followed her face as she got up to pace, and our conversation never waned. Eventually, I asked about her pacing in a warm, caring tone.

"Are you feeling better now that you have walked a little?"

"Yes, yes I am."

"Do you know what you were feeling when you first decided to start moving around?"

"I don't really know."

"Do you remember what we were talking about?"

"Nope."

"Well I think I do. You briefly mentioned your mom died when you were

---

[16]Often the body is used to relieve or process internal emotions and conflicts. This can be especially true of women with SSA. As Siegel (1988) notes, "this use of bodily communication made for tense, restless sessions. The analysands could find no comfort, or even a comforting and comfortable position on the couch" (pp. 40-41). Many of my clients have paced, sat on the floor, laid on the couch, asked to sit in my chair, covered themselves with pillows, thrown pillows, abruptly stood to their feet, and so on.

four. It must be very hard for you to talk about."

I lean forward, maintaining eye contact as she continues to pace.

"I didn't think it was *that* hard to talk about."

"What are you feeling right now?"

"I guess OK, but a bit bothered you're asking me all these questions."

Aware that my probing questions were increasing her anxiety, I decided to lighten up our interaction, asking, "Would it still feel good to walk a little more?" (I was attuned to her discomfort and I affirmed her need to pace. I wanted her to know that I *can* handle her. This might begin to eliminate any possible "testing" motive behind her pacing, and it may also distinguish me from others who have possibly shown intolerance for her physicality or "inability to behave.")

She responded, "Yeah, I'm all fidgety. I just can't sit down."

"That's fine," I said. "Take as much time as you need." I sat back in my chair and relaxed. After a while, I continued matter-of-factly in our original direction. "So, you were giving me an overview of your life. I think we were at age 5. Can you tell me what happened next?"

My intention in situations like this one is to allow my client to simply be who she is at this point in time. I want her to feel safe, yet I do lightly challenge her to connect with the inner impulse or emotion that first prompted her to pace. To relieve some of her anxiety, I choose to bypass the subject of her mother's death. There will be many more opportunities to explore that material. I also back away from the intensity of our attuned oneness, giving my client some needed breathing room.[17]

The experience of attuned oneness affords a woman the structure and support she needs to begin to connect with, regulate and understand—rather than remain victim to—her own emotions, reactions and behaviors. It also helps her acknowledge and integrate previously denied or neglected aspects of her self (Hughes, 1997), like her angry or hurt self. "The job of psychotherapy is not to de-emphasize, defuse, or discharge these moments of oneness, but to encourage, heighten, and embrace them instead. Only then will we be helping patients in their recovery from their detached, alienated core" (Walant, 1995, p. 122).

---

[17]Siegel (1999a) asserts that attunement includes the "capacity to read the signals (often nonverbal) that indicate the need for engagement or *disengagement* [italics added]," disengagement being defined as a person's normal need to be autonomous and not in alignment with another (p. 71).

PROTECTING HER FROM OVERPOWERING EMOTIONS

At one point in her journey, author Jeanette Howard could barely attend church. She said the environment was overwhelming: too loud, too crowded, too full of life. She made a habit of sitting in the back of the sanctuary near the door so she could leave when her discomfort became intolerable. Fearing God's disapproval and rejection because she was not a faithful churchgoer, she slumped into depression and shame. But one day she received a picture of God that changed her perspective of him forever. She saw God himself attuning to her fragile state. First she saw that her heart was so shriveled that it was almost lifeless. This was not a total surprise. But then she saw God gently extend a finger to massage her heart and keep it alive. She somehow knew that God's entire hand on her heart would have been too big and too heavy. She was amazed by God's sensitivity. She felt renewed in her strength—even if it was only enough to simply remain in the church building for the remainder of each service (2005, p. 54).

Attunement is especially powerful in helping a woman regulate and manage negative or overpowering emotions. Many of my clients seem to exist between two extremes: they either feel nothing, unable to connect with any stir of emotion, or they become completely consumed by an emotion such as despair and hopelessness, sliding into a subjective state of mind that makes it impossible to objectively process or rationally consider why the feelings arose initially. Jeanette Howard was struggling with this overwhelming subjectivity. She thought her only recourse to regulate anxiety and feelings of suffocation was to leave the building. These women often find no middle ground on which to healthily process ever-changing emotional states. I aim to tether myself emotionally to my clients and then lead them to this grounding point.

For example, a client beginning therapy may feel anxious and insecure. I try to intervene long before she begins to verbalize her discomfort or inability to proceed.[18] I may gently stop a conversation, saying, "You just told me a lot about your family. I know it was hard for you. I really appreciate the effort you are making. But I'd like us to take a break." After a pause, I say, slowly, "Why don't you relax back into the couch, take a deep breath in and then slowly let it out." Notice that at this point I do not *tell* her she is anxious, because this

---

[18]Jacobs (1990) stresses that in working with women with SSA, "the clinician has to be prepared to handle the eruptions of extreme anxiety by providing a holding environment (Winnicott, 1960) to sustain the patient through her panic" (p. 158).

would make her anxious about her anxiety.

"Let any tightness or tension you might be holding in just flow out as you slowly exhale." I do the exercise with her, exaggerating my breathing. She can basically mimic me. We continue identifying points of tension in her body, breathing into the tension, until she is fully relaxed.

"Okay," I say, smiling and leaning forward. "You are doing great work. We will continue your story next week. For now though, I would like you to just relax and try to connect with what you are feeling in your body." I will also want her to actively reflect by sharing what it was like for her to tell her story, to experience my interruption or to do the breathing exercise. This helps her to integrate these potentially new regulating experiences.

WHEN WE "MISS" HER

Even with my best intentions, I do fail to attune to my clients, and they are the first to point this out. They might ask, "Are you still with me?"

I reply honestly, "No, I'm not. I'm sorry. I was drifting there for a minute. Thanks for calling me back. By the way, it's not your fault I was daydreaming. It was rude for me to leave you. But I'm back. Thanks for being patient with me."[19]

Thankfully, both the positive and the negative impact of my personhood and behaviors on my clients is an essential part of the "realness" they must navigate and integrate into their framework for a healthy self and relationship. And it is through "the accumulation and reiteration of success and reparation" of attunement failures that an "infant establishes a positive affective core, with clearer boundaries between self and other (Emde, 1983)" (Tronick, 1989, p. 116). My goal as a therapist is not to be perfect but to be "good enough" in terms of securing an ongoing emotional connection that will elicit trust from my clients.

Sometimes I simply miss my client's cue. Once, during an obviously difficult moment, I tried to reassure a client that I was "with her" by sliding my

---

[19]"Unless repair of these disruptions in attunement is undertaken, toxic senses of shame and humiliation can become serious blocks to interpersonal communication" (Siegel, 1999a, p. 291). This is painfully true with my clients. Because their core self is fragile and precariously unstable, a breach in attunement with me through my dissociation or misunderstanding can catapult a woman into that dark hole of despair. She may believe she caused the breach. An overwhelming sense of badness and dread of annihilation may surface, overpowering her ability to articulate all that is taking place inside her. The best she can do at the time may be to withdraw or shutdown.

chair closer to hers and leaning forward. She continued to speak, but I noticed an increase in her level of anxiety. I assumed her anxiety was related to the topic. Thinking I was attuned to her, I reflected her strained facial expression and offered empathy, saying, "It must be so hard to talk about this. I can tell you are really struggling."

She reacted by sitting straight up and pushing herself back into the couch. Her eyes were bright and large as she announced, "*You* are making me nervous. I'm fine with talking about *this,* but *you* are getting too close!" Gratefully, her ability to be honest in that situation allowed us to quickly repair our connection and allowed me to reestablish safety by simply scooting my chair back.

As soon as I become aware of a rupture in attunement, I attempt to reattune to the client's emotional state. But to reattune on any level, she will have to be willing to open herself up enough to reconnect. If she is unable or unwilling to do so, I still affirm and respect her. I realize that her safety has been breached and her mistrust ignited. Hopefully, my ongoing patience and compassion will eventually reestablish an atmosphere of safety and coordinated interactive states.

When She Needs to Be "Missed"

The closer a client feels to me through our attuned oneness, the more she might worry about sexualizing our relationship, behaving inappropriately or, in the end, getting hurt. She may unconsciously disengage, instinctively attempting to create distance between us, or goad me into expressing disappointment or frustration with her. My rejection of her at this point would actually be a welcome relief.

I process her disengagement through gentle, nonshaming inquiry. I might proceed by saying, "I can sense that you need to back away a bit from our togetherness. Do you feel that?"

"Yeah, I do."

"How does that new place—a little distant from me—feel?"

"OK, I guess. I just needed a breath of air. I don't think I was breathing."

"That's OK. Why don't you just take a moment to take a deep breath and then let it out slowly?" I pause for a while and then say, in an energetic and positive tone, "You are doing great!"

In a more serious, focused tone, I ask, "What was it like for you to experience those intense moments of warmth and connection with me?"

Again, this opportunity to reflect allows her to integrate these warm moments into her greater experience and core affective self. We can then discuss what may have triggered her dissociation or need for nonattunement, such as fear or agitation. I typically direct these reflections in a very soft, tender, nurturing voice, inviting her to stay present to the deeper and richer places within her own being as she stays present with me.

Sometimes, after a few moments of experiencing warm connection, a client may disconnect through the use of hostile defenses, such as mocking my last heartfelt remark, abruptly changing the subject or coldly minimizing her emotions, saying something like, "Oh, it wasn't really that bad. You know, life sucks. But I'm over it!"

Many a time I have relaxed within a warm moment, only to be startled by a client's sarcasm or her analysis of our present moment, expressed in a comment such as, "Do you know that your forehead wrinkles when you look concerned?"

Over the years, I have learned to never interpret these defensive maneuvers as personal attacks or to react with harsh confrontation. Actually, at times I have to hide a smile. Indeed, my client's defenses provide an excellent opportunity for me to readjust my attunement and empathy to her fear, doubt or insecurity. I remind myself of the positive aspect of her character that I know and love, such as her dogged determination, and then, again, go where she goes. I allow her the freedom to relate, express and protect herself in the best way she knows how. When a woman admits that it would be easier to meet with me if "I wasn't so nice," I know she is emerging from fear and shame and entering a sense of safety. This does not necessarily mean that we are ready to fully enter grief work or directly tackle core beliefs or deep insecurities. We must first cultivate trust and a solid authentic attachment.

BALANCING ALL OF HER NEEDS

The opening stage of therapy can feel like a balancing act. Many women begin therapy amid very serious circumstances or emotional crises, such as ending a long-term same-sex relationship or facing severe adversity within a marriage. These situations require immediate attention. Yet the foundational processes of acceptance and attunement cannot be sidestepped in lieu of addressing emergencies and life difficulties. Once a woman finally makes a choice to allow herself, perhaps for the first time in her life, to *feel* safe and begin to allow another to enter her inner world, she is on holy ground. And when this happens, I, for one, want to be fully proficient to go where she goes.

CHAPTER SEVEN

Rebuilding on a
Corrective Relationship

Trust and Empathy

Once I knew only darkness and stillness. . . . My life was without past or future. . . . But a little word from the fingers of another fell into my hand that clutched at emptiness and my heart leaped to the rapture of living.

HELEN KELLER, *OPTIMISM*

Perriann Parks Beyers, a licensed clinical social worker, private practitioner and executive director of Counseling Centers of Utah, had worked with sexual abuse survivors prior to working with women with SSA. She hoped her previous experience would be useful in working with this new population, but she was not fully prepared for the differences. She immediately discovered that her approach with women with SSA (with or without a history of sexual abuse) had to be unique in terms of building trust. Through our personal communication, she explained that many of these women had specific challenges in connecting and bonding emotionally. She had to be far more overt and persistent in her caring behaviors than with other clients. Beyers realized that they needed to know beyond a shadow of doubt that she could and would continue to genuinely connect with them even if they could not fully trust or even *feel* a connection with her. She admits that securing this authentic connection on her part required a tremendous investment, but she was willing to do whatever it took to gain her clients' trust.

THERAPIST'S SECOND TASK: BUILD TRUST

Building trust with women with SSA is *not* the same as building theapeutic rapport with other clients. So difficult is this task, that when I first started my practice, I was tempted to believe my clients were intentionally and stubbornly resisting my exerted efforts to establish trust. It is not uncommon for new clients to openly question my sincerity and intentions. For example, even though they never miss an appointment, consistently show up on time and stay current with their accounts, in the initial stage of therapy, they may become angry and defensive when I ask about their week. They challenge me and sarcastically ask, "Why do you care?" or say, "You're just *acting* like you care." They seem to resist my interest, kindness and empathy, but when I challenge them about their readiness for therapy, they are offended by my implying they aren't serious about our work.

In time I came to realize that many of my clients had literally *never* experienced trust. As a result, they lacked a basic internalized *sense of trust*. And lacking trusting relationships, they missed the opportunity to develop their full *capacity to trust* and therefore to relate. Those who had a basis of foundational trust still often endured many trust-shattering experiences by adulthood or encountered damaging religious and social messages about homosexuality. Many came to believe that they would never be safe. I believe it is not true that my clients *won't* trust. They *can't* trust.

OPERATIONAL MISTRUST AND DEFENSIVENESS

As discussed in the previous chapter, an infant (or child) who is not provided with consistent emotional attunement or connection with another, as may be the case for women with SSA, may become flooded by her own negative emotions. To survive, a child will take whatever measures necessary to manage these feelings, such as

- disavowing selective feelings
- denying all feelings
- avoiding an "anticipated experience of negative affect, even in situations where negative affect might not occur" (Tronick, 1989, p. 117)
- indiscriminately disengaging from people and things
- dismissing opportunities for attachment (defensive detachment)

It is likely, then, that my clients' own unconscious denials and disengagements as small children further handicapped the ongoing possibility of an attuned connection with their parents and the development of a positive core self (Orcutt, 1995). It is also likely that my client's fledgling sense of self may have taken on traits not only of emptiness but also of *defendedness*—both of which are antithetical to the restful fullness and openness that typically characterize the life of a beloved child.[1] Indeed, a second striking common denominator of women with SSA is their heightened defensive posturing.

McDougall (1980) provides an example of how this defensiveness might look in the counseling office. Her client, Olivia, was complaining about how many of the women in her life criticized her appearance. One day in therapy, Olivia said, "I'm scruffy; I look like a grubby boy. I'm convinced you aren't interested in me either; I don't suppose you even want to go on with my analysis!" She then asked McDougall whether many attractively dressed women came to consult her, but immediately she dissolved into tears, saying she was "dirty, clumsy, and disgusting" and asserting it would be impossible for her to be otherwise (p. 99). She was essentially defending herself from an opportunity for McDougall to affirm her otherwise. She could not trust McDougall's warm acceptance. It is often heartwrenching to watch this level of self-contempt and relational ambivalence in my clients. Like Olivia, many women with SSA secretly long to be accepted and possibly seen as attractive, but they remain hopeless and closed off in their defensive core beliefs that they are unlovable and that no one could possibly view them as anything but repulsive.[2]

The task of building trust, then, is primarily *mine*. I must show (or in many instances, prove) that I—not counselors in general—am trustworthy. My efforts must extend beyond establishing my initial trustworthiness. I must also navigate through and compensate for my client's expectation that although I might appear trustworthy at this moment, I—like all of her other caregivers—will still fail her. Because of her mistrust, I must prove myself over and over. In the first stage of therapy, I am typically the one exerting energy, tracking

---

[1]Tronick (1989) notes that "what were normal self-regulatory behaviors become pathological or 'defensive'" (p. 117). As one might imagine, "the chronic experience of failure, nonreparation, and negative affect has several detrimental effects on developmental outcome" (p. 117). Winnicott (1965) concurs, claiming that "if maternal care is not good enough then the infant does not really come into existence, since there is no continuity of being; *instead the personality becomes built on the basis of reactions to environmental impingement* [italics added]" (p. 54).

[2]Not *all* women with SSA will present in such defended postures. Those who have reached greater levels of maturity and healthy development are able to accept my involvement and care, although they may still have vestiges of defensive detachment and other hidden defense mechanisms as described in following chapters. But those who have never fully entered into an experience of safety and trust will need to be convinced again and again of my safety and trustworthiness.

with emotions and setting the stage for connection. This does not mean my client is not exerting effort, but her energies are typically directed toward simply surviving the counseling hour and learning to enter into an attuned connection. Ideally, she is to become the recipient of the fruits of *my* labor.

ACCEPTING VERSUS BREAKING THROUGH THE DEFENSES

Because their defensive behaviors and relational style may be habitual, many women with SSA have confusedly and hopelessly concluded that this defensiveness is "just who I am." That a woman with SSA indeed *may* frustrate or infuriate others who attempt to draw close only confirms her beliefs that she lacks the ability to connect or that she could never be a good friend. Unfortunately, other professionals have often called her stubborn, belligerent, arrogant or resistant, further confirming her false beliefs and negative identities. Therapists should heed the following advice, given by a woman with SSA who runs support groups for other women: "No matter how mean they speak to you, no matter how mean they glare at you, they are just waiting for you to be the next person in their long litany of people who have given up on them. You have to be different."

I have found that one of the surest ways to be different and to show care is to honor my client's defenses. Ross (2000) suggests, "The defenses are part of the person. The therapist works *with* the defenses. They are part of the person just like the hopes, dreams, sense of humor and personal history" (p. 233). I therefore make it my aim to treat her defenses just as I would her hopes and dreams. I want to get to know them, to understand them and to discover their origin and her associated needs and desires. No matter how defensive or obstinately she may behave, I hold to the belief that a God-given longing for love and connection is hidden deep within her.

As I accept and work with her chosen modes of survival (which, to a client, is often the same as accepting *her*) rather than fight or challenge them, many of my clients report that they feel accepted and known, often for the first time. But since my clients' perceived survival has depended on their actual avoidance of trust and closeness, I do not expect them to immediately appreciate my efforts to offer acceptance and safety. They may remain disgruntled and closed off.

Week after week, I attempted to "enter" Lindsey's world. I expectantly asked her how she felt about our last session.

She coldly replied, "I didn't really think about it."

As we discussed her previous week and pursued more of her history, she spoke matter-of-factly, as if being sexually abused by the neighbor boys was a casual incident. When she shared how her first female lover left her for another woman, I softly replied, "That must have broken your heart."

Brushing me off, she sarcastically replied, "Oh, I got over it."

When I questioned her about her present loneliness, she exclaimed, "I am not lonely! Quit assuming you know who I am."

As I asked her what she wanted to get out of our session, she said, "Well, how the hell am I supposed to know? You're the counselor."

This went on and on, until one week, as we were talking about her dog, who was suffering from a serious illness, I saw her face flush briefly. I gently said, "This must be so scary for you—the thought of losing your dog."

She nodded. She had let me in.

I am so thankful that early in my training one of my supervisors reassured me that if a client keeps coming to therapy, she still wants something. In other words, I had a choice to believe either the message being sent by her faithfulness in coming or the message sent by her defenses. Unfortunately, the former message is usually quieter and more difficult to hear than the latter.

> *We spend all of our lives building these walls and trying to cover our vulnerabilities, and then what these therapists are asking us to do is to let them all down and allow our selves to be vulnerable. Right! I'll just do that tomorrow! No problem!*
> Sarah

THERAPEUTIC MISTAKES

At certain times I unintentionally leave my client feeling offended or questioning whether I am truly trustworthy. Because many women with SSA are deeply sensitive and hold negative self-images, I cannot shirk off these blunders. I have to address my mistakes and do so in a therapeutically beneficial way.

I can still vividly recall one such incident. I had been working with Randi for several months. She was 34 years old, extremely intelligent, an avid reader and well-versed in science, politics and philosophy. With a few minutes left at the end of a session, we entered into a rather intellectual discussion about certain pressing political affairs. Randi had a professional interest in politics, and I enjoyed getting to know this part of her. Eventually, however, she became extremely impassioned, laughed at one of my comments and made a few very dogmatic statements. Much to my chagrin, I reacted and defensively engaged her in a debate. Our session ended in tension and anxiety.

After seeking out consultation, I decided that to reestablish a sense of safety and trust, I needed to authentically interact with Randi in a discussion of my failure to keep her best interest in mind. Near the beginning of our next session, I apologized, taking full ownership of any negative reactions she may have had from our previous session. She sat speechless. She had actually come to the session believing she had done something wrong and was prepared to apologize to me. She later wrote me a note explaining how my apology affected her:

> I remember that when you apologized, you mentioned that you had felt hurt at some point in the "debate." You weren't blaming me for hurting you; you were just trying to explain why you reacted the way you did. But the fact that you were honest about your hurt was a big deal because you made yourself vulnerable to me. This leads me to the most important thing: in engaging with me and trying to pull me out from behind my fear, you put yourself out there with me to the point that you could be hurt. I was thinking that it was hard for me to be vulnerable and put myself out there . . . but you did it! I knew I could no longer keep you out. D***! . . . Also, I think the apology thing was so important to me because you weren't the only person in the interaction who was accountable and you took the high road. I was so used to being the only one to take the high road. I dropped my guard when I realized you were willing to do that.

MAINTAINING CARING BOUNDARIES, NOT BARRIERS

When a woman with SSA is beginning to trust and attach, perhaps for the first time in her life, she is especially vulnerable to a therapist's misuse of power, need fulfillment and unresolved personal issues. And if the therapeutic relationship is established on an authentic and real connection, as I recommend, the therapist will also experience some level of vulnerability. It is imperative that a therapist have the strength and personal integrity to set and clearly articulate the nature and purpose of professional boundaries. Professional boundaries do not exist to protect professionals from their clients or patients.[3] They exist to protect clients from their therapists.

I have counseled several women who have asked me, point blank, if I have adequate personal support in my life. They are genuinely concerned that my unmet needs may prompt me to become inappropriately emotionally or sexually involved with them. At a later stage in therapy, the same clients may admit that I am their closest friend and resent that we cannot have a relationship outside of therapy. It is normal throughout the process of therapy for a client to be confused about or question her boundaries. Therefore, as a therapist, I must assume *all* responsibility for maintaining boundaries for her sake. It is my opinion that therapists who tend to slide or compromise on professional boundaries should *not* work with women with SSA.

> *For me, as a struggler, boundaries are a humungous issue. That is why boundaries with my counselor have been useful for me in terms of trust and safety. I know what is going to happen. I know who and what she is going to be all the time. There is no ambiguity and no confusion. So much of life is filled with ambiguity and confusion, so that is why it's really important.*
>
> Ellen

The following therapeutic boundaries are extremely important in working with women with SSA. While they must be solid and consistently enforced, I acknowledge some inherent negotiable and flexible features.

BOUNDARY ONE: DUAL RELATIONSHIPS

I remain doggedly committed to never entertain a dual relationship with a client. Because many of my clients and I attend the same religious gatherings, it is very important that they know what to expect should our paths cross in public. Early in treatment, as I reassure a client of the boundaries to our relationship (always phrased in terms of my commitment to keep *her* safe), I ask her what she would like to see happen if we run into each other outside of the of-

---

[3]A therapist should never have to set personal boundaries within a session in an effort to secure his or her own safety or comfort. No matter how irritating, offensive or upsetting a client's actions or words are, the situation should be handled therapeutically. For instance, rather than saying, "You cannot speak to me like that," say, "I'm wondering what is behind the tone of voice you just used. Are you feeling hurt or scared?"

fice. We openly discuss the pros and cons of waving or saying hello. For example, if we greet one another, she may be put in an awkward situation when the friends she's with ask who I am. If her friends know me, she may be unduly exposed when they connect my work with women with SSA and her association with me. Another consideration is that offering a warm hello stirs relational longing. She may feel cheated or slighted by my simple hello, but my not saying hello may leave her feeling completely ignored or neglected. While discussions such as this may seem like overkill, my handling the implications of and subtle reactions to seemingly trivial matters of boundary clarification actually goes a long way in helping a woman to trust my sensitivity to all of *her* needs and expectations.

In relationally based therapy, the therapist's personal disclosure is vital to establishing an authentic connection. However, to remain faithful to professional ethics, I must consider these two points. First, I must make certain that my self-disclosure is *always* for the benefit of the client and associated with therapeutic processes, such as mutuality and mirroring, role modeling, normalizing or reality checking.[4] Second, I am also sensitive to the risks inherent in my self-disclosure, primarily the possibility that this information may confuse a client. For instance, she may be left asking herself questions like, *Now that I know these things about my therapist's life journey, what role am I supposed to take in this relationship? Am I supposed to care for my therapist the way I typically care for other important people in my life? Am I free to ask my therapist more questions about her life? What is my therapist's responsibility to me?* When a client articulates questions like these, I listen, address her concerns and reassure her that she has no responsibility to take care of me. She is to learn a posture of resting and receiving within our therapeutic relationship. I also reassure her that I *will* remain authentic and real within our sessions, but I will also remain wholeheartedly committed to our professional boundaries.

BOUNDARY TWO: TOUCH

The use of excessive touch, physical affection or holding therapies (outside of the involvement of an experienced therapeutic team, such as those specializing

---

[4]I may, therefore, disclose parts of my history in terms of my own healing and growth process or aspects of my personhood and ongoing internal struggles, but I do not typically share the actual data or activities related to my personal life.

in corrective attachment therapies) should be avoided.[5] Even a short hug at the end of a session or a kind gesture, such as holding a client's hand during prayer, may confuse many women. Touch is a powerful medium and can trigger a woman's sense of touch deprivation and need, not to mention create confusion about her therapist's ultimate intentions. Even the slightest affectionate gesture must be offered cautiously and with certainty that it is in the client's best interests, that she is capable of correctly interpreting it, and that she has given permission for such interaction.

I have worked with and interviewed several women who have entered into sexual relationships with their therapists during or immediately after terminating therapy. I have therefore learned to never underestimate the warm feelings I experience in association with a client's affection and undying loyalty to me. Dealing with these sorts of therapist reactions, both positive and negative, will be further dealt with in chapter eleven.

BOUNDARY THREE: TIMELINESS

I have come to understand that I must be punctual and available in terms of regularly scheduled appointments.[6] My arriving late to the office can create anxiety in a client as she becomes increasingly convinced that I don't want to be with her or that she is an imposition. It is imperative that I acknowledge my tardiness and allow her time to process its effects. If I go over time in a session (which is *not* a frequent practice), I communicate to my next client that I am running late. I use every opportunity I can to reassure my clients that I am aware of them and that I care about their predicaments.

Additionally, I give my clients advance notice if I am taking a vacation or a trip that will create a disruption in our regularly scheduled time. Not only may a woman need to prepare herself for my absence in terms of gathering outside support, but she may need to process deep feelings of abandonment or the temptation to internalize my absence as her fault. I am very conscientious about any promises I make to my clients, such as, "I will bring you that book next session." If I am not certain that I can keep a promise, I won't

---

[5]For an excellent review on the ethics of touch within psychotherapeutic settings, I recommend Zur (2007).

[6]This also means that I must end sessions on time, which can often be difficult when a client begins to experience a separation anxiety near the end of a session. I have learned to manage the time within sessions to accommodate these anxieties.

make it. And if I break a promise, then it is my job to apologize and repair the damage.

BEING CONSTANT UNTIL THE END

Building and growing in trust is a life long journey. Throughout our work together, my clients may still waver, repeatedly asking themselves, *Is she for real? Can I—should I—trust her? What if she lets me down, like everyone else? She is my last hope. If she fails me I will have nothing. Is trusting her really worth it?* But these moments of doubt can be overcome if I remain patient and persistent in my loving attitudes and protective care.

THERAPIST'S THIRD TASK: ESTABLISH AND MAINTAIN A SECURE ATTACHMENT

To not be attached is to remain adrift and empty in a cold and threatening world. In her book *Born That Way?* Erin Eldridge reveals that her "life became a cycle of stepping out into the cold, becoming unable to survive the storm, and running back to the only warmth and shelter" (1994, p. 13) she knew, the arms of another woman. Until my clients actually *experience* an attachment based on trust, my words *about* intimacy or relationship are merely academic. In response to a discussion about healthy intimacy, a client might say, "Yeah, whatever," or, reluctantly, "Well, I guess if that is what God wants, it must be good." She has no experience or internal representation of "healthy intimacy."

> *The first therapist I had was not helpful at all. She just gave me behavioral things, like don't hug a woman for very long, don't carry a pocketknife. It was all, "Don't do this," or "Don't do that." There was no attachment. I was more than ready. I was all blubbery and was really ready to delve into things, but it seemed she wasn't ready or willing to connect.*
>
> *Lauren*

Thankfully, as trust grows, so will a woman's healthy desire for intimacy and attachment.[7] This desire, although at times unconscious, is a sign of a growing and developing self; her *self* is designed to need and want connection. And the

---

[7]Moberly (1983) stresses that "it is this lack of trust which is central to the repression of the need for attachment" (p. 46).

more a woman experiences ongoing connection or secure attachments, the more she will come to know and develop her self. Rephrased in the negative, if there is no *other*, then there is no *me*. For women, attachment is the basis of a sense of self, life and love.[8]

In providing corrective attachment therapy, the therapeutic "focus is not about strategy, technique, or symptom removal. The primary healing aspect of the work is relational, not technical, and the success of treatment depends upon the quality of those relationships" (Rand, 1996, p. 24). Levy and Orlans (1998) stress that the following relational elements are essential to this therapeutic process:

- attunement (establishing safety)
- positive affect and support (dealing with defenses)
- structure (boundaries)
- empathy (basis of attachment)
- reciprocity (authenticity and realness in the moment)
- love (adapted from pp. 112-14)

Having addressed the first three, we now turn our attention to empathy and reciprocity, or experiencing realness in the here-and-now.

I FEEL YOU, I SEE YOU, I HEAR YOU

Therapeutic attunement is when I momentarily comprehend and experientially share in my client's psychological and emotional state, communicating my attunement through nonverbal gestures. Empathy involves attunement with the added component of verbalized validation and caring support. Female developmental theorists Jordan and Surrey (1989) define empathy as the "process through which one's experienced sense of basic connection and similarity to other humans is established. . . . Without empathy, there is no intimacy" (p. 85). The one receiving empathy recognizes it as the moment when she experiences the warm feeling of being completely understood and known. It can feel like relief and oneness, a thought like, *I am joined with one who understands.* Empathy is both the conduit through which care and compassion

---

[8]Researcher Beverly Wells (2003) discovered that self-identified lesbians, after receiving a minimum of three years of individual psychotherapy for relationship issues, reported lower levels of shame and a greater frequency of secure attachment styles than a similar but nonclinical sample of lesbian women previously studied by Wells & Hansen (2003).

flow and that on which secure attachment is based; it honors another's personhood. In their discussion of the significance of empathy, Jordan and Surrey (1989) suggest,

> Either we deal with the feelings that are inevitably present in our interactions by turning to each other—or we turn away. If we turn away from others without conveying recognition of the existence of their feelings, we inevitably leave the other person diminished to some degree. (p. 91)

As illustrated below in the dialogue I had with one of my clients, creating an empathic environment involves

- a primary focus on and identification with the client's inner needs and emotional experience (attunement)
- a release of focus on the *content* of the current discussion
- accurate mirroring and explicit validation
- genuine care and curiosity, with verification of accuracy
- encouragement and support

"Hi, Kim, how are you doing today?" I asked.

"Oh, I'm just fed up with everything," she announced in an aggravated tone. "I'm tired of processing, I'm tired of my depression, and I'm tired of counseling. Nothing is helping. It's no use."

"It sounds like you're feeling very weary and maybe hopeless. Am I close?" I focused on her emotional experience instead of the *reason* for her tiredness.

She nodded.

"Those feelings can be so heavy. Do you just feel weighted down?" I validated her weariness, verifying for accuracy.

"Yeah, It feels like I'm buried."

"So you just feel buried or under it." I paused and waited for her affirmation. "And you also feel like giving up?" Here I sought to unpack her emotional experience with care and curiosity.

"Yeah, I do," she answered, speaking more slowly.

Following a hunch that there is more poignant emotion to be revealed, I asked Kim, "What would giving up look like for you right now?"

"Well, you can be d*** sure I'd quit this counseling thing. What a *waste* of my time—and money I might add." She was instantly energized! She was going deeper.

"So you're feeling worn-out and hopeless?" Again, I paused for confirmation. "I think I'm also hearing anger." In this accurate mirroring and validation, I still did not pursue content or the reason for her anger. "Is that right?" I asked, seeking to verify my statement's accuracy.

"Yeah, I guess," she responded more slowly, perhaps feeling fear or shame.

"Kim, it's OK. You certainly have a right to feel anger if that is what you're truly feeling." I wanted to encourage and support her. "In fact, I think I sensed a bit of anger when you said you were tired of everything. So is *anger* the best word to describe your feeling, or is there another?"

"Oh, I don't know. I'm just mad."

"I know when I'm feeling angry, exhausted and hopeless all at the same time, I certainly feel buried," I shared, identifying with her experience. "You must be really struggling, Kim." I wanted to show encouragement and support again. "Thank you so much for being willing to share all these difficult feelings with me."

"Well, frankly, I'm really struggling with *you*," she retorted. Now that she felt heard and had the safety of an empathic environment, *she* took a huge risk and moved the conversation toward the content of her anger.

"Say more, Kim. I want to understand your struggle."

"Well, you made me mad last week."

"Kim, how I made you mad last week is really important and I want to hear all about it. But first I want to acknowledge how hard it must have been for you to carry this anger all week and come in and face me today." Saying this refocused the conversation on her emotional experience.

"It *was* hard. I didn't want to come."

"Yeah, I bet it was hard. Did you think about canceling?" I identified with her experience, communicating that if I had felt anger toward my therapist, I would have thought about canceling.

"Yes—but I decided, what the hell. If I can't tell *you* when I'm mad, then what good is it for me to keep coming?"

Expressing encouragement and support, I said, "You are absolutely right, Kim. I am so glad you trusted me enough to share your true feelings." I then added, out of genuine care for her, "I would have been *very* disappointed if you had canceled," and paused to see whether she wanted to say more about her process.

For empathy to have its positive, curative effect, I must set aside my reactions to a client's attitudes and accusations, even if she intends for me to take them personally. The content or story of why she is angry should not be completely negated, but it must be set aside until she first experiences the warmth and shelter of my empathic care and concern. Truth be known, Kim could probably have talked to anybody about *how* and *why* I made her angry, and she probably already had. I continued to use empathy even as we explored the reasons for her anger.

"So, Kim, do you feel comfortable telling me more about what made you mad last week?"

"I guess so. It was when we were talking about my relationship with Susan. At one point you were reminding me that I knew, even before she and I got involved, that she probably wouldn't stick around. But it wasn't *what* you said; it was *how* you said it. You pointed your finger at me. It made me feel like a child, like I was being scolded. I don't deserve that from you."

"You're right. You don't deserve that from me. I can see why you were upset."

"You reminded me of my dad. He used to wave his finger at me all the time."

"Oh, Kim, I'm so sorry to hear that. So I acted like your dad last week? How did you feel as a little girl when he pointed his finger?"

"Insignificant, small, ashamed. He always treated me like I was stupid."

"So did you feel stupid and ashamed when I pointed my finger like that?"

"Yeah, I did, but I was shocked, too. I didn't expect you to treat me like my dad would. The more I thought about it, the angrier I got."

"Kim, I want to apologize for my insensitive gesture. I feel so sad that you felt insignificant and ashamed. I shocked you by my behavior. I feel grieved that you thought I was scolding you. How difficult that must have been! I would surely feel infuriated if anyone treated me like a child or as if I was stupid. But I'm so thankful that you were able to tell me how I affected you. You have been very brave, and I know you took a huge risk in talking to me about this."

It is far more important for me to validate and empathize with my client's pain and anger at this point than to explain or defend myself. It is through this empathy that she will gain the sense that I am *with* her and *for* her, or, in other words, that I am attached.

"Kim, is there anything more you would like to say about last week?" She may have more to say, and I would use empathy as she unfolded more details about her feelings in the present and in the past.

"No, not really. But can you not do that again—the finger waving thing?" She was not that interested in *why* I did it, she just did not want it to happen again.

Smiling, I said, "You can be sure that I will certainly try my best to never do it again. But if I have a lapse and forget, you have my permission to speak up and tell me I blew it. I don't want to create another week of misery like this last one. Thanks for giving me a second chance. Some people may have quit without ever telling me why. Again, I feel honored by your trust and respect."

"Thanks for understanding."

If I want to be able to reach the very core of a woman's need, I must be able to affirm her and go *with* her into the many layers of pain and emotions through empathy.[9] And as each layer is uncovered and met with genuine care and acceptance, the shame of her emptiness and neediness will dissipate, allowing her to know and understand herself on the deepest level.[10]

To empathize is to offer my self as a distinct and solid presence. The majority of the experienced professional counselors I interviewed for this book agree that to be most effective with women with SSA, the counselor's *personal* development must take precedence over his or her *professional* development.[11] While I certainly participate in continuing education to build my professional skills and techniques, I also continue—through personal therapy and consultation—to challenge obstacles to strengthening my core self and to developing deeper connections and intimacies. I want to broaden and deepen my own inner world so that I can *connect* with my clients' rich inner worlds.

HERE-AND-NOW PROCESSING VERSUS INTERPRETATION

Empathy takes place within the here-and-now moment of a therapy session. As already indicated, the here-and-now approach "*de-emphasizes* (but does *not*

---

[9]While admitting there are risks involved in empathy, Siegel (1988), having worked with several women with SSA, agrees that "freely hovering attention, trial identification, and empathic immersal are the only means that have been found to grasp more fully the infantile needs of developmentally arrested patients" (p. 43).

[10]For other examples in which empathy can be effectively used with women with SSA, please see "Always Defer to Empathy" on the book website at www.ivpress.com.

[11]Jordan, Surrey and Kaplan (1991), leaders in the field of female development, stress that empathy requires a "high level of psychological development and ego strength" on the part of the therapist. "In order to empathize, one must have a well-differentiated sense of self in addition to an appreciation of and sensitivity to the differentness as well as the sameness of another person" (p. 29).

negate the importance of) the patient's historical past or events of his or her outside life" while emphasizing the curative power of a meaningful heartfelt connection with the client (Yalom, 2002, p. 46). "The here-and-now refers to the immediate events of the therapeutic hour" (p. 46). It is what *happens* in my relationship with my client—not the goals or outcomes of *my* agenda or treatment plan[12]—that is most substantial and important.[13]

I have learned that, at least in the first stage of therapy, I must let go of my multiple insights and simply enter into the process or adventure of building a real relationship with a real fascinating person. Besides, until a woman has a sense of attachment to and togetherness with me, she usually does not fully appreciate my "sagely wisdom" or insight. An intellectual understanding of her life does not necessarily resolve her deeper needs and will seem useless if she is still faced with traveling through life alone.

TO BE OR NOT TO BE

Analysis and interpretation require a client to work, to think, to dig up and put pieces together. She must remain in an intellectual *doing* mode. There is nothing inherently wrong with analysis or the intellectual "doing" side of therapy. But for the woman with SSA who has spent far too much of her life "doing" the work of survival and protecting herself against pain by intellectualizing, analysis is not the recommended primary mode of therapy, at least not for now. I've illustrated this below with two hypothetical exchanges.

Exchange 1: Using analysis and interpretation. Cautiously, Lauren opens our session, saying, "I wrote a poem for you. I brought it with me and would like to read it."

"Lauren, I'd love to hear it," I say with a serious but caring tone, leaning forward in my chair. "But before you read it, I'm wondering if we could process something."

Trusting me, Lauren replies, "Sure."

"I'm wondering if you have some underlying fear about our work together," I begin. "In the last few weeks you have brought in several books and read var-

---

[12]In person-centered relational therapy, goals or change might be measured in terms of a client using fewer pillows for protection, increasing eye contact, experiencing a fleeting connection with an emotion or being open to receive a warm caring comment.

[13]Schaffner (2003) points out that "a patient is more likely to respect a therapist who takes into account what occurs between the two of them, as well as the physical and psychological realities of the patient's life outside the consulting room" (p. 243).

ious excerpts. This week you bring in a poem. I am sensing that you need to place something between us, like a safety wall or protective blanket. What do you think?"

Squirming and squinting a little, Lauren finally replies, "No, I'm not aware of anything. I just wanted to read those things because I thought they were interesting. I thought you might enjoy them." She says this almost like it is a question.

"Are you sure?" I ask. "I just sense there might be something else going on."

"No, not that I know of," Lauren replies.

In a gentle but challenging tone, I suggest, "Well, we have been talking about your husband. Perhaps you are unconsciously wanting to avoid dealing with your strained marriage."

More sheepishly, Lauren replies, "I don't think so. Just last night he and I had a talk about where we were at."

Backing off, I say, "Well, all right, I just wanted to check it out. I'd love to hear your poem."

Now noticeably unsure of herself, Lauren mumbles, "Well, I don't have to if you don't think its OK."

By attempting to *analyze* Lauren's actions, which was not totally inappropriate based on her pattern of behavior, I have unnecessarily put Lauren on the defensive with my analytical directness. This chosen direction drew us into our heads rather than our hearts.

Exchange 2: Staying in the moment and deepening closeness. Cautiously, Lauren opens our session, saying, "I wrote a poem for you. I brought it with me and would like to read it."

"Lauren, I would love to hear it," I say. "But first, what are you feeling as we begin?"

"I'm really nervous. I've been working on this poem for quite a few months. It contains my heart. But I'm really afraid. I'm afraid that you will misunderstand me. I'm afraid that you will be scared off by what I share."

"Lauren, I can hear how much fear you have. It must have been hard for you to even ask if you could read it."

"Yeah, it was. I'm scared."

"Why don't you just close your eyes for a minute and take two or three deep breaths." I coach her in this process and take her through a brief "safe place" exercise. "How long have you been thinking about sharing this with me?"

"For the last month at least."

"So you've been afraid for *that* long?"

"Yeah, but I just couldn't get up the courage."

"Well, I knew there was something going on. I had a sense that you were avoiding something. I have felt very concerned."

Lauren, now smiling contentedly, "Oh, its nothing about you. It's about my fears. I've been both excited and scared about the thought of sharing this with you. I've been sort of working my way up to it."

"So that is what the other books were about?"

"Yep."

"Lauren, how are you doing right now—with the fear?"

"Well, I'm not afraid as I was when I came in."

"Do you feel safe to continue?"

"Yeah, I think so."

"Can I ask you a few more questions before you share your poem?"

"Sure."

"What are you imagining or hoping I will do as you read the poem?"

"Oh, I imagine you sitting up closer to me and just listening."

"Do you imagine me doing anything in particular when you finish reading?"

"No. I guess that's up to you!" she says with a laugh.

"But that's what has you scared! Right?" I ask, chuckling as I casually scoot my chair a bit closer to her. Teasingly, I say, "You're not sure *what* I'm going to do, are you?" Smiling, I settle into my chair, and ask, "Lauren, would you like me to pray before you read?"

"Yes, that would be really nice."

I say a short prayer asking God to help her stay connected with her heart and emotions as she reads. I also ask for his protection. Then I tell her she can start whenever she is ready.

Lauren is open and ready to share her heart. She has owned some of her past hesitancy and slight stalling in therapy and is feeling known, understood and safe—contained.

As it turned out, Lauren's poem was so tender and meaningful that we were both in tears by the time she was finished reading. At this point I had a choice: I could swallow my emotion and revert to being an objective, analyzing therapist (the poem's lines provided plenty of material), or I could stay in the moment, mirroring her vulnerability by showing my heart as it related to her pain.

I chose to stay with Lauren. We exchanged affirming smiles, tears and words. I thanked her for the poem and for the experience. Even though this was one of the warmest moments I can remember with a client, I *did not* touch Lauren. But I *did* hold her with my care, eye contact, mutuality and empathy. The connection was life changing for us both.[14]

GIVING INSIGHT, INTERPRETATION AND FEEDBACK

As therapy progresses, interpretation and insight become more important. Yet I continuously ask myself, *Is it more important for my client to analyze the source of her confusion about intimacy or for her to simply be open and unguarded in an intimate moment with me?* When I decide that insight would be more beneficial—as in the following interaction—I open the doors of the unconscious slowly and gently, always relying on empathy.

"Caitlin, I so appreciate what you are sharing about your brother." Caitlin is enraged by how her brother has been treating her. "I think I am learning some new things about you. Do you think that you can handle some of my observations?" If she declines my offer to share, I respect and affirm her decision and suggest that there will be another day and time for that.

If she is open to listen, I proceed. "I sense two things. It seems to me that you care a lot about your brother. You always seem willing to be there for him. You have expressed compassion and understanding with respect to his situation, and you seem to offer help in whatever way you can. Frankly, I think that you would do anything for him." I pause and wait for her confirmation.

"But I sense that your brother is not able to return all of your favors, and it seems hard for him to thank you in the ways that you might deserve," I continue. "When I put myself in your shoes, I feel angry and hurt too. And then I think of how your dad was never able to affirm you or tell you how special you were. I wonder if some of the intense anger and frustration you are feeling is really more about your dad. Do you think that's possible, or am I totally missing it?"

STAYING ATTACHED

Attachment is not a one-time event; it is an ongoing process that requires attention and maintenance. If I am indeed the first person to whom my client

---

[14]An additional step to Lauren's and my process would be to reflect on her experience of my listening and response to her poem. The client's active process of reflection helps her fully integrate this corrective experience.

has ever felt connected or attached, her fear of loss or abandonment will be immense.

> *I know I'm dying for connection, but there is still ambivalence about connecting with my counselor. It's hard to let yourself attach and care and be cared for when you know you can't be friends and it won't last forever. I don't know if I can handle that sense of abandonment, so I feel ambivalent at times and know I shut down.*
>
> *Alaina*

I do not expect my clients to trust or attach in a way that disallows the normal ambivalence and anxiety of human relationship. I walk with her through these seasons. However, if a woman's ostensive ambivalence and anxiety begin to interfere with our current therapeutic process, I will revert back to empathy in an effort to hear her and understand her deeper fears. This always takes priority over any other set agenda.

As I accept and attune to my clients, just as they are, they begin to feel known, respected and safe. As I prove myself trustworthy, offering her my protection, reliability and genuine care, she will begin to trust me. It is then that she can allow herself to rest within a secure attachment. Within this relationship—one based on attunement, empathy and authenticity—she will have a home in which to solidify her unique self and inherent value.

CHAPTER EIGHT

Four Basic Blueprints

Understanding the Various Profiles

The world sets in to making us into what the world would like us to be,
and because we have to survive after all, we try to make
ourselves into something that we hope the world will like better
than it apparently did the selves we originally were.

FREDERICK BUECHNER, *TELLING SECRETS*

I open the door to my waiting room unsure whether the client waiting will be a man or a woman. The name given on the phone was androgynous, and the voice sounded male, but I have prepared myself to greet a female. My assumptions were right. She is wearing a Mickey Mouse sweatshirt with colored tennis shoes and heavy athletic socks under light blue slacks that don't match her ensemble. She has a difficult time looking at me, so she watches the floor as she enters my office. Conversation is arduous, but she is finally able to admit she wants help with her relationships. She has no friends.

My next client saunters into my office wearing a man's white T-shirt with the sleeves rolled up, a leather flight jacket thrown over her shoulder, dark blue extra-long jeans and heavy black boots. I invite her to sit on either couch. She chooses one, turns to face me and literally drops her body free-fall onto the couch. She spreads her legs, leans forward and with a smirk demands, *I'm here. Now fix me.*

I welcome my next client. She has long, beautiful blond hair and is wearing eye makeup and sensuous, dark lipstick. She has a lovely smile and is dressed in feminine, casual professional clothes. She is friendly, open and engaging. We chat about her day and her drive over to my office. I ask how she feels about starting with a new therapist. She smiles and with much animation replies, "Oh, I don't *feel*. I don't feel anything. It was a real frustration for my last therapist of three years!"

I am at the end of the day, prepared to meet with my final client. I open the door to my waiting room and spot an attractive woman with great taste. As she walks into my office—wearing expensive female sportswear, cool shoes and a stylish short haircut—she smiles but speaks curtly as she hands me the paperwork I had left for her in the waiting room. "I won't sign this one for personal ethical reasons," she says, "and just to let you know, if you ask me to end my lesbian relationship, I'll quit."

BLUEPRINTS PROVIDE GUIDELINES

Even though each woman I meet is wonderfully unique and special, over the years I have observed certain diagnostic and behavioral or personality patterns among women with SSA. This has made it possible to conceptualize four distinct profiles—captured in the above vignettes—for the purpose of understanding and establishing appropriate treatment guidelines and goals. The four common profiles, which are the focus of the remainder of this chapter, coalesced as I considered clinical presentations, common diagnostic categories, attachment styles, defensive maneuvers and other personality attributes of my clientele as a whole. They are primarily descriptive in nature and should *not* be rigidly construed: indeed, many women *may* identify with one profile over another, but will most likely see parts of themselves in each of the other profiles as well.

The profiles overlap and are perhaps better understood as various personas within each individual woman based on her salient needs and the therapeutic themes experienced at different stages of her process. Generally speaking, then, the needs and treatment suggestions for all four profiles will benefit every woman in due time.

Furthermore, the words used to identify each profile describe characteristics or traits that have most likely emerged out of a woman's unique survival modes and defenses, compensations or false selves. They are *not* descriptive of a woman's truest and fullest God-given self, although they may highlight some of her true strengths and authentic inner conflict. For this reason, I am not apt to share these profiles, at least not explicitly, with my clients. If a client comes across them in my writings or my recorded lectures, I help her through any sense of judgment or confusion that may arise. As I address these profiles or psychological patterns, I do so with the *utmost respect* for my clients, acknowledging that they are *unique* women who cannot be ultimately contained by a diagnostic label or category.

Profile 1: Empty, Depressed, Withdrawn and Isolated

These women often have profound developmental deficits arising out of perceived and actual *emotional* absence or neglect. Their basic physical needs were met, but they nevertheless internalized the message that their existence was an inconvenience and a nuisance. Their lives are severely empty and lonely. They may have a few friends, but the friendships lack mutuality. They feel more attached to objects or animals than to people. They are uncomfortable in their own skin and know that they are not "normal," at least in social settings. They may show marked inability to follow standard social cueing or comprehend— let alone articulate—inner emotional or psychological dynamics. They are often overweight and tend to be nondescript in appearance.

These women live life robotically, often without meaning, a sense of purpose or any heartfelt connection. They are numb. Some perform better than others, but that is the basis of their existence—a perfunctory doing, following the rules, taking the next step. Yet they are often incredible writers, poets and artists. They have well-developed imaginations and secret fantasy worlds. The therapist may be the first person to see their true self and phenomenal gifting. The therapist may also be the first person to call them out into a real, tangible human connection.

Case study. Sophie is an only child of elderly parents. She does not remember spending much time with either parent. Her dad was absent, her mother preoccupied. Her dad yelled at her mother, calling her stupid and useless. Sophie tried to make herself invisible during these fights. She had few childhood friends; she was rarely allowed to go over to other kids' houses or to have friends over. When she was at school, she played by herself. Sophie has flash impressions of being sexually abused. She was often mistaken for a boy. She didn't intentionally *try* to look like a little boy, but to save money, her mother would buy her used boys' clothes. Sophie was always close to her female teachers. Sometimes she wished they were her *real* mothers. As she grew older, she would often imagine being best friends with one of the prettiest girls in school. She didn't fit in with any particular peer group. She was a loner. A committed Christian, Sophie has never been sexually involved with another woman. She had one emotionally dependent relationship with a woman after college, but it didn't last. She has a desire to have a close female friend, but she fears closeness with women since she is afraid it might become sexual. She entered therapy because she doesn't want to be lesbian.

The following table outlines my clinical assessment of and treatment guidelines for profile 1.[1]

Table 1. Profile 1

Developmental Issues
Negatively resolved (often up to *three* standard deviations) in the following developmental stages:

- trust vs. *mistrust*
- industry vs. *inferiority*
- identity vs. *identity confusion*
- intimacy vs. *isolation*
- generativity vs. *stagnation*
- ego integrity vs. *despair*[a]

Clinical Symptoms

- major depression
- dystymia
- generalized anxiety
- possible eating disturbances (overweight)[b]
- thought disorders

Characterological Patterns

- avoidant (with schizoid features), depressive, dependent, and masochistic (self-defeating and borderline) disorders and traits
- high comorbidity of Axis I and Axis II

[a]A high score in despair often indicates the presence of depression.
[b]For research related to weight and eating disorders amongst lesbians, please refer to the section "Homosexual Women and Weight" on the book website at www.ivpress.com.

---

[1]The following applies to the tables for all four profiles. *Developmental issues:* The terms listed here are identified in Erikson's (1980) eight-stage model of psychosocial development. These findings are based on my clinical observation and the formal psychological assessment tool: Measures of Psychosocial Development (MPD); see Hawley (1988). For research findings on developmental issues in women with SSA using the measures of psychosocial development, please refer to the book website at www.ivpress.com. *Clinical symptoms* and *characterological patterns:* These findings are based on my clinical observations and the formal psychological assessment tool: Millon Clinical Multiaxial Inventory-III (MCMI-III™); see Millon, Millon, Davis & Grossman (1994). The MCMI measures Axis II involvement along a continuum of severity in terms of inflexibility of any given pathological personality pattern. A person can be assessed as having possible *features*, considered the least severe, *traits*, moderately severe, or a *disorder*, the most severe and possibly justifying a formal diagnosis of a personality disorder. For more information on Axis II issues and women with SSA, please refer to the section "Characterological Patterns and Women with SSA" on the book website at www.ivpress.com. For a more complete discussion on pathology and homosexuality, please see the website.

Table 1. continued

Attachment Patterns
• avoidant/fearful (defined by distrust of self and others and avoidance of closeness) • ambivalent/resistant (defined as the combination of excessive anxiety and perceived neediness *with* resistant and defensive behaviors in close relationships)
Unique Therapeutic Approaches and Recommended Techniques
• psychotropic intervention • use of symbolism and metaphor (story) • drawing or poetry journal (pictures vs. words) • play therapy or playful therapeutic attitude; reading children's books • psychoeducation to improve communication, social skills and self-care; assertiveness training • body work (accessing and releasing emotion, impulses, blocked energy or reactions through tracking sensation in body) • personal disclosure of therapist used for reality checks and role modeling
Contraindicated Approaches and Techniques (at least in first stage of therapy)
• direct discussion using psychological terms or concepts • direct confrontation • intellectual analysis and interpretation • any technique that creates initial fear or discomfort (at least until trust is solidly established)
Treatment Considerations
• dependency on therapist may be profound but secretive • self-defeating and depressed undertone may persist
Treatment Goal
"Bringing her to life"

Finding a self to accept. I worked with one woman who, after months of attempting to identify her core self-image, finally declared that she was a piece of Plexiglas. This negative self-image surfaced after she explored why she didn't feel the ostensive loneliness of her life. She chose the metaphor of Plexiglas rather than ice, because ice *felt* cold. Several other negative beliefs and adaptive features were also associated with this image: If she is Plexiglas, then she isn't human. If she isn't human, then she doesn't matter, she doesn't feel, and therefore she can't hurt. If she is Plexiglas, she is merely an object to be used; she can neither relate nor be responsible for human relatedness. Some time later, when I asked her to draw a picture of her self, one that would reflect her current core identity, she drew a figure that resembled a monster or an animal-like creature. We had moved from the inanimate to the animate, though it was still not of the nature for which I had hoped.

Negative self-images, especially those that are part of a woman's overarching strategy for survival, are often the starting place for many of my clients in terms of dealing with core formational issues. I cannot jump the gun and expect a woman to practice self-acceptance or to integrate new aspects of her self if she sees that self as Plexiglas or monstrousness. I must be patient, allowing our warm attachment to have its positive formative effect. I season my communication with indications of my undying conviction that she is indeed fully human and uniquely made.

In my work with women, I observe the following progression in building a self:

1. identify and understand initial negative self-representation and associated negative core beliefs

2. begin to view and accept self as flesh and blood (vulnerable) and as human

3. accept self as something of value

4. accept and integrate unique and special characteristics of self

5. accept imperfections and weaknesses

6. integrate imperfections and needs (especially relational) with positive traits and strengths

7. accept biological sex

8. embrace inner femininity

9. consolidate full adult feminine identity

Until a woman reaches step 3, she will necessarily present with an extremely fragile ego.[2] A woman with a fragile ego will not be able to integrate affirming statements with respect to her personhood. Several women have informed me in no uncertain terms that until they are assured that I "know" and accept them

---

[2]Quinodoz (1989) speaks of a woman with SSA who may have fit profile 1: "She remained silent most of the time because, she told me, 'when I talk to you, it tears me into little bits, and I find it hard to put them together again into a whole'" (p. 61). So unconsolidated was this woman that even her attempts at self-assertion created overwhelming anxiety and depression.

at step 1, they consider my affirmations as nothing but careless or clueless judgments on my part.

What is a relationship? These women, unlike some other women with SSA, are not asking themselves, *How do I have* healthy *instead of emotionally dependent relationships?* They are asking the most basic question possible: *How do I do* any *kind of relationship?*

I must answer this question *with* relationship. And as we relate, connect, and journey together, I begin to reflect on our interactions to explain what just occurred or what certain things mean. I provide instruction and teaching within the context of active relating.

For example, Lisa and I had just finished talking about a recent trip I had taken. She had initiated the conversation by asking me about it. After sharing I said, "Thank you for asking me about my trip, Lisa. That meant a lot to me." Note that I did not share my feelings with Lisa because I rely on her to take care of me. I am sharing my feelings so that I can model a real-life intimate exchange.

"Oh sure," she said. "I was just curious."

"Lisa, what you just did—asking me about my trip—is what a good friend would naturally do. I sensed your sincerity and true interest. It made me feel important. Sincerity and interest are very important in relationships. So, how about practicing these two things? I want you to come to our next session with at least one more question that you would like to sincerely ask me."

Lisa smiles and fidgets a bit. "Anything?"

"Yep, anything. But there's something else. I noticed that while I shared, you sort of turned away and didn't have much to say in response. Were you uncomfortable?"

"Well yeah, I never know quite what to say. I don't want to interrupt you or say something stupid."

"Oh, that would be the least of my worries," I said, with genuine warmth and affection. "You have a long way to go before you interrupt anyone. You've got to at least start making noise, saying *something*, anything." We exchanged smiles. "A response helps me to know that you are listening and understanding me."

I continued, "Also, something else that feels really good when I am talking to people is their eye contact. When people look at me, I know they are connected and interested in what I'm saying. Like right now, you're looking at me and smiling. That feels great! So next week, as I answer your question, I want you to work on looking at me while I speak and then saying a few words in response. OK?"

"OK, I'll try."

Turning process into play. Life is not all about pain, but unfortunately, many women with SSA missed out on good clean fun in their childhood and adolescence. Because of this, I frame much of my time and work with my clients in terms of play. In a session with one client, I pulled out a pad of paper and told her we were going to play a game by making a list of her positive characteristics and traits. For each characteristic that she listed, she got one point. For each one I listed, I got *two* points. The one with the most points at the end won. Sadly, my client had a difficult time coming up with even one positive thing to say about herself, but I kept our session lighthearted and animated with smiles and an exaggerated affirming tone. It helped her feel more comfortable with the therapeutic process and lifted the heaviness that could have invaded such a revealing session.

Progress for most women associated with profile 1 will be arduous and slow—yet it is not without hope. The therapeutic environment must be replete with ongoing encouragement, support, affirmation and a commitment to remain constant and longsuffering.

PROFILE 2: TOUGH, ANGRY, SARCASTIC AND BARRICADED

These women often have the worst histories of trauma and abuse, frequently involving severe physical or emotional abandonment, although this is not always the case. For some, the environments in which they were raised were not hostile, but the women nevertheless sensed and were negatively affected by the underlying relational dysfunctions within the family system. Both groups of women carry a deep belief that the world is not safe. They have relied on toughness (rather than the deadness found among profile 1 women) to protect their tender hearts. They are often overwhelmingly disillusioned to discover that their method of survival— severe defensiveness—actually starves them of intimacy. Unlike those associated with profile 1, they can *feel* their inner agony and therefore aggressively and continuously "cut off" all vulnerabilities. They work hard but are demanding; they are impatient but also deeply committed. *If* they decide that you are safe, they will do anything in the world for you. They have an endless ability to care and take care of others, all the while denying their own needs.

They view the world as black and white. People are all good or all bad. They are hypervigilant. They know if people get it or don't, and they have great contempt for those who don't. They are unabashedly honest, blunt and direct. They are smart and determined to survive, yet they can be explosive, petulant and sometimes downright difficult, as often exhibited in their tumultuous and even violent same-sex relationships. There is deep relational ambivalence within them. They are often masculinized in their dress and appearance and display masculinized gestures and body postures as well.

> *I was a hard-nosed, hard-hearted, and overtly masculine woman with a huge chip on my shoulder, just daring anyone to come along and tell me I couldn't do something because I was a girl (though there wasn't much "girlishness" about me). My tough exterior worked at keeping everyone away from discovering that I was in reality: lonely, afraid and hopeless.*
>
> *Mary*

Case study. Cathy, because of her religious beliefs, has not actively sought out same-sex relationships for more than three years. As the oldest of four, she had been everyone's protector. Dad, a successful lawyer, was a secret alcoholic. When he drank, he became violent. Eventually Cathy would be the one to confront him, even when she was as young as 5 years old. She often took the blows that were meant for her siblings. She thought that she was strong enough to handle his rage and that her sisters were not. She knew her mother, who often spent entire days on the couch, was weak and depressed. Throughout Cathy's childhood, an uncle forced her to fondle him when he snuck into her bedroom at night during his visits. All of the men in her family used sexualized teasing and offensive remarks to display virility and power. Cathy hated being a female. Her first same-sex relationship was with an older friend during high school. Cathy felt safe with her. Unfortunately, Cathy eventually became suspicious and accused her girlfriend of being unfaithful. Cathy also drank heavily and had a volatile temper. After the other woman broke off the relationship, Cathy dived into the gay bar scene, entertaining one-night stands and many short-term relationships. Although very smart and talented, she struggles with employment and her living situations.

She entered therapy to heal from past abuses and explore God's greater purposes for her life.

The following table outlines my clinical assessment of and treatment guidelines for profile 2.

Table 2. Profile 2

Developmental Issues
Negatively resolved (often up to *three* standard deviations) in the following developmental stages:
• trust vs. *mistrust*   • ego integrity vs. *despair*
• identity vs. *identity confusion*
Positively resolved (up to *two* standard deviations or elevated above all other scales) possibly indicating compensation for their underlying fear and empty core[a]
• *initiative* vs. guilt   • *industry* vs. inferiority

Clinical Symptoms
• generalized anxiety   • PTSD
• depression   • dissociative disorders
• bipolar

Characterological Patterns
• depressive, dependent, masochistic, and borderline disorders and traits[b]
• high comorbidity of Axis I and Axis II

Attachment Patterns
• ambivalent/resistant (defined as the combination of excessive anxiety and perceived neediness *with* resistant and defensive behaviors in close relationships)
• avoidant/fearful (defined by distrust of self and others and avoidance of closeness)
• anxious/preoccupied (defined as an excessive preoccupation with and anxiety over attachment needs, resulting in clinging or overdependency in close relationships)

[a]For further discussion, see research findings on women with SSA using the measures of psychosocial development on the book website at www.ivpress.com.

[b]Zubenko, George, Soloff and Schulz (1987), after studying the frequency of homosexuality among patients diagnosed with borderline personality disorder, found that "homosexuality was 10 times more common among the men and six times more common among the women with borderline personality disorder than in the general population or in a depressed control group" (p. 748). While Paris, Zweig-Frank and Guzder (1995) confirmed this finding for males, they were unable to do so with inpatient female populations.

Table 2. continued

Unique Therapeutic Approaches and Recommended Techniques
• psychotropic intervention
• containment (safe-place work) and supportive therapies
• concrete, matter-of-fact, no-nonsense language used with great sensitivity (These women *cannot* handle what they dish out.)
• honesty with complete authenticity
• Dialectical Behavior Therapy (DBT)[a]
• coping-skills development, specifically anger management
• cognitive therapies *used with much caution and care* (Overwhelming anxiety can be created by exposing or disrupting too many negative or false core beliefs.)

Contraindicated Approaches and Techniques (at least in first stage of therapy)
• any technique that looks "stupid" or too exposing (threatening or embarrassing), like empty chair techniques, play therapy or role-play, at least until trust is securely established
• group therapy within opening stages of therapy (The client may be too hostile and unable to cooperate due to unresolved trust issues.)

Treatment Considerations
• dependency on therapist may be profound even though masked by ongoing ambivalence and resistance
• sexualization of therapeutic relationship may occur
• self-defeating and depressed undertone may persist

Treatment Goal
"Softening a hard heart"

[a]Marsha Linehan's strategies as outlined in her book *Cognitive-Behavioral Treatment of Borderline Personality Disorder* (1993) are superb in creating a positive and curative therapeutic environment for profile 2 women.

Walk softly but stand firm. When I first met Jan, she was mistrustful and suspicious. She brazenly announced she had the power to seduce me. I respectfully disagreed, explaining that she indeed may be powerful but that she underestimated my power. She asked me what I would do if she showed up at my house. I told her that I would ask her to leave but would promise to meet her at my office for our next scheduled appointment. She asked what I would do if she didn't leave. I said I would call 911. She smiled. She was not offended by my abruptness. It made her feel safe. Throughout our first two years of work, she struggled with the tension between wanting to seduce me (rather, conquer and devour me and therefore not have to connect with or deal with me) and wanting to be safely cared for by me without sexual involvement (which, unfortunately, she could not even imagine).

I never buy into the toughness projected by these women. Miller (1981) notes that the more grandiose an individual becomes in terms of her false self, the greater is her inner sense of inferiority and insecurity. So it is for these women. I have found that the easiest way to see past their tough persona is to literally look deeply into their eyes. Their eyes are often the softest characteristic of their face and will, more often than not, betray a hidden, tender, vulnerable little girl.

A tug-of-war of trust. Working with these women can feel like playing a game of tug-of-war. I pull firmly, inviting my client to step into a realm of safety and trust. She in turn yanks back, ostensibly hoping that I will let go or give up while secretly hoping that I am strong enough to hang on.

I regularly see dominant borderline characteristics as a client relaxes under my care in one session, only to arrive at the next session fuming with rage over how I said goodbye the week before. She can shun my kindness with sarcasm, open defiance or contempt.

I have learned that asking or even alluding to the question "Why can't you trust me?" is generally not a good idea. It exposes that I really *don't* know her. From her perspective, if I *really* knew her, I would know *why* it is so hard for her to trust. Instead, I simply acknowledge her mistrust by using empathy and encouragement.

After Jodie made a defensive remark, I said calmly, "It must be so frustrating to not be able to trust me."

"You're d*** right. But I just can't," she responded. Looking dejected, she added, "Sometimes, I'm not even sure I want to."

"I can tell. Sometimes you feel open and other times you just seem so barricaded. But I understand. Trust will take time. In the meantime," I continued, "I know we will both keep doing our best. Just promise to keep me posted if I'm pushing too hard or am presuming on your trust level."

At times, these clients may become disappointed with themselves, apologizing for how little they are changing. Many women have asked me, "How do you do this? I can't believe you want to stay with me. Why don't you just dump me and find a better client?" During this long phase of trust and relationship building, I continually bolster them, reassuring them that I have no intentions of quitting and that I will hold onto hope when they can't.

Caring enough to confront. Honoring a woman's defenses doesn't preclude confronting them lovingly and naming them for what they are. In fact, these women will lose respect for me if I withhold *any* truth from them, even if they can't handle the truth in a mature manner. So I've learned to prepare a client for the soft punch before I throw it. I ask her whether I can share with her how I'm feeling in the moment as I listen to her talk. She may smirk and give me an "I dare you" look, but when she concedes and I go on to share with her how her defensiveness makes me feel, she often relaxes under the warmth of my authenticity. For example, while dialoguing with one of my clients about our favorite movies, I shared how a particular scene in one movie had deeply touched me. My voice was filled with emotion as I spoke. My client quickly retorted, "Oh that's stupid, Janelle. That movie was so cheesey." After regaining my composure and asking for permission, I shared with her that I was feeling deflated because of her last comment. I felt as if I had been punched in the stomach. I felt sad because the warm connection we had as we chatted about movies now felt broken. By being authentic and vulnerable, my client then felt safe to reflect on what she had been feeling prior to making her comment. She realized that she had become uncomfortable with our closeness and that her anxiety had become unbearable. She found relief from the anxiety as soon as she "threw the punch."

After empathizing with a client's true feelings in situations such as these, I move ahead, rarely coming back to the defensive behavior. I do not want to shame or humiliate her; I just want to interact with the real person behind the wall. Once I have her, we can move on.

PROFILE 3: ENERGETIC, CARETAKING, DRAMA-ORIENTED, AND NEVER "HOME"

Even though these women are less likely to have traditional trauma or neglect in their background as compared to women associated with profiles 1 and 2, they still suffer from severe, subtle and negative relational dynamics such as familial enmeshment or rigid gender roles within their families of origin. Due to their attuned sensitivities and perhaps their deeper relational needs, they felt that they were neither acknowledged nor affirmed as special, particularly as a girl. Although they felt close and loved, they also felt obligated to support or take care of other family members, including mom and dad. Nevertheless, their basic needs were usually met, and they experience the greatest level of stability among the four profiles. They are active, often athletic and typically overachieving women.

Their outstanding features are their busyness and their seeming addiction to relational drama. They are rarely "home," literally and metaphorically. They rarely take quiet time and rarely reflect on how they are feeling via homework assignments or journaling. Actually, they aren't aware of feeling anything. In fact, they may miss the normal physical or emotional cues associated with exhaustion, illness, sadness or the onset of depression. If they become overwhelmed by one of these hidden culprits, life will turn into an event, rather than a quiet place of recovery and rest. There is never a dull moment in their lives or their therapy. They are openly appreciative and more demonstrative (especially in terms of warmth and affection) than the women in other profiles. Nevertheless, they still need to be constantly challenged on their tendency to escape their own hearts. They wear sporty and sometimes basic feminine clothing.

When I was in high school, I was on the diving team and track team and in softball and volleyball leagues. I was in the journalism club, I was president of my 4-H group, I worked a part-time job, and I babysat my nieces on some weekends. I usually got pretty high grades, so was in the honor society and joined a speaking group for Spanish. I thought it would look good on my resume. So, yeah, I guess I was a little busy.
Connie

Case study. Sandy had an almost idyllic childhood. Her kind parents gave her many rich opportunities and experiences. She felt loved and knew she came from a good family. Growing up, she enjoyed activity, adventure and sports. In fact, she was her dad's favorite. He was her coach, cheerleader and biggest fan, although he often criticized her and pressured her to rise to the top of her league, so to speak. She had two younger brothers whom she loved and cared about. She recalls an older neighborhood boy inappropriately touching her when she was 10, and she avoided him after that. By junior high, she had many friends and was involved in everything, but she never had a best friend. She would notice her loneliness at night in the quiet of her room. She always hoped that the next year would be different, but it never was. Her heart ached for deeper connection.

College was as different as she had hoped. However, in the thrill of experiencing a kindred connection with a girl friend, her boundaries fell. The physical involvement they shared felt normal and natural. After several subsequent relationships, Sandy entered therapy not because of sexual involvement with women (this was a minor piece of her relationships), but because of an ongoing pattern of emotional dependency. She shared that she feels split. A normal, smart, healthy woman, she becomes insecure, demanding, and possessive in most of her friendships. "It's like it's not even me. I can't believe some of the things I say and do. I hate being in that place. I want to figure out how to keep my relationships from becoming dependent," she told me. She has also admitted that one day she would like to marry a man.

The following table outlines my clinical assessment of and treatment guidelines for profile 3.

Table 3. Profile 3

Developmental Issues
Normative ranges for most scores but *spiked positive resolution* (possibly indicating overcompensation in the world of performance vs. the world of being) in the following developmental stages:
• *initiative* vs. guilt
• *industry* vs. inferiority
Clinical Symptoms
• periodic depression   • anxiety
Characterological Patterns
• histrionic traits with dependent, compulsive and narcissistic features
Attachment Patterns
• anxious/preoccupied (defined as an excessive preoccupation with and anxiety over attachment needs, resulting in clinging or overdependency in close relationships)[a]
• dismissive (primarily defined as a posture of self-reliance and independence as a means to escape pain associated with closeness)[b]
Unique Therapeutic Approaches and Recommended Techniques
• focusing and feeling work
• here-and-now processing and *experientially based therapies* in tandem with interpretative and cognitive therapies (These women are able to benefit from a broad range of therapeutic techniques once a foundation of trust has been securely established.)
• direct confrontation (with empathy and sensitivity)
• teaching and instruction regarding SSA framework
• reprocessing therapies, such as eye movement desensitization and reprocessing (EMDR) *once the woman is internally connected*
• therapy group and outside support group
Contraindicated Techniques
• purely interpretative, behavioral or cognitive therapies (These women may insist that this is all they need therapeutically.)
Treatment Goal
"Slowing down a racing horse"

[a]"The key features of the histrionic personality disorder overlap to a considerable extent with a preoccupied attachment orientation" (Bartholomew, Kwong & Hart, 2001, p. 215).

[b]This attachment style is further explained in Bartholomew (1990) and Fraley, Davis & Shaver (1998). Several studies have found a high occurrence of dismissive attachment styles amongst lesbian women in comparison to homosexual men and heterosexual populations. See Ridge & Feeney (1998); Wells (2003); Wells & Hansen (2003). Wells and Hansen (2003) speculate that the true nature of the "positive self" for dismissing individuals is actually defensive and fragile, developed as a means of self-protection.

Don't be fooled. The first impression these women make is that of a warm, connected person who is optimistic about changing some of her unhealthy relational patterns. However, as time progresses, I find myself struggling in our therapy sessions. She is more than willing to "do" work but is often so disconnected from her true heart's desire or inner emotions that she loses track of where she is headed or what she has been working on. While most of these women lack the theatrical, animated, attention-seeking relational styles typically associated with histrionic traits, they do exhibit the other associated traits of shallow emotions, lacking depth of introspective thought and speaking in impressionistic generalities. They are hard to get a hold of and steer in meaningful directions. It's almost as if, between sessions, they lose themselves in daily responsibilities and stressors. It takes a counseling session for them to wake up, so to speak, and reconnect with their inner self. If this pattern of disconnection continues, they may eventually become frustrated about their slow progress, even concluding that counseling is a waste of time and money.

A woman identified with profile 3 is still unsure whether her true self is valuable enough to elicit another's commitment and ongoing presence. At her core, she is deeply afraid and insecure. While she may admit that she fears abandonment, she is generally not in touch with the feelings associated with fear, such as anxiety, mistrust or insecurity. However, she *is* in touch with the positive desires associated with secure attachment and connection. She *really* wants deep connectedness in her relationships. She wants to *feel* special. These powerful desires often turn into a profound and desperate neediness that transforms a casual friendship into a sexually charged emotional dependency.

Connecting: A journey inward. Once coached, it is not difficult for such a woman to identify or articulate her deeper emotions (as well as thoughts, dreams and hopes); it is difficult for her to remember to do so on a regular basis. She needs constant encouragement and reminders within and outside of the counseling setting to verbalize, describe and unpack her feelings or inner thoughts.

At the beginning of each session, when I ask her what she is feeling in that moment, she will likely smile and say, "You know, I don't know."[3] Our conversation may proceed like this:

---

[3]Striegel-Moore, Tucker & Hsu (1990) found that lesbian women tend to have greater difficulty than heterosexual women in identifying with their own emotions.

"Well, now, that's a new one!" I say jokingly. "Sylvia, I know you *can* connect and figure out what you're feeling. So let's just take a minute. Why don't you close your eyes and see what you find going on inside."

"Oh, I know!" she declares excitedly.

"Well, share!" I insist.

"I'm feeling excited. I think something *is* changing inside of me. I feel hopeful, but scared at the same time."

Pausing. "Is there more?" I ask.

"Yeah. I feel sad, too, because I'm not sure my husband is on the same path as I am. I'm not sure he understands how to meet my heart. I guess I'm afraid that as I continue to grow, we will actually become further and further apart."

"Sylvia," I say, "this sounds like a very heavy burden. I want to talk more about it. But first, I have to say that you just did a fantastic job with connecting with your emotions. You are feeling excitement, hope, sadness and some fear—all at the same time! You have an incredible capacity to feel and hold many things. You did a great job!"

"Thanks."

"OK, close your eyes again and get back to that sad and scared place." I pause a moment and let her recenter herself. "Tell me more about the turmoil inside related to your concerns about your marriage."

Relaxation: An admission of need. A woman with this profile has a very full life. She can do many things well, so there is never a shortage of activity and possibility. However, her basic existence is more frenetic or hyperactive, jumping from one activity to the next, than warm or rich in times of solitude and soul searching. It seems frightening to her to enter quiet places alone. She has discovered, however, that she can meet her inner self when she is in the arms of a special female friend. I want, therefore, to help her connect with and deepen her inner world while calming her outer world and supporting her growth toward healthy self-nurture, autonomy and individuation.

Marcia came in for her regularly scheduled appointment. There were many circumstances in Marcia's life that were competing for her attention, so I knew she would want to give me an update. But as she shared, I began to feel a palpable exhaustion. So much was happening in her life that my head began to spin. I noticed Marcia, too, had a hard time centering. She would jump from one subject to the next. And then, as if it were simply an everyday occurrence, she said, "Oh, and I'm feeling vulnerable with one of my female friends. We might be getting too close." She didn't even pause. She started in on the next subject.

I had attempted several times to slow her down so that we could spend some time focusing, but she was too distracted. As she chattered, I thought I could either confront her many defenses operating against intimacy (such as rapidness of speech), address her shallowness of affect, which was a common issue to her, or tackle something even more unconscious. I chose the latter.

"Marcia," I gently interrupted. "I want you to do something. I want you to slide back and relax into the couch. Get really comfortable." I got up and brought a chair over to her. "Here, I want you to put your feet up on this chair. Now, your job for the rest of the session is to relax. You have such incredible amounts of energy; I'm not sure how anybody, let alone *your body*, can keep up with you. I am sure you feel extremely tired at times. And with everything happening, I suspect you just need to take a break. So I want you to sit back, close your eyes and take a few deep breaths. Let's just sit quietly for a minute." Twenty seconds passed. She lounged contentedly, but not fully relaxed.

I spoke softly and slowly. "Marcia, keep your eyes closed. I just want you to listen. I know that you know there are no quick or easy resolutions to any of the situations you mentioned today. So I've decided that rather than keep talking about them, we would do something else. But I want you to know how much I care about what you are going through. You have a lot going on.

"But right now," I continued, "I want you to listen to your innermost heart and soul. They must just be exhausted, not to mention broken and hurting. I'm sure you can feel the heaviness and pain at times. I'm going to play some music and read to you. You can keep your eyes closed or open, whatever is comfortable. I just want you to keep breathing, slowly and deeply."

I started playing a CD of slow-moving instrumentals (New Age-style music), excellent for calming a client or filling a room with a sense of presence or beauty. I grabbed my Bible and joined Marcia by scooting my chair a bit closer. I flipped through the Psalms until I landed on one that spoke of God as being our resting place and our hope. I read slowly and softly. Remarkably, Marcia was able to remain relaxed and receptive. She kept her eyes closed, but I could see tears and a slight smile on her face.

I then slowly prayed for her. I prayed as God led: that he would fill her with his peace, help her enter into deep rest and tranquility, and provide her with special times in his presence. When I knew we were running out of time, I asked Marcia, "How are you feeling right now?"

She replied, very slowly, "*So* relaxed. Oh, I needed that. Thank you."

Growing up, Marcia had played the family role of "the together one." Even though she had a good family, she rarely experienced nurturing. She could not remember an occasion where someone took her in his or her arms to say, "It's going to be OK." Everyone assumed she *was* fine. She admits that she felt unnoticed and devalued by her parents. She had always been quick to defend them because they weren't (truly weren't) abusive, but she was now facing the sadness and reality of her unmet needs as well as her habit of ignoring the truth—that she wasn't as strong as she thought. She longed for someone to nurture her. Since Marcia was on the brink of developing an inappropriate relationship, I decided to guide her toward self-nurture versus emotional dependence on another.

Profile 4: Pragmatic, Perfectionistic, Distant and Smugly Self-Assured

Women with this profile have various backgrounds but typically compensate for their losses and defend against their pain by avoiding all vulnerability and identifying with their ability to pursue excellence and success. They are often the movers and shakers within their field of expertise and find their kudos through achievement. They are very intelligent and extremely gifted. But because they are often so accomplished, they are also arrogant and contemptuous of others (especially men). They may unconsciously use others to serve their own purpose or meet their own needs.

They are excellent communicators and are committed to their beliefs. They enjoy a good debate; however, their head knowledge often betrays their lack of actual experience in life and love. It is difficult for them to admit that they have *need.* They maintain a veneer of control and management within their social settings and their intimate relationships. As clients, they are often stubborn, silently musing, *I don't buy that,* or *I'm not going to do that!* And they don't! Rather than use the defensive toughness to mask deep insecurity and inferiority as in profile 2, these women don the persona of superiority and dominance.

They have a severe split between their little girl and their successful adult persona. In the public realm, they are competent, confident and strong. Yet privately, they feel empty and desperately alone. Within their emotionally dependent relationships, they unconsciously live out of the neediness and desperation of their little girl, often displaying severe borderline-like tendencies. They rarely feel known or cherished apart from these relationships.

Case study. Kristine grew up in an upper middle-class family with working parents who saw themselves as pillars in the community and held high expectations for Kristine and her two younger sisters. Her parents were controlling, demanding and emotionally disengaged. Both parents drank, sometimes more than just socially. The constant activity in their home bordered on chaos. Kristine's parents divorced when she was 12, but she wished they had separated a lot sooner. She now knows that her dad was having an affair when her parents divorced. Kristine can recall several instances when her father would parade around the house in his underwear and would want Kristine and her sisters to sit on his lap.

Kristine always felt that she had to do everything well. Luckily, she had many talents and excelled in school and extracurricular activities. During high school, she dated some but was more interested in academics than in romance. It wasn't until graduate school that she experienced her first emotionally close relationship with a woman. She didn't want to admit that it might be a lesbian attraction, but nevertheless they became fully sexually involved. Something inside of her shifted because this was the first time in her life that she didn't feel empty or alone. Her partner was on a similar academic track, pursuing a Ph.D. in biology. Kristine is ambivalent about therapy and uncertain that she wants to give up same-sex relationships. She believes she cannot survive without a partner but is now a devout Mormon.

The table on page 178 outlines my clinical assessment of and treatment guidelines for profile 4.

I thought I was "fixed." Sally was tense and distraught during our first session. She was absolutely exasperated with what was happening in her life. Almost seven years had passed since her last same-sex relationship. She had worked hard over these seven years to obey God and live according to his principles on sexuality. She was doing everything right: going to a support group, seeing a counselor, reading books, attending church and a small group, and setting boundaries.

About a month before she came to see me, she met a woman at church with whom she shared many of the same interests. As their stories unfolded, Sally discovered that this woman had also had several same-sex relationships in her past. She could feel the pull to draw closer to this woman and to spend more

Table 4. Profile 4

Developmental Issues
No set pattern except *elevated positive resolution* of many developmental stages, especially • *initiative* vs. guilt   • *industry* vs. inferiority

Clinical Symptoms
• depression and anxiety during and after relationship breakup

Characterological Patterns
• narcissistic traits with histrionic and borderline features

Attachment Patterns
• dismissive (primarily defined as a posture of self-reliance and independence as a means to escape pain associated with closeness)[a] • ambivalent/resistant (defined as the combination of excessive anxiety and perceived neediness *with* resistant and defensive behaviors in close relationships) • anxious/preoccupied (defined as an excessive preoccupation with and anxiety over attachment needs, resulting in clinging or overdependency in close relationships)

Unique Therapeutic Approaches and Recommended Techniques
• concrete, matter of fact, no-nonsense language always moving toward language of emotions, feelings, visceral feelings and philosophies of life • reflective listening (start with repeating rather than rephrasing what a client says) • little-girl work • interpretative and analytical work only for containment purposes (The client will feel more comfortable doing this type of work, but it will not reach her vulnerable side.) • therapy group and outside support group

Contraindicated Techniques
• anything that looks "foolish" or potentially humiliating • reprocessing therapies, such as EMDR (Client may be too split in beginning stages of therapy.)

Treatment Goal
"Humanizing the woman, embracing the little girl"

[a]This attachment style is further explained in Bartholomew (1990) and Fraley, Davis & Shaver (1998). Several studies have found a high occurrence of dismissive attachment styles amongst lesbian women in comparison to homosexual men and heterosexual populations. See Ridge & Feeney (1998); Wells (2003); Wells & Hansen (2003). Wells and Hansen (2003) speculate that the true nature of the "positive self" for dismissing individuals is actually defensive and fragile, developed as a means of self-protection.

time with her. She hadn't felt these feelings for many years. She felt panicked by her own vulnerability. She knew she would give in if the woman made any movement toward her physically. She was also overcome with disappointment and discouragement. She had worked so hard, she explained. Why hadn't this part of her changed? Why was she still so vulnerable to the attention of another woman?

Often when a woman with SSA commits to recovery or a healing journey, her same-sex feelings become dormant or at least marginal while she focuses on the broader aspects of her life. It can come as quite a surprise when these feelings return. But usually, there is more to the story. I observe two common themes here, especially in the stories of women associated with profile 4.

First, as a woman with profile 4 comes to trust me, she often admits that over these years of recovery she has had few close friends. She may explain that her travel or business schedule prevents her from attending regularly scheduled events where she might meet new people. She may express disappointment in her friendships with married women because they are often too busy to connect because of family-related commitments. Perhaps because of her superior skills and professional status, a woman may admit that she rarely finds women whom she likes or who meet her standards; sadly, her polite contempt for others may be shielding her from opportunities for connection. Even if a friendship does form, this woman is often reluctant to share about her deepest feelings or needs, let alone her struggle with SSA. She fears public exposure or humiliation. She may also fear that if she becomes too close to a woman, the relationship might become sexualized or emotionally dependent. Needless to say, she has often been living in isolation, and unbeknownst to her, harboring an ever-increasing deprivation of emotional connection, affirmation and attention.

Second, through our time together, it becomes apparent that she may still not truly *know* or like herself. She often lives with veiled self-contempt and inner division. She *hates* the weak, soft, tender, needy places of her soul (her "little girl") and so remains in an ongoing state of self-disavowal, accessing only the skills and talents that bolster her performance orientation or high achievement.

I had just spent a long weekend with my partner. I remember worrying on my drive home that I would lose her. I sobbed the whole way home. I could hardly control the pain, feeling like I would lose this love and acceptance. But as soon as I pulled into my office, I had an appointment. And immediately, I became another person. I acted as if nothing was wrong. I can compartmentalize anything.

Ellen

These women were never meant to endure such hiddenness, division and relational deprivation. Their desperation—arising out of the lack of integration and unmet relational need—will eventually be revealed, leaving even the strongest of women feeling like putty under the loving gaze or hug of another woman who cares and desires closeness. Naturally, such tenderness would seem like a drink of cool water to her parched soul. It would be crazy to refuse it.

Presenting these deeper truths to a woman who fits this profile must be done carefully. The techniques identified in chapter eleven for little-girl work are important, although they are often met with suspicion. A profile 4 woman prides herself on her intellect and her ability to manage her life—as well as on her ability to control others. Suggesting that she may be missing something— that she may be disconnected from her vulnerable little-girl self or that she is unconsciously living her life out of fear, not competence—communicates to her that she is wrong (bad) or has made a mistake. Often her ego strength cannot handle such disequilibrium. She must be supported with attunement and empathy. She will also need to be directed to face her pattern of defensive detachment and her fears of closeness as discussed in chapter nine.

SEE THE WOMAN BEHIND THE PROFILE: THERE IS HOPE FOR HER

During a break at a recent conference, several women approached me to say that they had watched a video of my lecture on the various profiles. Each announced, gleefully, the profile number she felt described her. They giggled and laughed at how closely they fit their (self-assigned) categories and wanted to talk to me about their patterns. While I am thankful that they found these descriptions useful, I still shudder at the thought of a woman reduced to a profile rather than seen for the unique individual she truly is. The *woman* can grow and change; the profile cannot.

CHAPTER NINE

Discovering Her Own Home
Opening Doors to Healthy Intimacy

You find power when you are at home because it is there that you are loved,
cherished, and accepted just as you are, with all your frailty, fears, and flaws.
The call from God is to come home,
to embrace both our littleness and our greatness and come home.

MACRINA WIEDERKEHR, *A TREE FULL OF ANGELS*

The first stage of therapy, involving the primary work of inner *formation*, is far less conscious on the part of the client, occurs largely within a curative environment based on a therapist's attitude and personhood, and requires a tremendous investment of emotion and energy on the therapist's part. The second stage of therapy is focused on growth and *transformation*, and requires a conscious desire and motivation on the *client's* part. Although it incorporates a variety of therapeutic interventions requiring technique and skill, it does not require the previous level of emotional investment from the therapist.

I say this as a word of caution. If I am tired or nearing burnout, it is easier for me to play the role of an analyst or technician than an empathic mother. At these times, I am apt to challenge my client to enter a more deliberate working stage before she is ready. I have learned that when I encounter client resistance, I should check my motives and reassess her readiness, especially if I am directing her into this next stage of therapy. Many women will require ongoing bolstering of their ego strength as they attempt to step into the work described below.

SECOND STAGE OF THERAPY: TRANSFORMATION

The overarching goal of the second stage is to help a woman begin to transform and exchange her dismissive and self-protective posturing for new capabilities and competencies related to healthy and meaningful intimacy. This means, first, that she discover, connect with and integrate her true self and, second, that she equip her *self* to authentically and mutually connect with others.

"I DON'T *KNOW* WHO I AM!"

Many women with SSA have a history of controlling self-expression and self-assertion, measuring how much they will reveal to others in any given situation. They unconsciously control what or how much they feel, relying on numerous defense mechanisms to avoid uncomfortable or overwhelming feelings, especially anxiety and shame. They may control or moderate their felt needs, desires and expectations, guarding themselves from more disappointment or shame. They have also unconsciously controlled their own identification process, eliminating potential role models (like mother) and selecting, often by default, with whom they will identify. These patterns of self-control or repression keep a woman from knowing who she is and apprehending a true sense of self and identity.

In order for a woman to know herself, the therapist must help her to explore (open her eyes to) her hidden positive traits and assets, to count (embrace and take ownership of) them as treasures and, finally, to offer them as a gift to others (walk in vulnerability and authenticity). I cannot stress enough how difficult this journey is for most women with SSA. Many have formidable blocks to this process of identity redelineation. They must confront negative core beliefs, habitual defensive patterns and primal survival strategies. As her protective walls are dismantled, a woman will feel precariously exposed. And because her inner riches have been "safely" hidden from herself and others, the thought of retrieving them creates both terror and shame.

It often comes as an unwelcome shock to a client that I *can* actually see glimpses of who she truly or *already* is. My mirroring smiles and facial expressions, which communicate that she is enjoyable, lovable, funny or intelligent, may initially unnerve her. Because she may associate being seen with a greater chance of humiliation or rejection, I pace my mirroring and affirmative statements. In the first stage of therapy, I want the possibility that she has positive traits to linger or take up residence in her subconscious. But in this subsequent stage, as she is ready, I will challenge her to increase her conscious awareness of these strengths. I will involve her in many practical exercises, such as the following, where *she* verbalizes and explicitly discusses them.

Point out her character qualities and traits in the midst of other discussions. As opportunities arise, I will affirm her character traits with comments like these: "That was very insightful of you. You are very perceptive." "You are brave to acknowledge that you are still tempted to abuse alcohol." "It seems you often carry a burden and concern for people who are oppressed or mistreated. You have a wonderful heart."

When our discussion is over, I might ask her to reflect on my affirming comment: Did she notice it? What was her internal reaction? Did she think my comment was accurate or inaccurate?

Pay attention to her compliments and affirmations. Many of my clients are openly appreciative of *my* actions and personhood. I have come to believe that they are most often appreciative of those traits that they tend to deny in themselves. I pay close attention to their compliments, sensitive that they may affirm in me what they cannot affirm in themselves. Many women are also often sensitive and responsive to my needs, especially those that match their own presently disavowed needs.

Allow them to identify with me and role model my positive attitudes, characteristics, and behaviors. Whether or not it is ever acknowledged, my clients are likely to begin identifying with me when they come to trust and admire me. This identification process does not necessarily instill *new* characteristics and traits within my clients; rather, it affirms and validates their preexisting underdeveloped characteristics and traits as good and normal.

One of my clients, a woman who enjoyed drawing pictures as part of her journaling process, unconsciously launched an identification process with me by imagining herself and me as little girls riding rocking horses together. She then imagined me as an older friend, like a babysitter, who would let her sit in my lap as we read her favorite book or watched her favorite video. She felt acceptance as she crafted and unconsciously internalized these images. Shortly after she drew a picture of me holding her as a little girl, I was surprised to see a picture of both of us as adult women: we were facing one another, and I was holding her hands. In this picture we were peers, and she was comfortable with both this thought and this image. Throughout this process she experienced herself as acceptable and lovable and believed she was growing up to be like me, a feminine, friendly being.

Offer honest feedback when requested. My clients want the truth. Because they trust me, they often take great risks in asking for my opinion or viewpoint with respect to their attitudes, behaviors or personality traits. I never fabricate compliments, nor do I decline to offer responses that may be negatively slanted. But I cushion all difficult words with supportive empathy and humility, processing any reaction with openness and graciousness.

Assign journaling exercises. Below are some of the journaling exercises I assign to encourage a client's identity redelineation. Initially, some clients will not be able to complete these assignments alone (or they can't be alone long enough to complete them) but need to work on them with my help and encouragement. I am also not surprised if a client's journaling homework is exceedingly brief or contained on a scrap of paper. I know her courage will increase as her self-disclosure is met with acceptance and compassion. In fact, many of these assignments will take months—even years—to complete and process. I spend substantial focused time reviewing and discussing each assignment, always aware of the presence of shame and continually mirroring, validating and encouraging. I usually assign two of these lists a week.

- What are my positive traits?
- What are my negative traits?
- What things do I like?
- What things do I not like?
- What am I good at?
- What am I not good at?
- What are my favorite movies?
- What is my favorite music?
- What is my favorite food?
- What are my favorite places to travel?
- What are the masks that I wear with others?
- What do I want to hide from other people?
- What was my family role as a child?
- What role do I typically play in my current relationships?
- What were my mom, dad and siblings like when I was growing up?
- How am I like my mom, dad and siblings?

- How am I different from my mom, dad and siblings?
- Who is my hero?
- What do I admire in others?
- What do I most dislike in others?
- What are my special talents and giftings?
- What are my desires?
- What are my passions?
- What is my purpose?
- What are my dreams or hopes for the future?
- What are my established goals in life?

When a client has completed a list, it is very important to ask her to read it aloud. She will usually prefer that I read her list silently to myself, but I firmly yet kindly stress that it is important that I hear her voice and emotion as she reads. This can frighten a client and might draw out what has been referred to as annihilation anxiety—the fear that she will be silenced or punished if she asserts or expresses her true self. Further, she may feel embarrassed and even shame at the thought of talking about herself. Supportive attunement and empathy will help regulate her anxiety and bolster her ego.

A second exercise is developing a life chronology of all significant personal and family incidences. This chronology is best done on a computer so that a client can insert new information as it surfaces. I ask her to create two columns: the first will include dates or ages, and the second will include brief descriptions of monumental events, such as births, deaths, moves, schools, divorces, instances of abuse, awards, romantic or sexual experiences, seasons of friendships and so on. Many women have never taken a step back to see or understand their lives in light of their broader story or family history. This gives them a sense of rootedness, even if many of their memories are sad, for this provides a context for understanding current struggles. As we review a time line, I also help my clients identify repeated themes and identify the impact of certain events.

A third exercise is constructing a genogram or family tree with as many members of her extended family and generations as possible. I instruct my client to draw a family tree of sorts on a large piece of poster board, with herself at the very bottom. Females are represented with *circles*, males with *squares*. The name of each family member is written next to the appropriate symbol. I have my client draw a line (the tree) branching upward and outward to her mother and father and then to their mothers and fathers. Different colors and markings are added to the symbols to indicate certain characteristics as applicable:

- addicted: solid red shading in lower half
- recovering from addiction: red slashes in lower half
- often abusive: solid red shading in upper half
- occasionally abusive: red slashes in upper half
- deceased: black X from corner to corner
- critical: black slashes in upper half
- emotionally unavailable: black slashes in lower half
- rageful: blue slashes
- divorced: black D between adjacent symbols
- safe: solid green outline

By reviewing a chart of this nature, a woman is able to see the overarching emotional and relational patterns that contributed to her development and identity formation. For instance, all three generations of circles (women) may be marked as being abusive and critical whereas the only green (safe) symbol on her page represents a brother. This may explain, for example, some of her difficulties relating to most women and her unconscious identification with the masculine.

Using charts such as these is extremely powerful in a group setting. I instruct each woman to share a 20-minute narrative of her family history as she reveals her genogram. Group members often have incredible insights and, after seeing a woman's family tree, are usually compelled to affirm and highlight her strengths and assets.

In a fourth exercise, a client interviews friends and asks them to share what they see as her strengths and weaknesses. For this assignment to be effective, the friends must have a substantial history with the client *and* must have proven themselves compassionate and trustworthy.

SHE *Is* WHAT SHE BELIEVES

In general, I have found that my clients cling to sophisticated and self-perpetuating cognitive frameworks that form the basis of their internal self-representation or identity. Here are some of the most common negative core beliefs:

- I am not real. I am nothing.
- I am wrong. I am not understandable.
- I am alone and I can't survive
- I am ugly. I will never be loved.
- I am not safe. People cannot be trusted.
- Vulnerability is bad. I am the only one who can protect myself.
- I can handle it. I don't need anybody.

For a woman to redelineate her identity, she must recognize and challenge these core beliefs. However, because many of my clients have lived in their heads—analyzing, deducing and rehearsing their beliefs and theories since they were young—their cognitions are usually guarded and inflexible to change. Her beliefs have provided a means to understand and explain why things are the way they are (and why she is the way she is) and are therefore intertwined with her core strategies for survival. For instance, when a woman is put off by a man's condescending attitude, she can find immediate relief from her humiliation by telling herself, *Oh yeah, men are jerks.* This "truth" brings relief and is reinforced by her experience.

While cognitive restructuring therapies are very effective, they must be used in conjunction with attunement and empathy, cycling between the two therapeutic styles. It is difficult for many women, particularly *smart* women, to be open or to assimilate new information or transforming truth, especially if they are proud of or have formed an identity around their cognitive skills. It is not unusual for a client to complete a session focused on faulty cognitions to then obsess over our discussion and develop a defense and justification for the next session.

Once a woman begins to learn how and why her beliefs were formed and to experience my unconditional acceptance in spite of her ongoing distorted thinking, she will be able to engage more fully in a cognitive process. Yet even then, change will be slow. I find that we circle through her negative beliefs: weakening a belief in one context only to see it reemerge in another with a slightly different slant.[1]

---

[1] Reprocessing techniques such as eye movement desensitization and reprocessing (EMDR), visualization exercises and forms of healing prayer are extremely powerful in dismantling negative core beliefs and cementing positive cognitions and deeper understandings of difficult moments or harmful environments. For more information, see chapter 12.

Eventually, the negative belief system will become less entrenched and replaced by positive cognitions that allow for growth, hope and relationship.

"AND WHOEVER OR WHATEVER I AM, I DON'T LIKE IT!"

It is easier for a child to blame herself for life's disappointments and abuses ("I am the problem") than for her to integrate the truth of her parents' imperfections. She is helpless to manage or change her mother's neglectfulness or her father's emotional unavailability. But if *she* is the problem, she might be able to at least manage or change her self.

For many women with SSA, the core belief "I am the problem" typically translates into "I am bad." So to rid herself of the "problem," she unconsciously starves or supresses her self. When her self refuses to ultimately die or vacate—as is usually the case, thankfully—she often responds with her next best weapon, hatred: "If I can't *kill* me, then I will *hate* me."[2] To return to her true self or her inner home, she must expose and challenge her ingrained patterns of self-abdication and self-hatred.

Many of these women may also be trapped in the dangerous habit of self-introspection (Payne, 1991), picking herself apart and becoming her own worst critic. No matter how hard she tries, the inner voice of shame and contempt says something akin to *Not good enough,* or *You missed it again,* or *There is something wrong with you,* or *You are not normal.* I find it helpful to objectify these voices, speaking to my client as if they *are* an audible voice outside of her head.

For example, a client might say, "I'm just so stupid. I can't get anything right."

"There's that condemning voice again, Maxine. That voice sure is hard on you. When did it start speaking to you that way?"

"Oh, I don't know. As long as I can remember."

"Who does that voice remind you of? Did anyone in your life have that voice?" I ask.

"Hell, yes! It sounds just like my dad—always criticizing me. He'd tell me I could be the best but then tear down everything I did on the basketball court. You'd think I was the worst player out there." (She actually received a college scholarship in basketball.)

---

[2]Harry Gershman (1975), dean of the American Institute for Psychoanalysis of the Karen Horney Psychoanalytic Institute and Center, cautions that "the therapist must be perceptive and alert to the ever-present factor of intense self-contempt in these patients [lesbian women]" (p. 309).

A woman may also find it helpful to make a list of all her hostile internal messages or judgments and then to create a list of affirmative truth statements in response. Self-negating or sabotaging behaviors—such as neglecting self-care, binge drinking or eating, or not buying groceries on a regular basis—should also be identified and slowly challenged. If self-hatred is not directly dealt with, any process of self-acceptance and identify formation will ultimately be derailed.

After working with me for over two years, one client was finally able to recognize how much she despised her self: She had been appreciating a red rose that a friend gave her for her birthday. One morning, she awoke to find the rose wilted and drooped. Her heart sank. She wondered whether God felt sad about the wilted rose as well. It then dawned on her that God looked on *her* as she had looked on the rose. She wrote this in her journal:

> Oh, God, I confess my sin of not wanting or believing myself to be something of beauty in your sight. I give up the fight to hold on to a false, ugly identity. If you care about the wilted rose in my front room, then how much more must you care about me, a beautiful human rose that didn't bloom?

She also realized how she had been unconsciously fighting off my affirmations and validations. Later she discovered that she had also resisted identifying with me, continually repeating the belief that she was different and couldn't be like me in any way.

I have found that for many women, it is essential that they verbally confess and renounce, in someone else's presence, the habit of self-hatred and shaming self-condemnation. For instance, a client might say something like this:

> I admit that I have hated my self. I admit that I have believed that I don't deserve to live, that I don't deserve anything good. I admit that I believe I am ugly and worthless. But I no longer agree with these beliefs. I no longer want to hate and condemn myself. I want to live. I want to thrive. I want to enjoy good things in my life. I want my life to matter, to count, to have value. I want to love and give of myself. I choose to receive and embrace goodness and life. I choose to receive God's love and his truth.

Reciting words such these may seem rote to some, but when a woman speaks them *out loud,* deep emotions and the pain of her self-rejection and self-inflicted deprivation often surface, allowing her to truly grieve her self-hatred. An emotional shift may also occur as she speaks the words affirming her desire to live. She may emotionally connect with that deep place inside of her that has fought so hard to survive. Her spoken words begin to resonate with her true heart, empowering her to begin taking a stand against all that is false or that would seek to extinguish her life.

"WHAT? YOU WANT *ME* TO FEEL?"

To know one's self is to know one's own thoughts *and* feelings. Sadly, as discussed in previous chapters, women in conflict with SSA are typically profoundly disconnected from or defended against their emotions and visceral sensations. It is not that they merely refuse to *talk* about their feelings; they truly *can't* feel[3] or at least lack the self-awareness of feeling.

> *I would talk about my abuse like I was reading an article from the newspaper, but my counselor would start crying. It totally freaked me out. Twice I got up and walked out because I didn't know how to handle her emotions. They scared me. We did this for a long time before I actually felt anything. I was so detached.*
>
> *Mary*

As illustrated with women associated with profile 3, when asked what they feel, many such women will respond with a blank stare and exclaim, "I don't know!"

When asked, "How did you feel when your mom forgot you at the grocery store?" they say, "I don't know. Should I have felt something?"

When asked, "How do you think your dad's absence affected you in those early years?" they say, "I don't know. Is there something wrong with his being gone? Frankly, I was glad."

When asked, "How do you think you were affected by your dad's control when you were a teenager?" they say, "I don't know. That's what I know. That's the way life is. Are you trying to tell me that it's not OK and that it's not normal?"

Even though these women have developed superior analytical and cognitive processing skills, they lack the reflective thought connected with the affective processing of their emotional lives. To never feel is to be flat, monotone

---

[3]Research has shown that the inability to communicate one's inner world is directly linked to insecure attachment patterns (Hughes, 1997; Siegel, 1999a).

or, even worse, devoid of inner color and texture. To be nonfeeling and non-reflective is to be frozen or empty. A therapist can help a woman thaw and reconnect and thereby reintroduce depth, richness and warmth to her existence.

I use many different techniques to help my clients begin to connect with, identify and articulate their feelings and reflections. For example, I might

Give her an extensive and categorized list of feeling words. When a client is struggling to figure out what she is feeling, I make suggestions.[4] This gives her an opportunity to test the waters, so to speak, and at least identify what she *isn't* feeling, thus narrowing the focus to what she *is* feeling.

Interrupt discussions and ask how she is feeling in the present moment. The oft-repeated question, "How are you feeling?" may become an irritation or even a joke to my clients. I regularly reassure and gently remind them that I truly want to know how they are feeling and joyfully announce, "practice makes perfect," as I duck in preparation for the pillow that may come flying in my direction.

Confront her "I don't know" answer. When she says, "I don't know," I might offer attuned support: for example, "While we were talking, I was beginning to feel anxious. I felt a tightness in my chest. Were you feeling this too?" I may ask her how it feels to not know how she is feeling. This question often dislodges strong feelings of frustration and hopelessness. It often surprises women that they do indeed feel.

Help her to find the feeling in her body. If a client is unable to articulate a feeling word, I may ask what she is sensing in her body. Can she feel tightness, pressure, discomfort? Once she identifies a sensation, I ask her to describe it, giving it a shape, color, intensity level. I might ask her to listen to what the sensation or associated body part is "telling her." I may ask if she can remember another time she felt a similar sensation. All the while I am supporting her to identify additional visceral sensations or actual emotions.

Help her to distinguish a thought or judgment from a feeling. I might say, "How are you feeling as we talk about your sister?"

"Well, I think that she was mean."

"How does the thought of her meanness make you feel?"

"Oh, I don't know. She was just so selfish."

---

[4]Siegel (1988) observes that when a client was given a word for her feeling state, it "allowed her to recognize it as something bearable, even understandable. The semantic bridge I offered her permitted her to grow into a more fully communicating person" (p. 210).

"And how does the thought of her selfishness make you feel?"

"Mad, I guess."

"Great job! So you felt mad when your sister acted mean."

Use a focusing technique. The goal of focusing is to land on a feeling that actually invokes emotion in the present moment.[5]

I ask, "How does it make you feel when you are mad?"

"Overwhelmed," my client responds.

"And what is that like? How does it make you feel when you are overwhelmed?"

"Frustrated."

"Being frustrated—how does that feel?"

"Helpless."

"And how do you feel when you are helpless?"

"All alone," she says, tearfully.

I then support the client as she unpacks and holds the sad feeling as long as possible, connecting it with a past memory or the incident being currently discussed.

Openly share my feelings as they pertain to her story or my story. Many of my clients have never had people model healthy expressions of feelings, let alone directly share their heartfelt feelings about her.

Encourage client to join a support or therapy group that focuses on affect and expression.

In group settings, use role-play. When a woman has difficulty identifying how she felt in a situation, I invite other women to act out the circumstance. As the client watches the role-play, I ask her what she thinks the woman playing her role is feeling. The group members could also share what they were feeling as they watched or participated.

Assign homework assignments that might help a woman engage with her feelings. Have her maintain a daily "feelings" journal in which she documents the different feelings she experiences throughout the day and the different sensations or aches and pains she feels in her body. Suggest that she write poetry and then reread it to identify the emotional content. Or encourage her to rent children's movies focusing on animals or little girl characters that evoke strong emotion.

---

[5]For more information, see *Focusing* by Eugene Gendlin (1981).

It is always important that I monitor and contain a woman's potential anxiety as she cooperates with these exercises. Having been shut down for so many years, she may find it unsettling to realize that she does indeed have many feelings, that they often surge uncontrollably through her body, and that she has little ability to identify, describe or manage them. Given her lack of experience in expressing or self-regulating her emotions, she may begin to feel foolish, out of control or frightened. Women who are connecting to a wide spectrum of emotions, perhaps for the first time, may also exhibit childlike behaviors and attitudes. Many actually need to be taught how to separate their feelings (which might be spontaneous) from their actions and reactions (which involve intent and volition). Ultimately, I want them to cultivate healthy self-regulatory containment and coping skills.

"ARE YOU SURE I SHOULD FEEL?"

For a woman to fully embrace her emotional life and then eventually healthily connect with someone else's emotional life, she will have to consciously confront her familiar and habitual defense mechanisms. Defense mechanisms are used to block feelings, not necessarily relationships, although at times they appear to be frontal assaults. Considering the possibility that many women with SSA have very high IQs, are acutely sensitive and are gifted with expansive imaginations and creativity, I suggest that as infants and young girls, they were able to develop a complex and highly creative defensive infrastructure—for their very survival. And the more they succeeded in erecting walls around their inner self, the more they unknowingly impeded their own emotional growth and intimacy (Miller, 1981, p. 54). Just as her negative core beliefs can potentially derail the process of encountering her true self, core beliefs such as these can fuel a woman's defenses against feeling:

- I don't or can't feel.
- It is the way I was made.
- Feelings are weaknesses. They are bad.
- It is not OK to feel.
- I will be overwhelmed if I feel too much. I will lose control.
- Feelings don't matter. They are good for nothing.
- No one cares how I feel.

In the beginning stages of therapy, I merely take note of a woman's most common defenses and the underlying emotions they are functionally covering. For instance, I may notice that she cracks a joke every time she begins to feel sad. In this second stage, I begin to bring this material to her attention directly. It is key that she get to know and even befriend her defenses (offering herself understanding and compassion) while she begins to challenge the underlying sabotaging beliefs, such as, It is weak to feel sad. To help my clients, I have developed a fairly comprehensive list of defense mechanisms. I share this list and ask them to circle any defenses that they think they use on a regular basis. In both individual or group settings, each woman identifies a defense and shares examples of when and why she has used it. I also ask her to reflect on what she learned from her family about feelings and how to handle them. Following are what I believe are the five most common defense mechanisms employed by women with SSA.

Intellectualizing. To avoid feeling, these women analyze, rationalize, minimize, theorize, assess, calculate, construct excellent explanations and debate.

Sarcasm and contempt. When a woman relies on a cynical, mocking, condescending style of relating, I believe she is subversively mocking and demeaning her self—especially her tender, warm and softer (possibly feminine) parts and emotions.[6] Essentially, as she fills with fear as her tender sides emerge, she bolsters her tough angry self.

Humor. I am careful to affirm a woman's gift for humor, but I gently point out that its misuse as a defense is counterproductive to a fuller emotional life.

Caretaking. A focus on caring for others likely cloaks the shame of a woman's felt sense of neglect. It is likely that as a little girl she was never asked, *What do* you *like?* or *What do* you *need?* or *How do* you *feel?* Often my clients are flabbergasted when I ask these simple questions, but ask them I will, over and over until their responses become spontaneous and free.

"What were you feeling just then when you offered Suzie advice?" I ask in a group setting.

"Oh, I don't know."

"It seemed really important to you that Suzie get the help that you think she needs. What were you feeling as she shared about her fears?"

"I just think she would be better off if she talked more to her church group

---

[6]Siegel (1988) believes this type of overt hostility arises out of a woman's deep self-hatred and drivenness to numb or annihilate her self and all of its supposed weakness.

about her needs instead of hiding them."

"And what were you feeling as Suzie spoke?"

"Frustrated and angry."

Following a hunch, I probe gently, asking, "With whom?"

"With myself, I guess. I just realized I don't talk to people about my needs either."

Busyness and performance orientation. When I assigned reading homework to one client, she not only had the book read within one week, but she also outlined each chapter. Yet when I gave the same assignment to another client, she would come to her sessions, week after week, complaining about how busy she was. Both women have an ingrained pattern of sidestepping quiet reflection and emotions—one through industry and the other through a frenetic sense of busyness. Each struggles with a deep sense of emptiness and isolation.

Restful quiet moments are not only essential to her connecting with her heart and emotions, but fundamental to her process of being and becoming. Here are some practical ways that I guide a woman in confronting her busyness:

- document her weekly schedule
- evaluate all extracurricular commitments
- prioritize involvements based on whether or not they move her toward either greater inner connection and self-reflection or intimacy[7]
- review her moving pattern and, if she moves every 9 to 12 months, have her resolve to stay in her current or next residence for at least two years
- encourage her to create a "special place" within her home to have quiet times (starting with 5 minutes of quiet time every other day) for reflection, journaling, reading poetry and so on
- explore her restlessness and sense of boredom once she cuts something out of her schedule

Once a woman is personally aware of her defense patterns, I can confront them directly as they arise in our sessions. I always do so with a lighthearted, compassionate tone, making sure that she is not unduly overwhelmed by shame.

---

[7]Activity-oriented events must begin to be curtailed. If she sleeps more than usual, I point out that sleeping is a common nonproductive *activity*.

"BUT I CAN'T LET *ANYONE* SEE ME CRY"

A woman with SSA usually has strong defenses against crying. She may say that crying is a sign of weakness. She might be able to cry alone or with her partner, but she is terrified at the thought of crying in front of another. It may be that she cannot cry at all, and this makes her so frustrated that she tries to force herself to create tears and wonders whether she is deeply flawed.

In this case as in others, I offer ongoing empathy and support around her feelings of flatness or her inability to shed tears. I also point out and empathize with the visceral feelings associated with tearfulness, such as a lump in the throat or an inability to speak, or with her feelings of foolishness, childishness or fear that she may never be able to stop crying once she starts. I affirm the courage it requires to be so vulnerable, especially in front of others. I let her know that when I observe her showing deep emotion through her facial expression, I do not view her as weak but as very strong. I also suggest that it is possible she actually *feels* more deeply than many other people, so it may take tremendous strength and courage on her part to step into the depths of her heart.

"AND I HATE TO BE *NEEDY*"

As a woman connects with her inner world, she will eventually encounter her *need*. The word itself is so repulsive that many of my clients refer to it as the "N-word." They hate need and they hate feeling needy. They react to it as if being needy is immoral or is a sign of utter and complete weakness. Women who lack a sense of trust and secure attachment with others or a solid sense of self do not find it easy to cope with the reality of need. Neediness is simply too vulnerable and horrifying. So, as they do with their emotions, they expunge their neediness or any hint of weakness or vulnerability. Jeannette Howard (2005) notes that to choose "to live from a point of need promotes dependency on God" (p. 68). I fully agree, but this dependency or trust is exactly what many women don't want or can't do, at least not at the beginning of therapy. It will require a major paradigm shift in a woman's thinking and experience before she can fully embrace and integrate the needy, dependent, frail side of her wonderful humanity; and for the sake of her wholeness and health, this shift is exactly what she must pursue. This will be explained further in chapter eleven.

TAKING OFF FALSE COVERINGS

False selves not only deceive these women with respect to their inner true identity, but also become a direct defense against real relationship or intimacy. A false self has no *real* substance. It is an illusion. It is a fabricated persona that often has evolved from the magical thinking of little child. It cannot enter into authentic intimacy with a real person. Unfortunately, my clients' defenses and their false ways of being and relating add, unintentionally, to their growing loneliness and emptiness.

I help a woman face her false selves in the same way that I support her as she dismantles her defense mechanisms. (Often they are one in the same. For instance, her pattern of intellectualizing may eventually coalesce into an analytical false self or persona.) She must first recognize, describe and possibly name the fragmented part of her self. It is essential that she become familiar with it. She must then seek to understand the needs, emotions and authentic longings associated with each false persona. For instance, behind the tough persona may be a legitimate need for safety or a hidden longing to be seen as significant. This persona may also disguise a broken heart filled with sadness and pain. As a woman integrates these underlying needs (and points of grief)—instead of splitting them into fortified fragments of her self—a deep restoration of her true being begins.[8]

I often use a voice-dialogue technique to help a woman become more acquainted with and ultimately integrate her "tough girl," for instance. By objectifying this persona, I give it a voice outside of the woman, offer it respect and treat it as a legitimate part of her personhood. I first ask a client to draw a picture representing her "tough" part. After thoroughly discussing the insights gained from making the drawing, I ask her to assume the part of "tough girl" by sitting in another chair and holding her picture. I give her a brief introduction to the voice-dialogue process, explaining that she and I will be dialoguing but that she will be speaking as the "tough girl." When my client is ready, I begin by thanking her (the "tough girl") for agreeing to come and talk to me. I might ask her how long she has been helping my client, how she helps, what she wants, what she feels, what she believes (magical or distorted thinking may be exposed at this point) or how old she is. I ask her how she

---

[8] "Awareness of the destructiveness of the false, defensive self, as well as awareness of the impairments in the real self, are the necessary primary building blocks in the development of a real self" (Klein, 1989, p. 39).

specifically feels about my client and what she thinks my client needs. We essentially carry on a lengthy dialogue. If the part is young, I speak to it as if I am speaking to a young child. Throughout this exercise, my clients, by acting out the "tough" part, often access deep emotion and even repressed memories. For some, it is the first time this part of their experience has ever been shared or exposed to another.

When I am assured that the "tough" part has felt heard, I thank her for helping me to better understand my client and gently close our discussion. I then ask my client to resume her original chair, taking a few deep breaths to recenter and to continue to integrate her emotions. The client is then instructed to speak directly to her "tough" part. We place the picture of "tough girl" in the empty chair. The client may want to thank this part for helping her to survive all these years or acknowledge what she learned as she listened. Many clients will gently tell the part that they are ready and willing to feel their pain and no longer need to be protected and covered with toughness. They may ask the tough part to now please cooperate in allowing her to continue the work of healing and recovery. Through this dialogue, my client is essentially regaining control of her life and destiny by integrating this fragmented part. I encourage her to continue to dialogue with this part if it once again attempts to reassert control and prevent my client from feeling her pain.

Howard asserts that "bravery is required to step out from the fig leaves of falsehood and allow the true self to emerge" (2005, p. 56). I therefore make it a point to show great compassion and affirmation, sprinkled with praise and encouragement, as my client dares to understand and relinquish a false persona that has felt like her only resource for need fulfillment or for a sense of self.

"BUT THIS RELATIONSHIP THING IS NOT FOR ME"
These are the voices of a lifelong pattern of defensively detaching from relationship and intimacy:
- I don't belong. I don't fit in.
- I'm not like them. I'm different. I don't want to be like them.
- I don't know how to connect. I can't do that chit-chat stuff.
- I'm not sure what I have to offer.
- Besides, who really cares? They won't understand me.
- And if we did become friends, I would probably become emotionally de-

pendent or get sexually involved. So why bother?

Originating from a place of mistrust, disrespect and disidentification (as outlined in chapter 3), separating, defensively differentiating[9] and isolating have become unconscious patterns for many women with SSA.

I observe a progression of sorts in a woman's (girl's) development of defensive detachment or relational ambivalence (dismissiveness):

1. As an infant or child, she avoids an "anticipated experience of negative affect, even in situations where negative affect might not occur" (Tronick, 1989, p. 117).

2. She develops a pattern of indiscriminate disengagement from people and things.

3. She refuses to reattach or identify with mother (Moberly, 1983).

4. She detaches from inner characteristics such as femaleness and other aspects of her true self.

5. She detaches from all that is feminine externally.

6. She detaches from and denies natural longings for relational intimacy because of risk of disappointment.

7. She detaches from or does not know how to attach to her same-sex peer group.

8. She develops a default "attachment" or "identification" with the aggressor, her dad, her brothers or boys and simultaneously detaches from emotional or sexual closeness.

9. She detaches from or disidentifies with her own self.

10. She detaches from life-giving forces or energies related to spontaneity, creativity and God.

If a woman has experienced this type of global detachment, her relational need and internal fragmentation will be severe. Yet as she dares to connect to her longings and needs—which I must encourage her to do—she connects as well to the fear of disappointment. She will grow ambivalent and be pulled in two directions. Until a woman can fully recognize and confront the features

---

[9]Defensive detachment must be distinguished from a girl's natural process of differentiation as a unique self apart from her mom. Unlike the boy who differentiates through separation from his mom, a girl must differentiate *within* an ongoing attachment. Paradoxically, defensive detachment will derail a girl's ability to fully differentiate.

within her long-term ambivalence, her relational needs are often unconsciously expressed through demands such as wanting to be the "special" someone versus a friend among many friends or wanting the intense feelings associated with a romantic encounter versus those associated with an ordinary friendship. All-or-nothing thinking is often at the core of her relational ambivalence.

I know now to listen closely whenever a woman begins to despair of her lack of friendship or community. While I want to empathize with what she might be feeling, I am also aware that she may be despairing because of her unconscious habit to defend against, disqualify herself from or control all relationships.

Regardless of its form, a woman's defensive detachment and resulting ambivalence must be gently exposed as she commits to greater levels of maturity and wholeness. I agree with Elizabeth Moberly (1983): "Healing for the homosexual is not just a matter of meeting unmet needs, but [a matter] of dealing with the barrier that blocked their fulfillment in the ordinary course of growth and can continue to prevent such fulfillment" (p. 48). But for some women, it is not only their defensive postures that have prevented the emotional connection for which they were made, but also the lack of opportunity to *learn* the most basic relational skills.

"BUT I REALLY DON'T KNOW *HOW* TO DO IT!"

Many women with SSA, depending on the degree of insecurity and trauma in their backgrounds, lack the ability to empathize, recognize social cuing or mutually engage within relationship. One night in group, Laura tearfully shared about a hurtful interaction with her mother. Most of the group members were engaged with good eye contact and attentive body language. However, a few women were nonchalantly looking around the room. As soon as Laura concluded, one of these distracted (and perhaps dissociative) women, Jody, piped up and, without acknowledging Laura's story whatsoever, asked if we could talk about how to have healthy relationships. I took advantage of this moment to ask Jody what she was *feeling* (self-awareness is a starting point for connection with another) as Laura shared.

Jody responded, "I don't know."

"Jody," I said, "Try to imagine yourself in Laura's place. What would you feel if your mother said those angry words to you?"

Jody bluntly replied, "My mom is dead. I don't talk to her. Now can we talk about how to have healthy relationships?"

Although I felt sadness at her response, it was hard not to grin. I feel such fondness for women like Jody. Jody had many developmental deficits, lacked a positive sense of self, lived much of her life in isolation and therefore presented with little ego strength to cope with even the slightest levels of emotional intensity within her own soul, let alone within another. She had never learned adequate social cueing or higher processes like empathy. Jody had no concept of how she affected others, either negatively or positively. She didn't believe that she was *real* enough to even *make* an impact.

My goal is to nurture and affirm my client's true emerging self and to ultimately encourage the natural development of an other-centered or generative posture in her life, instead of perpetuating immature self-centeredness or stagnant self-absorption. As a woman becomes rooted and established in *my* love, she will begin to love herself. As she experiences my empathy, she can learn to use self-empathy or "make empathic contact with some aspect of the self as object" (Jordan & Surrey, 1989, p. 100). And as she loves and empathizes with herself, she will begin to love and empathize with others. As a woman matures in her self-actualization—openly participating in something bigger (the relational universe) outside of herself—her sense of dignity and value will also increase.

In the meantime, however, many women with SSA need practical help making eye contact, assigning meaning and receiving from others.

Making eye contact. As Tobi shared in our group meeting, I noticed she was engaged in her typical pattern of staring at the floor. I intervened and asked her whether she was aware that she rarely made eye contact when she spoke. She explained that she became anxious and self-conscious when she looked at us. Because she was new to the group, I reassured her that she could continue to look at the floor if she needed to but that she was missing out on our smiling faces. She looked up at me and asked, "What do you mean?"

I then asked the group whether they had noticed how other members were showing care through their body language and facial expressions. They all emphatically exclaimed, "Yes!" and then took turns sharing with Tobi what they had seen in the other women that demonstrated care and concern. Tobi was shocked to discover not only that others cared, but that she had missed it all.

One of my favorite group exercises is to instruct one woman to look into the eyes of each of the other group members, holding each gaze for at least three to five seconds. This often brings women to tears. Outside of a romantic relationship, many of these women have never seen the affirmation and love that can be communicated through another's eyes and face.

Assigning meaning. Many women also miss the meaning behind another's casual kindness or caring gesture. When they do notice, they can't seem to hold on to the meaning or be blessed or nourished by it. I might interrupt a client when I sense that she just missed a meaningful comment, saying something like, "Joanie, stop for just a minute. Did you really hear what I just said? You didn't seem to flinch, so I just wanted to make sure you heard me."

"Yeah, I heard it."

"Well I'm glad you did, but what did you do with that comment? Did it have any meaning for you?"

"Well, yeah, it was nice."

"Joanie, I just said you were amazingly brave and very kind. What is it like for you to hear me say those words to you?" I wonder: Did it made her pause? Was she grateful? Did she *feel* blessed or honored? What blocks her from *taking it in?*

Receiving from others. Many of my clients have no idea how to take in goodness. They readily internalize negative experiences, messages and emotions, but they have little or no capacity to receive that which might be life-giving. Like a child whose stomach has shrunk for lack of food, these women must be fed kindness one spoonful at a time, until their soul expands and adjusts to accommodate more nourishment. They must also be convinced that this "nourishment" is going to continue. They do not want to allow themselves to enjoy it or become reliant on it if it will only be short lived. They would rather starve than be jerked around.

On the other hand, many women with SSA are conditioned to expect love to be passionate, desperate, exciting and dramatic—like the powerful spray of a fire hose—rather than ordinary and moderate. Within a romanticized same-sex relationship, a woman often lowers her boundaries and literally loses herself in the exciting flood of her partner's love and affection. This form of emotional abandon becomes the standard for how to *receive* love. When she is presented with a healthily boundaried friendship or simple act of kindness, she may not recognize it for what it is: a normal portion of healthy nourishment. A normal friendship or gesture may seem flat or boring. She needs help to begin redefining love, affection and care while also learning to recognize, receive and hold the small "meals" of warm connection within the counseling office. I regularly invite my clients to recall and reflect on our warm moments together or meaningful times they've shared with other people. A woman learns that she can continue to nourish herself by recalling these good memories.

To develop their capacity to receive and hold, I encourage my clients to practice articulating an acknowledgment or "thank you" in response to a person's kindness. For some women this sounds much easier than it actually is. Verbalizing an authentic "thank you" requires them to first admit that they are valuable and that they deserve good things. This may still disrupt their inner equilibrium based on negative self-representations and beliefs. Even after practicing these simple words, it may still take months for them to feel comfortable in using them.

NAVIGATING HEALTHY FRIENDSHIPS

To be sure, these women want to connect and be accepted and loved. They don't want to be alone. They would like to come home to another. They want to be cared for and to be able to care for another. These are not "lesbian desires" but natural relational desires that reflect their intact humanity and authentic core self. These are the very desires that I want to affirm so their fears and defensive compulsions will begin to pale in light of their relational hunger and need.

> *For so many years, I spent all of my time nurturing my one special friendship. I never developed much of an outside community. What a huge amount of life I've lost. But during these last years of counseling and Living Waters [a Christian organization for people pursuing healing from relational and sexual brokenness], I have finally come to realize that I am a likable person. I believe now that people in general—not just the woman I am with, but other people—genuinely like me and want to spend time with me!*
>
> *Joyce*

Besides providing a client with an opportunity to practice vulnerability in therapy, I encourage her to seek out other relational opportunities where she can start to understand her defensive posturing, practice letting her guard down and explore healthy friendship. Becoming involved in a small group,

such as a special interest club or church Bible study, allows her to practice relational skills at a safer distance, since the spotlight will not always be on her.
But eventually, it will become important for her to identify a few specific
women with whom she can build a friendship or mentoring relationship.[10]

Many women with SSA have a long line of broken relationships. They have
ended relationships because they feared becoming sexually involved or decided
to leave relationships because they *have* become sexually involved. Relationships have ended because either woman may have become emotionally dependent and decided that breaking up sooner would be easier than doing it later.
Some women live within a constant state of relational ambivalence with their
closest female friends or have been the brunt of another's ongoing relational
ambivalence. The thought of "trying again," often surfaces their deep disappointment and relational despair.

So my clients will have many things to process with me once new friendships begin to grow, especially regarding what is "normal." I therefore instruct
and coach my clients on the healthy stages of intimacy, expectations for the
various stages and what is typical in most female friendships with respect to
the following:

- the amount of time spent together as the friendship builds or becomes
  established
- the amount of time spent communicating (via phone, e-mail, text messages
  or instant messages)
- mutuality in terms of initiating contact
- the level of self-disclosure
- the nature of physical affection or comforting touch
- the awareness of similarities and dissimilarities
- fears, doubts or insecurities
- feelings of genuine affection, curiosity or excitement
- interdependency versus codependency

---

[10]To help my clients find healthy and safe female friends, I encourage them to listen to the quality of
a woman's words and sentiments, versus focusing on her external looks or even her interests. I coax
them to pursue women of substance and passion as well as with women who are self-aware and able
to admit their own sin and brokenness. For more ideas on helping women with SSA build friendships, see Howard (2005), Paulk (2003) and Whitehead (2003). For resources on healthy female
friendships, see Apter & Josselson (1998), Brestin (1997), Cox & Dant (1999), Gilligan, Lyons &
Hanmer (1990), McGinnis (2004) and Sheehy (2000).

It may be useful for a woman to interview some of her existing friends or mentors about their friendships, exploring, for example, what each friendship means to them, why they like their friend, how they met, what they do together, how much they touch or how often they talk.

On occasion, a client will experience sexual arousal once she relaxes into a warm friendship with another woman. This is not a reason to terminate the friendship, but she may need to understand that her arousal may be a defensive maneuver to thwart closeness and non-erotic intimacy. She must learn how to separate sexual feelings from emotional closeness (as discussed in the next chapter) and how to reestablish the beauty and innocence of a warm human connection. The bottom line is that a woman's unhealthy detachment patterns do not just need to be extinguished; they need to be replaced by healthy attachment patterns.

CHAPTER TEN

Leaving the Home of Another

Dealing with Same-Sex Attractions

My soul is restless until it rests in you, O God.

St. Augustine

At some point, almost every woman with whom I work comes to a place in her journey where she desires to break her patterns of same-sex relating and emotional dependency.[1] Having been through the disappointment of personal compromise as she tried to "fit" into another woman's home or life, she is now ready to exert effort to establish her own home and find an independent sense of security and stability. It will only be within her *own* home that she can truly "come out" and fully be her unique self. This means that she wants my help to exit an existing same-sex relationship or to challenge future same-sex attractions so that she will not become romantically involved with a new female friend. This in turn means that she will have to confront, understand and intentionally choose a different course of action in response to her same-sex desires.

GETTING READY TO "MOVE OUT" AND "MOVE ON"

Contrary to popular belief, these women *can* choose a course for their lives that is counter to their feelings, wishes or desires. Many of us do this every day. We roll out of bed when the alarm rings even though we feel tired and desire to be independently wealthy so we don't have to go to work. We have the freedom either to let feelings such as these become the dictating voice

---

[1]This has not happened as of yet with some of my new adolescent and young adult self-identified lesbian clients. Their current goals in therapy are to stabilize family relationships, overcome depression and anxiety, or bolster their self-esteem.

for our life (and therefore stay in bed) or to allow something else to determine the outcome. For years I was told that the "something else" should be my will. But I always had difficulty understanding *how* to operate this thing called my volition or will. Nothing seemed to happen when I *willed* to be good, for instance.

What I eventually discovered is that in using my will, I simply needed to choose *which* wish or desire I wanted to live in accordance with. For instance, as I'm rolling out of bed there is a part of me—a deeper and perhaps far less accessible part of me—that feels hopeful for a new day and desires to please God in all that I do and say. The key for me, then, was to access and integrate these deeper and probably truer parts of myself so that I could have other options, rather than feeling ruled or victimized by my lesser desires such as staying in bed. If I am only connected to a single driving feeling or aspect of my life, such as a craving for sleep, I really have no choice apart from deciding *how* to fulfill my craving. This is not freedom. My clients need to discover this same truth and then determine which part of themselves they want to choose to live from. Is a woman's lesbian desire the most fundamental or important driving force in her life, or does she have deeper desires? Are her desires mutually exclusive or compatible? Each woman must come to her own conclusion.

> *I tried to rationalize or justify my lesbian relationship with God and the Bible. I came up with things like this: Other people live in sin all the time, and they are still Christians. It's not really wrong; it feels so natural. I don't lust after women; I just want to be close to some of them. I'm not really gay. We're not doing everything sexually that gay people do. But somehow I just couldn't figure it all out. There was no peace. I did have seasons of what felt like peace, but they never lasted. Without lasting peace, I knew I couldn't live this way. I knew I wanted peace more than I wanted a lesbian relationship.*
>
> *a client*

A CONFLICT OF DESIRES

When a woman of faith is in the midst of a same-sex sexual attraction that seems to have the power to draw her into a relationship against her will, the division within her heart is often clearly exposed, as I've illustrated here:

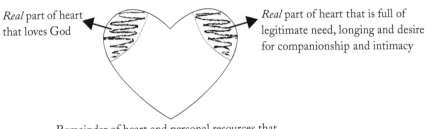

Real part of heart that loves God

Real part of heart that is full of legitimate need, longing and desire for companionship and intimacy

Remainder of heart and personal resources that are unknown, inaccessible or not integrated into mature sense of self

Figure 10.1.

Each woman has a part of her that *wants* to obey God and draw closer to him, but she often finds her intimacy with God less than fulfilling in terms of providing a deep sense of being loved. This Godward side of her heart usually defines a major part of her external life and religious identity, but it is not necessarily effective in promoting growth or fulfilling her deepest needs for intimacy. This is an unfortunate but common reality for many of my clients. They know "obedience" hasn't been enough to fulfill them but can't put their finger on what is actually wrong.

Each woman has another part of her that is also true and real but typically has been disowned or denied: her relational longings and inherent vulnerability. These needs and longings may initially enter her consciousness at the first hint of mutual recognition or admiring gaze from another woman. She will feel helplessly exposed and powerless to deal with her own overwhelming desire. Sadly, a same-sex erotic or emotionally dependent relationship may be the only thing she has ever known that comes close to meeting her desires. She may, therefore, define her core longing for closeness as lesbian desire.

She now faces a heart-wrenching dilemma: she believes that she cannot survive without her needs being met in a lesbian relationship but that she also cannot survive if she is disappointing God. In choosing to follow God, she will languish in her unmet relational need. In choosing to be with a woman, she will languish in guilt and possibly lose her voice or personal freedom through enmeshment. I cannot stress enough how difficult it is for her to choose between these paths and how hard it is as a therapist to authentically empathize with her

as she comes close to collapsing under the weight of hopelessness and despair.[2]
This conflict often creates a perpetual cycle to a woman's same-sex relating:

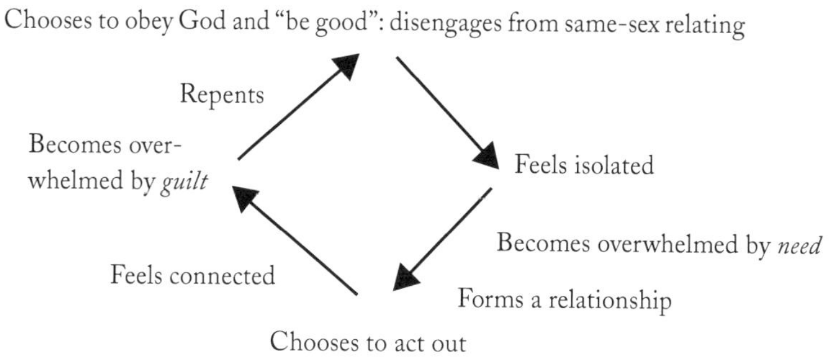

Chooses to obey God and "be good": disengages from same-sex relating

Repents

Becomes over-
whelmed by *guilt*   Feels isolated

                                                Becomes overwhelmed by *need*

Feels connected
                                          Forms a relationship
                    Chooses to act out

Figure 10.2.

A woman who chooses to refrain from same-sex relating potentially creates
for herself a sense of isolation *if* she is not able to build meaningful intimacy
with God, herself or others. Her relational needs naturally become overwhelming. She becomes desperate to relieve her isolation and emptiness. This
desperation may be the impetus for her to enter a new same-sex relationship
or to seek relief through fantasy and masturbation. In either case, she will gain
a *sense* of relief and connection.

The ensuing fear of enmeshment, her loss of self or her feelings of guilt become overwhelming, at which point she renounces her behavior or ends her
relationship. This may relieve her guilt, but she is left facing her inner and
outer desolation once again. She is alone. Naturally, her need grows. And the
cycle continues, reinforcing her belief that change is not possible.

But change is possible. As in any addiction cycle, points of intervention can
and do disrupt such patterns. For instance, as a woman comes into an experiential understanding of God's unconditional love and abiding presence or
heals memories related to abandonment, she may no longer become overwhelmed with feelings of desperate loneliness or existential need. As a woman
acknowledges her value and surrounds herself with healthy community, her

---

[2]Frankly, I have come to believe that if I do *not* sometimes find myself wishing that a client could feel
loved and live happily ever after in a relationship with a gentle and kind woman, then I am not allowing myself to truly empathize with her deep pain and confusion.

sense of isolation may be mitigated, shifting the vulnerabilities perpetuating this cycle. A woman can also directly shift the cycle by altering her same-sex behaviors or her chosen method of "acting out."

CHALLENGING A SEXUALIZED ATTRACTION: MORE THAN BEHAVIOR MODIFICATION

Challenging a woman's sexualized attraction or helping her transform an emotionally dependent relationship into a non-erotic, nondependent friendship is complex. It will require intentionality and candidness on both of our parts. She will need the freedom to openly and frankly discuss her same-sex longings and her specific same-sex attractions and behaviors. She will need to openly discuss her struggles with God and her general ambivalence and confusion with respect to her future and future choices.

I want her to be able to freely speak about her friend, their conversations and their behaviors for the sake of her self-reflection and growth. I do not show any disrespect or bias that would give the impression that I think her friend is "bad" or necessarily the unhealthy one. I don't want my client to feel she has to defend her friend or her attraction to and enjoyment of her friend. This will distract her from the task at hand.

> *My therapist sat and listened for a long time. And then she gently suggested a different course of action. I never ever felt like she was saying, "You've got to do this." I didn't ever feel like an action on my part was mandatory. Her work with me was not conditioned upon my ultimate decision. I felt wholly loved and accepted.*
>
> Joyce

At this stage of therapy my client may need the freedom to integrate and openly proclaim a lesbian identity, even as she makes decisions about ending a present relationship or foregoing a new relationship. This does not dismay me, nor do I think this is a step backward in her process or an act of brazenness toward God. This admission brings her a sense of relief and freedom. Sometimes it's as if she is saying, *Now that* this *is settled, I can get on with it and sort through the rest of my stuff.*

> *For the most part, I like me, even with my lesbian feelings. I couldn't have*

said that at all a few years ago. I don't always like the lesbian struggle, but I believe that God is present with me as I navigate through my journey. So, I'm OK with me and have accepted my lesbianism as a piece of me where I get to rely on God's strength. By living in God's light, I am being true to myself. I am not less of a person because I have lesbian feelings. I choose to acknowledge my lesbianism openly without engaging in lesbian relationships or behaviors. I attempt to faithfully follow Christ and serve God, not because he will change me, but because he loves me. I know that God embraces me—not in spite of my struggle, but because of it.

Terry

NAVIGATING A NEW SEXUALIZED ATTRACTION

Below are recommendations I might suggest to a client as she moves *through* a new same-sex attraction. Following is a section that will address the common steps of exiting an existing emotionally dependent same-sex relationship.

Do not run. Many of my clients experience uninvited sexual feelings as they attempt to build non-erotic friendships with women. When these feelings arise, a woman may be tempted to abruptly end or avoid this new friendship.[3] But avoiding a potentially rewarding friendship (especially if the other woman does not struggle with SSA) out of fear is not typically beneficial, because it reinforces both her pattern of defensively detaching or dismissing intimacy and her core negative beliefs about herself, such as *I am dangerous,* or *I always screw things up.* She has a true need for healthy friendships, so she is going to have to resist the urge to detach, take risks in establishing new relationships and face the reality that life can be messy.

Do not share. I advise my client to refrain from communicating her romantic sentiments to the other woman, even if she intends to do it in a spirit of confession. If the other woman is also struggling with same-sex issues and feels attracted to my client, an admission like this may catapult them into unbearable longings to be close, sexual fantasies or even a sexual relationship. Just the thought of being wanted can weaken most women's resolve. Even if the other woman does not struggle with SSA, she may not have adequate information

---

[3]Assuming that my client's stated goal is to refrain from same-sex relating or behavior, "running" may be in her best interest if this new friend is explicitly pursuing her for a sexualized relationship or exhibits no commitment to refrain from such relating or behavior.

or support to know how to react or continue to walk out a friendship with my client. Once the other woman is known and trusted, my client might want to revisit a possible confession, but only as a disclosure of a same-sex struggle, not as an admission of a personal attraction.[4]

Rather, I encourage my client to talk to *me* about their longings and fantasies for the sake of deeper understanding. Of course this does not feel nearly as good to her as it would were she sharing with her friend. Talking with her friend would give her a sense of relief from the pressure of two needs: the need to be known and the need to know whether her friend feels the same. While such a confession may feel as if it meets or relieves these needs, it only does so on a shallow level. These two women are so much more than their sexual feelings or attractions. They deserve (and need) to be known and seen for their entire personhood, not just their fleeting sexual desire.

Face the shame. A therapist's nonmoralizing attitude combined with a matter-of-fact discussion style helps many women combat the shame and guilt often present in the midst of a sexual attraction. Some women feel so disappointed in themselves that they can barely engage in a conversation. Others are naturally embarrassed by discussing such personal issues as sexual fantasies or behaviors.

For instance, during a group meeting one night, Suzette writhed on the couch as she attempted to talk about her new friendship and the rising desire she had for a physical relationship, "Oh, it is so shameful to talk about this!"

First, I explained that her "shameful" desires probably point to some innocent longing or need. It was important for her to know and understand these longings. I then reassured her that as I listened to her words, I would hear not just sexual content but the symbolic expressions of these deep longings and needs.

I then gave her a nudge by opening up a frank discussion about what I speculated was one of her hopes within her sexual fantasies. "Let's say that sex would be *great* with this woman," I prompted. She and all the others in the group let out a big sigh of relief as I put into words what she had indeed been wondering but was reluctant to openly admit because of its "sinful" content. I

---

[4]These recommendations do not necessarily apply if a woman is developing a mentoring relationship. In that case, explicit processing of her feelings and thoughts would be more appropriate since the relationship itself is not intended to be fully mutual. The mentor is to retain somewhat of an objective role as "big sister" or "teacher."

have found that raw honesty is far better than prudish sidestepping.

"What needs do you think would be met by having *great* sex?" I asked her. Suzette was taken back by such a direct question but was able to at least crack a smile. After she stammered out a few more words and after I told her she was doing a great job, I addressed the question to the entire group. There were others who were also uncomfortable discussing such private thoughts, but a few were more than willing and able to share. They admitted that sex gives them a feeling of connection and deep attachment. They feel wanted and loved and enjoy being touched and held. They also acknowledged that, as adult women, they simply want and enjoy sex.

When Suzette heard their words, she was finally able to admit that she too wanted this sense of connection. She shared more of her story about the deprivation of healthy touch in her family. She also concluded that some of the shame surrounding her sexuality is related to her history of sexual exploitation and abuse. For a woman to fully gain the benefit of understanding her deepest longings and desires such as a need for connection, she must face her shame.

Understand the infatuation. Women with SSA are not the only people who tend to have romanticized notions about life. Many of us believe, or at least hope, there is a perfect someone out there who can take away the pangs of our fallen existence through his or her constant love and undying devotion. If we meet this person, we will feel complete, life will be great, sex will be great, and we will live happily ever after—never to feel lonely again. Western culture has flaunted this myth, which includes the premise that this idealistic bliss is not only attainable but also that each and every one of us deserves to attain it. Most people, once they've pulled their head out of the clouds, agree that attempting to build a relationship on the foundation of this myth is foolish and even dangerous.

Besides idealizing intimacy, many of my clients also have a pattern of sexualizing intimacy. As mentioned before, as soon as warm feelings emerge in a relationship, so do sexual fantasies. These fantasies then consume a woman's thoughts. She often objectifies the other woman, wanting her for what she can give rather than for who she is. So quick are some women to transfer their affections into the sexual realm, the relationship barely has time to progress into a casual friendship. This is why some women with SSA have never had platonic friends. Every potential friendship turns erotic.[5]

---

[5] For a spiritual perspective on overcoming the temptation of same-sex feelings, see Paulk (2003).

Yet every woman needs female friends. We can live without sexual partners, but we cannot live without friends. I therefore encourage my clients to take a step back from a developing attraction to examine their hearts, emotions and beliefs as they proceed by asking questions along these lines: *What is really happening here? Is this new friend really my true love, or does she remind me of the mother I never had? Is my heart crying out for friendly attention and affection or for sex? Do I believe that she is the only one that will ever love me?*

I invite my client to objectify her infatuation by gathering as much unconscious material as she can, regardless of its confused or sexualized nature. I reassure her that I will not judge her for her thoughts or feelings. I treat this process like a brainstorming exercise: that is, I do not initially offer my analysis or interpretations. For now, I want *her* to practice asking herself important questions and making the connections that are within *her* ability to make. The following questions can be directly discussed or assigned as journaling homework.

- What were you feeling prior to meeting this woman?
- What were you looking at or working on in counseling prior to meeting this woman?
- What were your top three felt needs at the time?[6]
- What do you like about this woman?
- What was the first thing that drew you to her?
- What are her special features and characteristics?
- What does she do, what are her passions, and what does she believe in?
- Does she remind you of anyone you have known in the past?
- How are you alike?
- How are you different?
- What do you feel when you are with her?
- What do you like to do together?
- Is there anything about her that frightens you?
- Is there anything about her that you dislike?

---

[6]Just prior to meeting her new friend, a woman may have been battling severe loneliness or processing deep grief over past losses. It is important that she begin to acknowledge her painful feelings or vulnerabilities and to assess whether she is subconsciously seeking to avoid or find relief by pursuing a romantic liaison.

- What do you want out of your relationship with her?
- What are your hopes and desires for this relationship?
- What relational longings have been stirred in you as a result of meeting her?
- What do you hope to experience if your sexual fantasy is fulfilled?
- What do you fear if you enter into a relationship with her?
- What do you fear if you don't enter into a relationship with her?

When a woman answers these questions methodically and honestly, rich symbolic material usually emerges.[7] Katie, one of my clients, noticed an interesting woman at a business event. She was immediately curious and felt a strong emotional draw. They finally had an opportunity to chat, but Katie was shocked and disappointed to hear that the other woman was about to move to another state. Katie thought, *She's leaving!* As soon as she returned to her seat, she glanced again toward the other woman and immediately had a sexual fantasy. Katie eventually realized that the sexual fantasy warded off her unwanted feelings of abandonment.[8]

The level of insight a woman gains will depend on her motivation and ability to objectively sort out this material. Regardless, the process of asking and answering questions such as these can help her stabilize her powerful emotions. She will typically alternate between a centered place of objective analysis and a powerless state of subjective need and strong emotions.

I am getting to know the wife of one of my husband's friends. We have had lunch together a couple of times, and it's been really nice because she has called and invited me to do it again. First, it has felt good that I can actually admit to myself that I am attracted to her. But second, and more

---

[7]Breaking the idealization is extremely challenging for a woman who has never consummated her longings for touch and physical closeness with another woman. She is faced with a constant curiosity and secret hopefulness that maybe, just maybe, a physical relationship *will* meet her unmet needs. It is my job to empathize with her deep ache and longing and to simultaneously invite her to face the past relational losses or deficits that may be confusedly expressed as physical need. I must affirm her desire to be someone special to another even as I gently challenge the myth that all will be well if she can just get physically closer to her friend.

[8]Moberly (1983) refers to sexualization or same-sex attraction as a reenactment or reparative urge: the impulse to "make good earlier deficits in the parent-child relationship" (p. 6). To sexualize, however, is to essentially introduce sex into a parent-child relationship. Acknowledging that heterosexuals also enter into reparative relationships, she still nevertheless emphasizes it is not "appropriate to any relationships which, however adult in other respects, is significantly determined by the attempt to meet non-adult attachment needs" (p. 20).

important, I can clearly see why. She is where I want to be in my life. Knowing this or being honest about it helps me to stay committed to my personal journey instead of unconsciously stepping into hers. It helps to remember this so I don't get lost in a fantasy about her.

Teresa

If the new relationship continues to develop over time, I will not be surprised if her felt need and her attraction to her new friend become stronger. Frequently, as these positive feelings peak, she reaches the brink of a deep desperation or a fear of abandonment, feeling that she will die if she can't be with her friend. Needless to say, at this point, she may not be able to regulate and process all of her inner pressures and turmoil. She may begin to contact her friend more frequently, wanting to know whether her friend is OK or whether her friend still wants to be friends. The contact could be as brief as a short e-mail or as engaging as a sexual interaction. Any, and I mean *any,* sense of connection will feel like a relief. She may require additional stabilizing support during this phase

Create a pathway for genuine non-erotic friendship. Because of the possible emotional intensity in establishing a new friendship, my clients usually need to be introduced to or reminded about the concept of boundaries.[9] Some find setting boundaries far from straightforward. Setting a boundary can bring to the surface a woman's deep fear of abandonment or isolation or the belief that to *say no* is mean. As we discuss the necessity of boundaries, I rely on the following list of key process questions. A corresponding "reality check"—the way I would explain what is considered normative in terms of personal investment and limits within friendships—follows each question below.

- *How much time do you spend talking on the phone? How often do you communicate each day (through phone, e-mail, instant messages, etc.)? How much time are you spending together in a single day? Across the week?* Friends do not typically speak to each other every day, but if they do, they usually don't speak three to four times a day. Some friends might only speak once a week or even once a month. Also, a healthy woman will have a full life and therefore will not be available every time her friends call. She does not wait at home, hoping her friends will call.

---

[9]Cloud & Townsend (1992), Hemfelt, Minirth & Meier (1989) and books on codependency are very beneficial in introducing clients to this topic.

- *Who is initiating the contact?* Friendships are mutual. Friends take turns calling each other. If you called your friend today, then it would be appropriate for you to wait for her to initiate the next time. By waiting, you are letting her set the pace that is most comfortable for her. However, if she is initiating multiple contacts each day, perhaps a boundary should be established.

- *What kind of things are you doing together? In private or public? At what hour?* Friends are comfortable with meeting for dinner at a restaurant or attending a social activity together. They do not require the majority of their time to be spent in private settings or late into the night.

- *What kinds of things are you telling her about yourself? What kinds of things is she sharing with you?* Friendships take time to develop. Usually, at the beginning, new friends talk about factual details about their life. They may gradually open up and share more personal information. But rarely do they talk about their deepest darkest secrets within the first week.

- *What do you feel as you think about your friend or anticipate seeing her?* It is normal to feel excited about meeting a person that you really like. It feels good to discover that the interest in getting to know each other is mutual. Building a friendship should feel fun, rewarding and pleasurable—otherwise, few people would remain friends. However, friendships are not usually defined by intense levels of drama and intrigue.

- *Is the relationship moving too fast? Too slow? Why?* If a new friend assumes the role of long-time best friend within the first month, the relationship is probably moving too fast. As Cox and Dant (1999) explain, "Genuine friendships form and deepen over time through the sharing of interests and experiences. The more we share with a friend, the more rewarding the relationship becomes. Building friendships requires patience and a willingness to invest" (p. 2).

- *Are you regularly assessing and discussing your relationship?* In *The Four Loves*, C. S. Lewis (1960) contrasts two kinds of love: eros (romantic) and platonic (friendship). He says, "Lovers are always talking to one another about their love; Friends hardly ever about their Friendship" (p. 91). Friends do not feel a need to constantly talk about their relationship. They allow it to simply unfold and become whatever it will naturally become. There is no single definition of a friendship. One woman may have a friend she sees at the health club, a friend she sees at her Bible study, a friend who is a work associate and a friend with whom she shares her deepest heart.

- *What other friends are you seeing right now? Are you maintaining your regular social commitments?* If a friendship does not provide an opportunity for each woman to have *many* other friends and time with family, husbands or children, then the relationship has become exclusive. As the quote from Lewis in chapter five explained, a true friendship will open its doors to others.

- *Are one or both of you giving small gifts, sending cards or offering acts of service on a regular basis?* Friends might give a small gift apart from birthday or Christmas, but this happens only once in a great while. Cards are typically sent on birthdays or other special occasions, but some friends do not exchange cards or gifts at all. A woman certainly helps her friend when she finds herself in a bind, but typically she is not involved in every problem or difficult situation her friend may have. They will both probably have other friends to rely on as well.

- *Are you keeping up with your daily responsibilities?* Usually, new friendships do not interrupt or circumvent an individual's regular schedule or responsibilities. Friendships adjust to these important factors within a woman's life. Close friends can enjoy a tremendous amount of closeness, but they can also leave when its time to go home and get back to their personal lives.

- *How are you self-nurturing right now?* A friendship can never replace the benefits of self-care and self-nurture. Only a woman herself knows what she needs.

- *Are you physically affectionate? If so, how is that being expressed?* Friends might hold hands or hold one another when one needs comfort or reassurance through a difficult time. Friends might hug hello and goodbye. Affectionate gestures such as touches on the arm or shoulder are common. Friends might give each other short neck rubs or therapeutic foot rubs. Typically, friends do not linger in each other's arms.

Face and deal with any sexual involvement. When a client becomes sexually involved with the woman to whom she is attracted, she may feel completely defeated. I become very intentional in my interventions at this point. I offer unconditional acceptance as I attune and empathize. She will have many mixed feelings. I do not moralize (unless she draws me into a discussion on biblical morality) nor do I show disappointment. I continue to encourage her to reflect on her situation and reassure her that she can still learn and grow. I do not want her to sink under the common sabotaging belief that all is lost or that she can never change.

If at this point, or any other point in her process, a woman decides to remain in a same-sex relationship or integrate and affirm a lesbian identity as God's best for her, I will reassure her of my commitment to journey with her as long as she wants me along. While I neither affirm that her homosexuality is an inborn trait nor that it is blessed by God, I do respect her decision. My goal is to always honor a woman's autonomy and bolster her ego strength so that she can choose and change decisions based on new desires, circumstances or insights. If we proceed in therapy, I will provide the same level of emotional support as I have in the past while we continue to address the underlying issues that were already at the forefront of our work together. Therapy with a woman such as this is never terminated simply because of a change in her stated goals. It is terminated when we have reached her therapeutic goals or she becomes convinced that it is in her best interests to terminate. As long as we are engaged in a therapeutic process, my commitment remains unwavering.

> *Believe it or not, God graciously used my same-sex relationship with my girlfriend. It brought up so many triggers in me, and then I was able to process those with my therapist. I gained so much understanding about myself. I was able to try new things and not simply repeat the patterns of my past.*
>
> Joyce

CHOOSING TO END A SAME-SEX RELATIONSHIP: "CAN WE EVER BE FRIENDS?"

Most of my clients are more interested in shifting their same-sex relationship into a non-erotic, nondependent *friendship* than in ending the relationship once and for all. Some lay leaders and professionals helping women in conflict with SSA doubt that a relationship that has been emotionally dependent can *ever* be transformed into a healthy friendship. But even if this is true, a client must be respected and given the time to reach this conclusion on her own.

> *When I first went to my counselor, she asked me what I wanted out of counseling. I told her, "I want out of my lesbian relationship, but I still*

want us to be friends and roommates." My counselor said, "Okay. We will give it a try." If she had said, "No, that is not possible," I would have walked out of the door and never returned.

Nicole

Since much of a female's sense of self and self-esteem arise out of the successful negotiation of relationships, risking or terminating a relationship is a direct threat to her core identity. It is therefore important to remind a woman that there is no mandate that says we, as women, *ought* to be able to be in a healthy relationship with *everyone*. With some people we can, and with others we can't. We have limits. And when we can't sustain a healthy connection, it is our responsibility to set the boundaries necessary to maximize health and wholeness for all those involved.

Many clients, on the other hand, are extremely eager to terminate their same-sex relationships and do whatever it takes to change. I have worked with enough women to believe that meaningful, permanent change requires a tremendous amount of time, energy and long-term reinforcement; deep issues are rarely resolved by simply ending a same-sex relationship. I do not want to reinforce a woman's misplaced energy to find a quick fix by encouraging her to immediately end a relationship or deny herself her only friend or support system. Granted, some women will be more ready than others to transform or terminate an unhealthy relationship, but most will do so across time, self-reflecting and integrating new beliefs, behaviors and friendships throughout the process.

The remainder of this chapter provides a description of the preparations, boundaries and relational adjustments most women will have to make as they seek to exit or redefine a same-sex relationship. This process will not be linear, but it will progress while she addresses, repeatedly and concurrently, most of the issues below.

Strengthen support resources. If a woman's current same-sex relationship is indeed the *only* close relationship in her life, a gradual separation should occur only after she has gained a sense of emotional stability, and only as she also works toward inner formation and authentic relating with others.[10] Even

---

[10]Research has found that it is far more common for women with SSA to befriend a former lover and maintain this relationship even after becoming seriously involved with another woman than it is for married heterosexual women to maintain friendships with former partners (Solomon, Rothblum & Balsam, 2004, p. 282).

though a woman may be emotionally dependent on or sexually involved with her female partner, the relationship may still provide elements of authentic friendship, companionship and sense of family that are genuinely meaningful and valuable, as discussed in chapter five. Choosing to restructure an emotionally dependent relationship can be just as difficult as facing an unexpected breakup, or as painful as a divorce.

Finding good support is usually never easy for a woman with SSA. It will take time and much deliberate effort. Her therapist will need to assess whether she has ongoing compassionate support from an understanding friend, mentor, family member, support group, pastor or spouse (she may need support from all of these avenues); whether she is amenable to relying on psychotropic medication if recommended by a physician; and whether she is committed to regularly attending her AA meetings if she also struggles with alcohol or drug dependency.

Tell her friend. When my client tells her friend, "I think we need to change our relationship," or "I want to spend less time with you," her friend might react to these devastating words in one or more of these ways: she may exhibit rage, resistance and violence; she may immediately accept the news with a sense of relief; she may feel profound shame and a sense of worthlessness; or she may experience a destabilizing sense of abandonment and insecurity. Even though my client is the one deciding and bearing the bad news, she may also have similar internal reactions to her own verbalization. Therefore, we discuss all of these possibilities ahead of time in order to equip her for every contingency.

Once this declaration has been made, both women may feel frightened about the impending losses and separation, and the relationship is likely to become more enmeshed, clingy and sexualized. But ultimately, to implement the gradual process as set forth below, *each* woman will need to be able to recommit to the goal of establishing a non-erotic, nondependent friendship. If my client's friend does *not* want to redefine or end the relationship, adjustments to the process will need to be considered. My client may have to courageously and single-handedly set and maintain all new boundaries.

Gradually separate. Some women can make a decision to immediately cease all sexual activity or to move into their own place within weeks. However, it is still important that she be encouraged to stay in touch with all that she is feeling and experiencing. Changing behavior or apartments does not necessarily indicate deep or lasting personal or relational change. Most women will need to approach the thought of separating slowly and methodically.

> *I could have never done it cold turkey. It has taken time. When you live with someone for so many years and are used to talking to each other every day, it has to be a process.*
> Sarah

Women move through the separation process in different stages and in various time frames. Rarely is this process straightforward; but in general, the two women will need to begin separating their

1. physical and emotional time together[11]
2. beds and bedrooms
3. clothes and closets
4. finances and joint property
5. apartments or living space
6. custody (if both women have assumed parental responsibility and rights for a child)
7. jobs (if they work together) or churches
8. social community (if, as one would expect, they share the same friends)

In the end, each woman will need to establish personal space and an identity apart from her partner. This is a huge undertaking. One should never presume this to be easy or even possible for every woman. Most women will suffer from severe separation anxieties (Kaufman, Harrison & Hyde, 1984) and even fear of annihilation. Further, most of these women will need to navigate their ongoing need for touch and affection once a physical boundary is set within their relationship. But by enacting these painful separations and facing the underlying core beliefs and fears, as addressed below, a woman will not only distance herself from the patterns of enmeshment, but be healed of past wounds, gain a sense of her unique self and restructure the entire foundation of her future relationships and intimacy.[12] This journey will be painful but life-changing.

---

[11]Kaufman, Harrison and Hyde (1984) suggest that women wanting healthy distance in their relationship will have to increase territorial, temporal, financial, cognitive, emotional and social space (p. 532).

[12]If a woman has been in an addictive pattern, she may end up working through multiple heartbreaking relationships before the pattern of dependency and sexualization is significantly altered.

Challenge the patterns of seduction and sexualization. Once a client has actively sought to understand the meaning behind her infatuations and emotional dependencies, she must also begin to understand the meaning behind any actual sexual or seductive *behavior,* especially if she is attempting to set a boundary within an existing relationship. For example, one woman admitted that she was sexualizing a mentoring relationship in which she was the mentor. She became conscious of several hidden dynamics: If she acted out sexually, then she could finally be rid of the pressure to continue to be the perfect one. But, if she successfully seduced her friend and became the perfect lover, then she would be the "best" or the "star." Through seduction, she unconsciously thought she could simultaneously meet her need for affirmation *and* find relief from the pressure of being good all the time.

Whenever a woman seeks immediate relief from painful feelings through sexual behavior, she makes deep healing and change impossible. This is why for some women it *will* become necessary to commit to periods of abstinence. They must stop anesthetizing themselves through physical *or* emotional contact and find the courage to face their losses or inner struggles. It makes me sad to think of all the women who are encouraged or affirmed to live out of the impulse of their same-sex sexual desires without being encouraged to explore their deeper underlying needs or internal dynamics.

Sexual fantasy or behavior can also be a form of defensive detachment—an avoidance of platonic or maternal intimacy in its purest form (Moberly, 1983). A woman may believe that true intimacy or emotional closeness could result in pain, so it must be avoided. Instead of pursuing a pure or innocent friendship, she sexualizes it, likely damaging the opportunity for "just a friendship." Many women may also need to reinterpret their compulsion for sexualized touch and understand it for what it truly is: a legitimate need for soothing or comforting touch.

My clients usually—not always, but usually—find that it is fairly easy to eventually stop blatant sexual contact within their same-sex relationship. But to stop all holding, snuggling and physical closeness is extremely difficult.

THE NEED FOR TOUCH

Needless to say, touch itself is an essential and legitimate need for my clients.[13] Primal attachments are formed on the basis of touch. It is at once affirming, reassuring, regulating and containing. It is vital to human existence and yet often minimized or overlooked for its formative and stabilizing forces. My clients have an immeasurable hunger for comforting and loving touch. Once they experience its power to comfort or affirm within a same-sex relationship,[14] it seems ludicrous to curtail or limit opportunities for more. Examining the benefits and drawbacks of the physical affection expressed within her relationship will be one of the most difficult steps a woman will undertake in redefining her friendship.

> *There were times my body screamed for a gentle touch—not a sexual touch, just gentle contact. . . . Sometimes I would stop acting out sexually for a few days, but each time I would fall back in. When I tried to pull away there would be days with no human contact, not even shaking hands. My body kept screaming at me, demanding to be touched.*
>
> *Lydia (as quoted in Eldridge, 1994, p. 175)*

As a woman curtails some of the physical affection with her friend, she may also need to learn about the varieties of touch that *are* available to her, rather than focus on the touch she "can't" have. She can explore working with a massage therapist, adopting a pet, taking dancing lessons or befriending children or the elderly. She might explain her need to a mentor, requesting that therapeutic touch be incorporated into their time together. Friends and mentors can have a significant impact in this area, provided a woman has invited or given permission for them to touch her. A lingering handshake, a pat on the back, hello and goodbye hugs, comforting gestures such as touching her arm or hand while conversing, a kiss on the cheek, a foot rub, brushing her hair, wiping her tears, holding her while she cries, the laying on of hands during

---

[13]It is possible that some of these women were rarely touched, even as small children. Researchers have found that "females are significantly more impaired in psychosexual functioning than males by deprivation of parental physical affection" (Prescott, LaFortune, Levy & Wallace, 1980, p. 169). Others, who appear to have had ample physical affection, still often failed to internalize a sense of emotional connection or touch.

[14]McDougall (1980) reports that some women used touch to integrate with their own bodies. They "would lavish on a female partner caresses, minute explorations, tenderness, and all the loving that they unconsciously demanded for their own bodies—believed to be ugly and deformed, physically weak, or unhealthy" (p. 112).

prayer, a neck rub—all are examples of mediating healthy touch that indeed can go a long way if a woman is open to receive. Nevertheless, most of these options will pale in light of the electrifying touch experienced in her past same-sex relationship. It will take time for a woman to reorganize her needs for and interpretations of touch.

UNRAVELING THE EMOTIONAL ENMESHMENT

When two women successfully end all sexual behavior, they may find themselves lethargically believing that the relationship is just fine as it is. However, they are usually only a few paces down a long path.

Challenge core beliefs. The following false core beliefs perpetuate emotional dependency and prevent a woman from discovering and moving into her own home: *I am no one apart from her. She's the only one who knows and accepts me. I am home; I feel safe with her. I will die if I lose our connection. I will be all alone for the rest of my life and I can't handle being alone.*

It is not uncommon for these beliefs to be the central organizing focus behind a woman's identity and style of relating. As she defies these beliefs—by creating distance or a separation in her relationship—her fears and anxieties will naturally increase. As she feels the need to contact her friend because of building separation anxiety, I invite her to identify and own the fearful inner voices but also to directly challenge them by framing the objective truth within her current situation: *Yes, I really do miss her, but no, she will not be able to meet all of my needs. Calling her right now is not going to solve all of my problems. I am feeling lonely and dejected because of some issues with my boss. I need to press into and deal with those issues. To call her would be to escape and avoid what is important and what would be best for me. It would not be healthy for me to get back into a pattern of depending on her to make me feel OK, and it is not going to help me accomplish my goals of building my own life and learning to like and take care of myself. Choosing to get back into a dependent relationship with her is choosing to not take care of my self.*

Know who is feeling what. When a woman does not have a solid understanding of her true self, and therefore has no solid ego boundaries, her emotions may become unconsciously fused with the other woman's emotions, believing, for example, that the other woman's pain *is* her pain. Unfortunately, when this type of merging occurs, neither woman is being truly understood or known; rather, each is essentially consumed or "entered" by another ego or person (Jordan, Surrey & Kaplan, 1991, p. 29). This is not true intimacy, though it may feel good to a woman who has lived with abject emptiness.

A woman will need to continually work on objectively separating her emotional state from her friend's. Revisiting the exercises in chapter nine that help her to first identify her own feelings will be useful. She can also speculate on what her friend might be feeling in any given situation, comparing and contrasting that with her reactions and feelings. But ultimately, she will need to develop true empathy, freely feeling and *knowing she is feeling* her friend's feelings while at the same time *knowing* that she may be feeling differently.

Differentiate from each other. Whereas earlier the aim was to help a woman delineate her own unique tastes, interests or traits, the focus at this stage is on helping her to highlight the *differences* or *distinctions* between her friend and herself—over and against slipping into the old pattern of focusing on their sameness or similarities. However, as noted by Nichols (1988a), the pursuit of individuality and differentiation within an emotionally dependent relationship can trigger her fear of abandonment and actual *loss* of personal identity if she has sought her security and sense of validation through the other woman (p. 399). As with most of these processes, a woman needs to be continually supported as she processes these deeper reactions and pursues the ongoing work of inner stabilization and autonomy. Once a woman grasps her distinctiveness, she will then need to begin acting on this uniqueness: for instance, she might volunteer at a woman's shelter—*all by her self.* The intention here is to help her stay connected with her own feelings, desires and personal responsibilities and activities versus those of the other woman.

Curtail the constant connection and the ongoing discussions about their process. So committed are many women to this process of relational change that it may become the main focus of their relationship. These women and their partners might spend considerable time discussing the shifts and desired goals of their relationship or share all the new insights and minute details of individual counseling sessions. This is a carryover pattern of emotional enmeshment. Formerly, they probably took large chunks of time to discuss their relationship in terms of jealousies, insecurities or unmet needs (and they still may); now they talk about their excitements, victories or new insights.

Smalley (1987) suggests that people with codependent patterns are often observed as having "long talks." These long talks are primarily devoted to "explaining and justifying positions" so that the other will thoroughly understand (p. 134). Being fully understood or known is indeed a motivating need for many of my clients, but as they ascertain on their own who they are, this will begin to shift. Curtailing these types of conversations may initially seem wrong to many women. They will feel as if they are forsaking the friendship and their friend. They will need to be gently reminded that *friends* typically do not spend time analyzing and processing their relationships; they just *are*, usually enjoying some activity or interest together.

Stop caretaking. The compulsion to caretake is one of the most insidious patterns to break within an emotionally dependent relationship. I believe that the power behind a caretaking role and style of relating is a woman's own fear of abandonment. She herself has a deep need to be taken care of and consistently attended to, but she has most likely distanced herself from or disavowed this need, projecting it onto her partner. She then becomes convinced that her partner cannot survive without her. So she becomes the hero, rising to the occasion and rescuing her partner from extinction. But as she caretakes, she is unconsciously and vicariously taking care of that needy and lonely part of her self. It is this pattern of projective identification that prevents many women, who are otherwise committed to living out a healthy friendship, from making the desired separations. A conversation like this one can help identify the roots of this tendency.

"So we drew these boundaries so that we wouldn't go too far," my client explains.

"But you kept crossing those boundary lines?" I ask.

"Yes. We would say, 'We can't do this.' But then we would say, 'We can do it tonight, but not tomorrow.'"

"I see."

"But she was crying and hurting," she justifies. "How can I not take her in my arms and comfort her? Am I supposed to just become this cold fish?"

I try to reflect her reasoning, asking, "So are you saying there is no way you can say no to her?"

"I guess what I can't say no to is the need. I might be able to say no to *her* but not to her *need*."

"Why can't you say no to her need?"

"Because if I don't meet her needs, then she would be upset with me, and then she would push me away, and I would be by myself."

"And what happens when you are by yourself?"

"I would hurt," she confesses.

"And what happens if you hurt?" I ask, probing deeper.

"That's not a good thing. I want to die—or I feel like I'm going to die."

Having pressed her into these deeper feelings, we can refocus our work on her fear of abandonment. It is not essential that a client initially connect her fear or underlying need with her caretaking behaviors, but such conscious awareness will become more important as she continues to attempt to break her caretaking pattern. Chapter eleven provides further suggestions for helping a woman resolve such projections and transferences.

Recognize and stop the mixed messages. Consider the mixed messages Rhonda and her friend were sending based on the following report:

> My friend and I [Rhonda] finally came to the conclusion that we had to stop communicating. I had met her online. We had never met face to face but were still very emotionally involved. That night, *after* we had said our final goodbyes, she sent me another e-mail. She said she is fixated on meeting me and was in love with me. I wrote her and told her that we couldn't communicate (again). She e-mailed me later that night and asked if I would log on and chat. I e-mailed back saying no. She e-mailed back saying, "Please." I e-mailed back saying no. She called. . . . I refused to discuss our relationship. She called again this morning saying she can't believe she was so stupid and would I please give her another chance.

In this vignette, Rhonda's friend was not intentionally manipulating her as much as she was indirectly communicating her deep panic and fear over the loss of the relationship. However, her incessant attempts at reuniting were manipulative, and she certainly intended to draw Rhonda back in. While Rhonda appeared to be unscathed by these attempts, she fully participated in the tug-of-war dance initiated by her friend. If Rhonda really meant what she said when they made their final goodbyes, then she should have never responded to her friend's follow-up e-mail. By writing her friend back, Rhonda essentially negated her promise to never speak again. She gave her friend a subtle message that she was also "still connected." Endless discussions or sidestepping firm absolutes such as "yes" or "no" whittle away at a woman's boundaries and sense of effectiveness, not to mention fuel a sense of drama that often distracts from her own process.

Discontinue the reminiscing and romanticizing. Without having real flesh-and-blood "love objects" to whom they can attach and develop a sense of selfhood, some women, at a very early age, develop a fantasy life to alleviate loneliness and lostness. They might fantasize about becoming best friends with the most popular girl in school, for example.[15] But when a growing girl is still relationally deprived or her own ability to regulate or self-comfort is depleted, her innocent fantasies can turn into romantic obsessions. And while she fantasizes (and idealizes her partner or object of affection) she may also masturbate,[16] strengthening the sense of attachment while also strengthening her confusion between intimacy and sex. She may linger over repetitive viewings of lesbian films or literature, imagining herself as one of the characters, or continuously relive "the good old days" with her current partner from whom she is attempting to disengage. While romanticizing and idealizing, she may inadvertently reinforce negative core beliefs such as *She is the* only *person who ever loved me.* These fantasies and thought patterns (and behaviors) must eventually be brought out into the light and explored in a way similar to exploring compulsive sexual behavior.

Courageously face the loneliness. I regularly hear the question, "Why should I work on my SSA if all it will lead to is being alone *for the rest of my life?*" This fear of being alone *for the rest of her life* is not an entirely irrational one. Yes, she will have relationships with friends, religious communities, work associates and perhaps family, but there is no guarantee that she will have a lifelong companion or a husband or a family of her own if she sets aside same-sex relating. So while I challenge any core false beliefs around this question, I also want to empathize with her feelings as she faces the possibility of singleness *for the rest of her life.*

A woman often needs to reposition herself toward loneliness. Feeling lonely is feeling her true heart's longing for relationship. Feeling lonely is to recognize she is not invincible but fragile and needy within an imperfect world. Feeling

---

[15] As noted by Schwartz and Southern (1999), a person bonds with the object of the addiction as a means of internal regulating and calming (p. 171).

[16] Michael, Gagnon, Laumann and Kolata (1994) note that 30% of women who periodically masturbate said they did it to relax (p. 166). A woman's generalized anxiety, separation anxiety and level of exhaustion should all be explored as she seeks to understand a pattern of compulsive masturbation. This behavior may have also developed in relation to a sexually abusive or traumatic event. Children often innocently discover that masturbation can give them felt relief from their inner pain, fear and loneliness. Exploring the symbolic nature of a woman's associated fantasy or the use of actual pornographic material will also be beneficial.

lonely is to recognize her camaraderie with the entire human race. It is in her loneliness—alone with her heart and God—that she can recenter and remember who she is as God's special daughter. Similarly, in *Reaching Out: The Three Movements of the Spiritual Life,* Henri Nouwen (1975) observes,

> As hard as it is to believe that the dry desolate desert can yield endless varieties of flowers, it is equally hard to imagine that our loneliness is hiding unknown beauty. The movement from loneliness to solitude, however, is the beginning of any spiritual life because it is the movement from the restless senses to the restful spirit, from the outward-reaching cravings to the inward-reaching search, from the fearful clinging to the fearless play. (p. 34)

Even as a women matures in her relationship with God, she will still naturally connect with her loneliness during our sessions. I will continue to attune to and empathize with her pain. And as she focuses on her deep pangs of loneliness, she may recall past memories and disappointments that can now be processed, leading to a fuller, more healed sense of self and, ultimately, a greater capacity for meaningful intimacy.

Feeling her loneliness and exploring all that her unique and special heart is longing for allows her to refine or redirect her steps and goals as they relate to her future. Many women may need encouragement to follow some of their wildest dreams, such as working in a refugee camp or considering adoption. It is indeed their heart's longings and desires that can direct them into incredibly fulfilling lives and greater opportunities for growth and intimacy.

Let go. To successfully navigate all of the above steps and processes, most women will need to initiate a formal time-out from their relationship. This is a season of at least three to six months where both women agree to have no contact for the sake of working toward emotional separation. The ultimate hope is that during their time apart, the old foundation of enmeshment, neediness and confused roles can dissolve completely, allowing for a new foundation to be built. The individual growth and change made by each woman as she lives her separate life will determine whether an additional "renewed" relationship is desirable, let alone doable. Further negotiations or time-outs may need to be made. For some, the relationship must come to a final end.

> *I had to end the relationship. I had to let it go and allow it to die. Was it difficult? Hell yes! But it had to end. I did not know myself apart from her.*

It was easy to stop the sex. We had done that many years ago. But when you have to stop the emotional connection—that's when the panic sets in. But I survived, and it feels real good to be able to stand by myself as myself before God, my friends and family.

Jordan

GROWING AND CHANGING

A woman's relationship may have survived the winds of change, or it may have died a gentle death. In either case, she will need to continually revisit many of the above processes and steps, vigilantly guard her heart, and make sure she prioritizes her deepest desires and life goals by giving them her time, attention and energy. She is worth it.

For years I was working on all this stuff, but it felt like I was taking two steps forward and one step back. I used to unload on a friend who would just listen. I would complain that I didn't think I was changing at all or getting any better in any area. She would say, "Yeah, well you used to talk about some stuff every day. Then it was every third day, and now it's only like once a week." Something was changing!

Shari

Living intentionally—pursuing health and wholeness—is a lifelong journey. Sadly, there are few people who will ever appreciate all these women have accomplished. Their rewards will be played out within their own peace of mind and hopefully into eternity as well.

CHAPTER ELEVEN

Forgotten Rooms

Transference and Countertransference

Not everything that is faced can be changed;
but nothing can be changed until it is faced.

JAMES BALDWIN

THIRD STAGE OF THERAPY: INTEGRATION

As a woman moves through the stages of therapy as outlined in this book, she will necessarily move into deeper and more unconscious material. For many women, this work becomes tedious and even frightening. But to eventually overcome the desperation that often fuels her emotionally dependent relationships, a woman will need to acknowledge, own and integrate her inner realities and the sometimes paradoxical sides of her true self. The woman who excavates her dark or unknown parts will experience the most profound and satisfying changes.

ESCAPING FROM THE "BAD"

For years, these women have survived the pain and confusion of their lives by cutting off needs, ignoring unresolved issues and relationships in their past, and avoiding inner pain and emptiness. As a result, they have accumulated a storehouseful of unconscious material. Besides relying on the common defense mechanisms discussed in chapter nine, three additional mechanisms have aided them in managing this material but are now destroying their opportunities for self-understanding and growth: *projection, transference* and *regression.*

Projection. This involves pushing outward or projecting one's own dis-

avowed or uncomfortable feelings, thoughts, attitudes, characteristics or defenses onto another person. It is more than repressing or cutting off (psychologically and emotionally) an emotion and more than denying an attitude.
Projection involves another person; it allows a woman to distance herself from
an emotion through an unconscious process of *dispossession* and *reassignment*.
A woman who is unconsciously projecting says to herself, *I don't have that feeling. It isn't mine. It's hers. It belongs to her.* Projection indicates a lack of psychological boundaries (McWilliams, 1994) and can become extremely damaging
to relationships. For example, a woman may project her jealousy out onto her
friend. She will begin to view and perhaps accuse her friend as always being
jealous. Her friend will feel unjustly accused or confused as she attempts to defend herself against the unfounded allegations that she is jealous. The woman
may then accuse her friend of being in denial, projecting her own denial (of
her jealousy) onto her friend. This can lead to endless and confusing debates.

Transference. A close companion of projection, transference involves trans-
mitting unresolved difficulties or damaging dynamics of *past relationships* (including all associated emotions, reactions and distorted cognitions) onto current relationships. In other words, a woman may read a present situation *as if*
it is just like a painful situation from her past that wounded her, or she may
view a friend *as if* the friend is just like the older sister who rejected her.[1]
Women who rely on projection and transference as a means to protect themselves against psychic pain or menacing situations typically *heighten* or increase
the very thing they are trying to avoid. They create emotional instability
within themselves by discovering sordid and threatening feelings or attitudes
in those closest to them, and they often re-create the relational difficulties that
they have experienced repeatedly in their past. This is, of course, one of the
reasons that many women with SSA habitually live in elevated relational and
emotional drama.

Projections and transferences can also involve positive material, often taking on the characteristics of a child's wishful or magical thinking. A person (or
situation) becomes wonderfully bigger than life and is unconsciously idealized
or expected to give more than any adult can appropriately give to another
adult. For example, a woman may transfer her unmet longings for mother,
nurture or a sense of safety all onto one woman and then feel irresistibly drawn

---

[1]For an excellent book on transference within friendships and church settings, see McIntyre (1999).

to her. She might immediately believe that this other woman is *the one* who can deliver her from all besetting emotions or needs.

Regression. Within the midst of experiencing a same-sex attraction, many women actually regress into a primal state of dependency (see chapter 5). Regression is an unconscious backsliding of sorts into the habits or the emotional or psychological condition of a prior maturational stage (McWilliams, 1994). This means a woman not only will unconsciously look to the other woman to meet her needs (transference), but will also *feel* and *experience* all of the subjective vulnerability, weakness and smallness associated with an infant or child who depends on her parents for her very survival. She is essentially reliving or replaying—unconsciously—her primal attachment needs involving complete dependency. This is why emotionally dependent relationships can be so much more emotionally intense, and the partners so much more psychologically fragile, than normative codependent relationships.

COMMON PROJECTIONS AND TRANSFERENCES

I am, therefore, always on the lookout for these potentially destabilizing unconscious processes within my clients and their relationships. I regularly assess whether my client is

- projecting her own disavowed *positive traits* and characteristics onto the other woman, thereby unconsciously attempting to affirm herself by identifying with the other woman
- projecting her specific *need to be loved,* wanted, admired or treated as special onto the other woman, vicariously attempting to meet her own need by loving and caring for the other woman[2]
- transferring her feelings of *mistrust, disrespect or contempt of men or women* from her past onto men and women (including her partner) in the present
- projecting her *fear of abandonment* onto the other woman, creating an unconscious hope that she can alleviate her own fear and insecurity by staying with or never leaving the other woman (which has the effect of barring the exit door to an emotionally dependent relationship)

It is no wonder that many of my clients often feel so out of control and crazy

---

[2]McDougall (1970) saw this dynamic playing out in the common pattern of a woman finding more gratification and interest "in giving sexual pleasure than in receiving it" (p. 207). The woman's rejection of her own body shows up in a fantasy of wanting to love another woman's body (p. 195).

and thus want something different for themselves and their lives. Gratefully, these patterns can change.

In order to help a client identify a possible negative or positive projection or transference, I tell her to look for situations in which her emotional reaction or response is disproportionate to the circumstance or in which a pattern can be observed, such as a repetitive argument or behavior. I have come to personally believe that many behaviors or emotional reactions that appear resistant to change are often also based on one of these unconscious dynamics. Once a client becomes aware of a possible projection or transference, she can then begin to explore the connections with her past or disavowed emotions and thoughts. She can also regain an objective perspective of the present. Following is an example of how one of my clients and I discovered an underlying transference within one of her relationships.

I had been stumped for quite some time with my client Jaimie. She was an attractive and intelligent woman who was open to almost all therapeutic approaches and techniques, but she returned cyclically to a traumatic emotional "dance" with one of her female friends. The dance would start with Jaimie feeling excluded or left out from some social event by her friend. She would accuse her friend of being insensitive or thoughtless. Her friend would then try to explain herself and reassure Jaimie that she was still her best friend. Jaimie would be consoled, but only for a week or so. The dance would then repeat.

Jaimie *knew* this pattern was unhealthy but couldn't seem to stop it. One day in therapy, I asked her to help me make a list of her mother's characteristics, inside and out, the good and the bad. She had done enough work at this point to be able to view her mother objectively with compassion. A few sessions later, I asked her to describe her friend, as if I had never met or heard about her. I made a list of her friend's characteristics as she spoke. I then read the list back to Jaimie. About halfway through the list, she looked at me and exclaimed, "Oh my gosh, she *is* my mother!" I quickly retrieved the list we had made of her mother's characteristics and started comparing the two. We were both shocked at the striking similarities. The lists were almost identical.

Jaimie's perceptions of and feelings toward her friend and her mother were the same. She was essentially transferring her primal feelings of being ignored and misunderstood onto her relationship with her friend. And to the extent that Jaimie was living out of this unconscious transference, she was blinded to the full reality of her friend and their friendship—in this case, to the *good* of both.

To break this transference, Jaimie needed to face, *feel* and process the losses and disappointments of both the past and the present as they pertained to her mother. She also needed to resurrect, so to speak, and *integrate* her innocent longings and desires for a tender, nurturing, attentive mom—or a stronger dad, or a kinder brother. These longings, including the desire to be known as loveable, albeit painful, can no longer be displaced onto a current relationship that promises the illusion of complete satisfaction. As these natural and legitimate longings, relational desires and associated grief are integrated for what they truly are, a healthy separation between the past and present can begin.

Ultimately, I have learned that it is not so important that my clients be able to distinguish between a projection and transference per se but rather that they learn how to redirect their attention away from their present relational drama and toward the underlying historic or subconscious material that fuels these very profound defense mechanisms. Processes that I have found most useful in helping my clients deal with their past and integrate their childhood losses *with* their adult self include

- corrective attachment experiences within individual or group therapy (as described in chapters 6 and 7)
- using counselor countertransference therapeutically
- effectively dealing with client projections and transferences that become a part of the therapeutic relationship
- little-girl work (voice dialogue)
- reprocessing techniques such as eye movement desensitization and reprocessing (EMDR)
- grief work

WHEN THE UNCONSCIOUS ENTERS THE COUNSELING OFFICE

Regardless of the stage of therapy or level of trust established with my clients, projections and transferences *will* be a part of our therapeutic relationship. A client may see me and *treat me* as her "bad" mother, her rejecting girl friend or her demanding father (Quinodoz, 1989). It is natural for me to have a reaction or an emotional response to my clients' unconscious projections and associated externalized behaviors or attitudes. However, I have found that my emotional reactions, commonly known as *countertransferences*,[3] are often stronger in my work with women with SSA than with other women. Elaine Siegel (1988) wisely emphasizes that a therapist working with women with SSA must be "prepared to withstand the vicissitudes of becoming a self-object for the patient (Kohut, 1971) and to bear the brunt of the concomitant countertransferences" (p. 203) and, like a mother, "be ready to accept sometimes stormy feeling states" (p. 204) within herself.

Below I've listed some of the most common feeling states or therapist countertransferences experienced in working with women with SSA. Many of these countertransferences may be a direct indication of how a client is actually feeling (a projection) or a reaction to how a client typically defends against closeness or difficult emotions. In other words, I may be feeling how many other people typically feel when they are with my client.

Severe anxiety. A counselor's anxiety may come in the form of feeling frightened by a client's dominating presence or extremely difficult circumstances; discomfort over a client's sexualized words of affection; or fear of losing control of a session, of doing something wrong (and being confronted by an angry client) or of losing of objectivity.

A deep sense of helplessness and inadequacy. I must admit, ashamedly, there have been times when, sitting with a client, I seriously thought to myself, *This woman needs so much help, I think I need to help her find a* real *counselor.* I often feel a mixture of panic and helplessness as I work with a woman in what seems like an impossible predicament in her life. I may be tempted to grope for solutions and quick fixes.

Defensiveness and anger. When a client is transferring or projecting negative thoughts and feelings, accusing me of having certain attitudes or beliefs, I can feel extremely defensive and angry. I may also feel discounted and frustrated when a client dismisses my efforts at caring or attempts to "tell me how to do my job."

Guarded or violated. When a client gropes for my personal data or for a certain emotional reaction in me, I may react by becoming guarded or feeling violated.

Fear of engulfment or exhaustion. On occasion, I struggle with feeling ex-

---

[3]Alice Miller (1981) encourages therapists to assume "that *all* the feelings that the patient arouses in his analyst, during his analysis, are part of his unconscious attempt to tell the analyst his story and at the same time to hide it from him" (p. 77).

hausted and fearing engulfment when a client depends on me to sustain her commitment to therapy or her will to live. Like an overwhelmed or depleted new mother, I may want to quit, withdraw and shut down emotionally.

To be able to use my countertransference in a beneficial way, it is imperative that I *know* myself well enough to distinguish whether my reaction arises out of my *own* unresolved issues, whether the client is evoking it, or both. Regardless, I must be able to check myself, regain my objectivity and separate from my feelings long enough to formulate a response that will be in my client's best therapeutic interests. My therapeutic aim is to *respond differently* than what she has come to expect. This will be very difficult if I have unfinished business related to the types of behaviors or attitudes that she is presently exhibiting. It is therefore important that I remain committed to my own healing journey, making sure that I have the tools to remain centered as my client's unconscious material comes flooding to the surface during a therapy session.

When I sense the presence of unconscious material on my client's part (usually through the awareness of my countertransference), I immediately attempt to slow down my internal processing. So powerful are some of my countertransferences that at times I must unobtrusively take a few deep breaths and practice meditative techniques in order to regain my center. Having taken note of my reactions, I must then exert all of my energy on attuning to my client's affective state and underlying unconscious dynamic. I remind myself that she is doing the best she can and that I am here to support her in her process, not my own.

I might invite my client to also pause and take a step back by observing and objectively reporting all of her words, attitudes or behaviors exhibited in the last 5 minutes. We document all of the previous details in a matter-of-fact way. This helps her to objectify or look at her behaviors and attitudes from a non-judgmental stance.

Ultimately, I want to shift attention off of these externals and onto an internal reflection between the client and her deeper self. *What was she feeling? Who did I remind her of? What was she wanting or needing?* We gradually move into a here-and-now process, focusing on the quality and nature of our relationship. *Did she feel connected? Did she sense distance? Is she being completely truthful with me, or is she holding something back?* Depending on a woman's ego strength, I may disclose my feelings or countertransference as a means to help her understand the possible unconscious purpose of her words or attitudes.

(My countertransference is never shared to shame or manipulate a client into changing how she behaves in my presence.) If she is able, I may also direct her to access the associated historic memories that may have evoked similar behaviors or underlying feelings.

It is extremely important to undergird these types of discussions with absolute unconditional acceptance and genuine curiosity and care. It is also crucial to continue to trust and follow my own feeling states—yet not get lost in them. If I become too analytical, I lose the creativity and spontaneity needed to move with my client into her ever shifting feeling states or unconscious processes.

DEALING WITH A POSITIVE TRANSFERENCE

As their unconscious material pushes to be seen and known, many of my clients, especially after establishing trust and feeling my care, experience an intense positive transference of affection and need.[4] Some clients will openly admit to their growing feelings of love and affection; others will not. A client may state that I am the best therapist she has ever had, that I understand her like no one else or that she doesn't know where she would be if she didn't have me. She might bring me special gifts, behave flirtatiously, have difficulty ending a session on time or offer to help me in anyway I might need. She may want to terminate counseling so that she can become my friend or generously offer her professional skills and services. She may pass through these strong warm feelings quickly or linger in them, deepening in a sense of attachment and possibly regressing into a primal state of dependency.

Besides feeling overwhelmed by a rising need to see or be with me, my clients may also be simultaneously feeling embarassed, ashamed or afraid.

There is just this overwhelming feeling like I'm so grateful you are in my life and I'm so grateful that I can talk to you. I'm kind of freaked out. I think I have become anxious because I feel differently about you after two years. I think I feel exposed. It doesn't feel comfortable, and I'm wondering how to get back to where I was. Maybe I need a break from counseling. I

---

[4]This type of transference is more common with female therapists, but it might still occur on a smaller scale with male therapists. A discussion of the unique concerns for male therapists working with women with SSA is found in chapter 13.

know I want you in my life, I want you to help, I want to be open so you
can help me figure some things out, but I don't want to feel this attachment
thing. I don't want it. So that's my question. How do I get out of it?

a client

Some clients may begin to withdraw or behave defensively for no apparent reason at all, warding off the fear that I will terminate or abandon her. My clients might feel ashamed of not being able to control their feelings, ashamed of being needy, and foolish for feeling like a child. She may become angry toward herself, secretly launching into self-destructive or sabotaging behaviors.

Understandably, it may not be easy for most women to directly discuss these feelings of affection. A conversation might proceed like this:

"I just think this whole counseling thing is stupid. I just don't see how it's going to get me anywhere," announced Bobbie at the beginning of a session.

After using empathy, I ask, "If I could grant you one wish, where would you like counseling to get you or what would you like counseling to give you?" I'm following a hunch.

"Oh, its just so stupid. I don't know if I want to talk about it right now."

"No, I mean it Bobbie, I really want to know. What would it take for counseling to be worth it?"

"Well, it's not really the counseling."

"It's not?" I say with surprise, although I'm not totally surprised. "What is it then?"

"I just feel so stupid."

"Bobbie, I'm pretty sure that I won't think your answer is stupid, but if I do, I promise I'll tell you," I respond, attempting to draw in some humor and lightness. (This must be done with caution, as it could backfire.)

"You don't have to do that," Bobbie says, letting out a deep sigh. "It's just that I'm not sure that I can do this."

"What do you mean by *this?*"

"I mean, I like you. I really like you, and I'm not sure that I can get all close to you and trust you when at some point you are just going to leave."

"So you're afraid that I will leave?"

"No, not now or anything. I'm afraid for later. Like when we have to quit doing this. Yeah, I knew it was stupid."[5]

"Bobbie, I want you to look at my face when I say this." I pause and then proceed with slow and deliberate speech, leaning forward. "Your feeling afraid that I might leave, at any point in your life, is *not* stupid. We have a real relationship here. You like me and I like you. That is how it is supposed to work. It is totally natural for you to be concerned about the future. In fact, I'm honored that you care. That means our relationship counts. It really matters for you and I'm so glad it does, because it sure matters to me. And because our relationship is important, I want to make sure that you continue to feel safe and free to process all your feelings and thoughts with me. We are doing great work together, and I am thrilled to be able to see a little more of your heart. Thank you so much for being honest."

If a client is eroticizing her feelings of affection and warmth, she may be thoroughly appalled and shocked that sexual feelings and thoughts have entered our relationship. She may be gripped with fear that she is dangerous and has the power to seduce me, that I have sexual feelings toward her, that our relationship may turn sexual, that I do *not* have sexual feelings toward her, or that she is disgusting and repulsive and deserves to die.

If I sense that a client is growing in discomfort as our relationship continues to increase in meaning and warmth, I might say to her, "Sometimes I have clients who feel warm and happy when they are with me, but it scares them to feel that way. Have you ever had sensations like that?" But I do not pry if she is unable to identify or own these types of feelings, and I *never* directly ask if she has erotic or sexualized thoughts or feelings. I also never push a client to articulate something before she is ready or capable of handling the additional emotions that come with such exposure.

A Gracious Response

When a woman with SSA enters into a positive affectionate transference within the therapeutic setting, even if she is unable to directly acknowledge it,

---

[5]If this discussion were to turn into details about our future relationship post-termination, I might gently suggest that she is projecting herself unnecessarily into the future instead of simply *resting* in what we have in the present. But if she insists, I will be honest about the fullness of my life and the unlikelihood of our being able to spend too much time together once counseling ends. I deliberately offer an authentic and personal explanation rather than a professional clarification of ethics. In the moment, I want to maintain a connection with her heart and emotions rather than appeal to her intellect. I would again reassure her of my present commitment to walk with her as long as it takes.

I have one of the greatest opportunities to provide a life-changing corrective relationship that is not enmeshed, violating her personal boundaries; sexual, violating her physical boundaries; or perfect—but good enough.

It is therefore essential that I proceed as I would with any other projection or transference: with sensitivity, groundedness and compassion. The positive transferences of affection and attachment (with or without sexualization) are a window into some of the most vulnerable and precious places in my client's hearts.

I show no shock or surprise. I do not display surprise when she uses words or gestures of affection. I thank her for taking the risk and affirm her decision to share her feelings. I tell her that her feelings do not make me uncomfortable and that I am not afraid of her or her emotions.

I validate and accept her feelings. I do not moralize or attempt to analyze the symbolic meaning behind her feelings. Initially, I want to attune, empathize, validate and accept her feelings and inner process, saying things like, "I hear how disturbing these feelings are to you. It must have been very difficult to share them with me." I want to understand how her feelings are affecting her daily life and her ability to continue to relate with me. I know that eventually she will begin to understand their meaning if I can continue to provide a safe, supportive environment.

I reassure her I will not leave or terminate our relationship. I tell her that her feelings are neither a bad sign nor something that requires us to end our professional relationship. I affirm her willingness to trust and cooperate with the uncomfortable process she now finds herself in. "It is great that you have been able to arrive at this place," I might say encouragingly.

I reassure her I will maintain appropriate boundaries. I tell her that I am strong and I know who I am—that I will not get lost in the ocean of her emotion, nor will I let her "crawl inside of me" for refuge. I gently warn her that she may even feel anger at times because I am not offering all of the affection or openness she desires. I remind her that my boundaries are firm and solid and that I will not cross physical boundaries. If she has admitted to sexual feelings, I reassure her that our relationship will *not* become sexual and that I will take full responsibility for assuring that our relationship will remain healthy and safe. I want her to be able to relax and process whatever emotions or thoughts surface without worrying about ruining our relationship.

COUNSELOR, BEWARE

Counselor countertransferences in the form of mutual affection or even sexualization should not be dismissed as mere possibilities in working with women with SSA nor minimized if they occur. I have worked with multiple women who needed to undergo recovery because of sexual involvement with previous female therapists. Collette was in her late twenties when she had her first same-sex relationship. She was frightened and confused and felt helpless to exit the relationship even though she was in great conflict over it. She decided to find a counselor. Her counselor was female with no previous history of same-sex feelings or behaviors. However, she and Collette eventually became emotionally and sexually involved. Collette reflects that

> I knew how to tap into a woman's emotions. I knew how to gain her attention and grab her heart. If she wasn't responding in the way I wanted, I would say, "F*** you," and walk away. I knew the challenge would pull her in even more. She would worry about me. Then I would apologize and share deep emotional things about myself. All of my interactions were carefully orchestrated. I knew what I wanted to share and when and how to share it. This was how I generally seduced women, emotionally and sexually. And that is exactly what I did with my therapist.

Even though Collette now recognizes her pattern of seduction, I am in no way implying that the boundary violation with her previous therapist was *Collette's* fault. I included Collette's words and perspectives to emphasize the intentionality and strength of some women's pull on a therapist's emotions and heart. Collette was simply acting out her entrenched pattern of survival and needs fulfillment. It was her counselor's responsibility to remain objective enough to protect Collette, so to speak, from her self.

It goes without saying how damaging a role reversal or, worse, a violation of a client's emotional, spiritual and physical boundaries are on a woman who has vulnerably risked seeking professional support and guidance. Sadly, most women with SSA will have nowhere to turn in the midst of their confusion and entrapment by a mental health professional. Should a woman decide to pick up the pieces and continue to pursue growth and health, it will take her several years to reestablish a basic level of therapeutic trust, let alone a vulnerable trust in which she can process some of her deepest dependency issues. Much to her credit, Collette was able to do just that. The typical warning signs of dangerous therapist countertransference include the following:

Unmanageable anxiety and sense of intimidation. These feelings can emerge especially if a client has a dominating personality, is making demands for more time or on how the time is spent, and is heavily sexualizing. A therapist might want to be honest and say, "I'm not sure how to help you right now, but please be reassured that I am here for you and I am not leaving. We will find our way through this together." It is recommended that the therapist seek immediate consultation and resolve any sense of intimidation or underlying fear. If a therapist is unable to regain an objective stance with the client, then they may have to make a professional referral, but only after they have clearly explained to the client that the referral is not being made because of something she did or said. It is being made because the therapist is not adequately equipped or qualified to handle her case. The client may still nevertheless interpret her therapist's action as a direct rejection of her personhood.

Sense of supreme power. Within a client's transference, she may have imbued her therapist with the illusion of the power of a mother, a father, God, a lover and even her own self. The sense of this illusory power can be both fearful and exhilarating. It is important that the therapist remember they are not the person their client has made them out to be and that they do *not* have power to affect change in her. They are only a tool—and an imperfect one at that. A therapist can provide support and guidance as a client continues on *her* journey of growth and change.

Anticipation or excitement in seeing a particular client or relishing in a sense of feeling special or being needed. The level of affection and admiration emanating from a woman within a positive transference can become intoxicating to a therapist who is vulnerable or needy to this type of attention.

Compulsion to give out one's home phone number, to share personal problems with a client or to increase client contact hours. Many clients will feel extremely frustrated that the therapeutic relationship isn't fully mutual in the sense of sharing personal data. The therapist must therefore evaluate all personal disclosure and discussions to ascertain whether it is in the client's best interests or the therapist's own.

Desire to hold or reassure client through physical touch. So strong is their felt need for touch, many women will request, cajole and even beg their therapist for some measure of physical comfort. Many therapists buckle under this pressure, thereby losing objectivity and control of the therapeutic process. To offer touch at this point is to collude with a woman's unconscious pattern of desperately depending on another for comfort rather than developing her own internal resources for self-regulation and security.

Therapists must pursue whatever measures necessary (including consulting and personal therapy) to assure that they are not, consciously or unconsciously, taking advantage of their client's fondness for their own pleasure or ego. If a therapist is unable to reach ongoing objectivity and centeredness, it may not be advisable for him or her to continue working with this particular client or population in the future. I believe strongly that counselors who have unmet dependency needs, attachment issues, unresolved abuse or trauma, or weak boundaries or vulnerability due to a personal struggle with SSA should seek ongoing therapy or professional consultation prior to committing to work with women with SSA.

REGRESSION INTO A STATE OF DEPENDENCY

As a woman continues to grow in her sense of safety and attachment to me, she may *regress* into a state of childlike dependency similar to how she might within an emotionally dependent relationship (Socarides, 2002). In order to help her break this ongoing cycle, I must offer something curative while she experiences these powerful unconscious forces.[6] Though this regressed state introduces unique and challenging therapeutic dynamics, it will, in the end, afford an opportunity to accomplish some of the deepest and most important work possible.[7]

As a client enters a regressed state of helpless dependency, she may become extremely frightened. She will not be able to stop or control her profound vulnerability or deep neediness in terms of wanting to be with or connected to me. Her longings and emotions will defy every former defense, fear and lifelong pattern of dismissiveness, isolation and self-protection. She knows that if I *were* to violate a boundary, she would be unable to resist. My emotional,

---

[6]Bowlby (1988) reports that when therapists allow free expression of "dependency feelings" on the part of their patients, an intense and anxious attachment to the therapist is often formed. But this phenomenon enables the "patient to recover the emotional life he or she had lost during childhood and with it to recover a sense of 'real self.' Therapeutically the results were good" (p. 54).

[7]A regressed state might also be played out with another woman, such as a mentor, while a client is in therapy with me. The same therapeutic measures and precautions discussed in the following sections will apply. Even though her strong sense of attachment is not focused on me, I will still want to reassure her of my ongoing presence and commitment.

psychological and physical boundaries must be firmly in place in order to guard her safety. It is during this stage that a great disparity should exist in our roles. This is not the time to develop mutuality or to encourage the formation of empathy; I must aggressively assume the role as protective and nurturing parent.

> *I remember being very embarrassed to tell my counselor that I wanted her to take care of me—like a mother takes care of her daughter. I was upset that I had even thought it and worried that I had ruined the counseling relationship. But my counselor said she felt honored that I would trust her like a mother.*
>
> *Linda*

This new sense of attachment and dependency may usher in an overwhelming primal terror. My client will fear that I might leave her or that she will lose me through my death, a geographical move or a tragedy in my life. She may also fear my rejection, unavailability or emotional withdrawal. I have become the lifeboat that keeps her afloat. Her life *depends* on me. There is no turning back.

In this profound separation anxiety, my client may begin to despair of life itself. She thinks, *If my counselor leaves, I will die.* The underlying premise is true: when an infant or young child is separated from her caregivers, she *will* eventually die. But my client is *not* an infant, although it is possible than an infant part of her has not been able to move past a primal sense of abandonment and terror.[8]

WALKING THROUGH THE SHADOW OF DEATH

During this phase, a woman will not be capable of deep interpretative or analytical work but will be focused on her daily survival. She will be doing well to just show up in my office or get out of bed every morning. She may persistently ask me questions about my commitment level and personal reactions to

---

[8]Siegel (1988) notes, "While it cannot be emphasized enough that no adult can ever recapture early infantile experiences in their entirety, the emanations of this distant past nevertheless made themselves felt over and over again" in her clients with SSA (p. 14). She also stresses how important it is to welcome "early infantile, possibly presymbolic phenomena into the therapeutic process" (p. 14) with women with SSA.

her desperate state. We will operate primarily in the here-and-now, focusing on our relationship and her ability to trust or regulate her feelings in the moment. We will work on building new coping skills, identifying self-defeating thinking and pinpointing triggers or signs of an encroaching panic attack, for instance. Quinodoz (1989) cautions that the therapeutic process at this point "calls for infinite caution and patience, but the slow rate of progress must be seen in the light of the intensity of the anxieties which these patients must confront" (p. 62).

He makes another equally important observation: many clients will begin to question the efficacy of continuing in this process. "They fear that, by reliving these early anxieties in the transference, they have everything to lose and nothing to gain" (p. 62). They will ask themselves whether this is worth it if, in the end (when the professional relationship is terminated), they will be alone again. Therefore, a client's possible growing depression or impulse to quit therapy must be monitored. It is not unusual for my clients to also seek the support of a medical professional, if they have not already done so.

At this point I must be even more sensitive as I seek to attune to the most fragile and innocent primal places of need and longing within my client's soul. Janine Puls, a licensed clinical social worker, relies on the rich metaphor of mothers and infants in her clinical work with women with SSA. She explains that as long as a woman is consumed with a palpable separation anxiety, she will not be relaxed enough to take in the nourishment and comfort that is being provided in the therapeutic setting. She mentions how common it is to feel, as a therapist or a helper, the disappointment of offering the most wonderful, rich, pure "milk," only to realize that the client is unable to keep it down. With each emotional feeding, her tiny stomach contracts as another wave of terror and fear surges through her body. One of the most curative aspects of our work will be my ability to remain patient. I want her to experience unwavering love and support even as she "spits up" or resorts to her lifelong defensive behaviors and attitudes.

Practical Supportive Measures

Besides needing to learn relaxation and containment skills,[9] many of my clients need to develop a sense of *object constancy.* Influenced by their impending

---

[9] See Davis, Eshelman & McKay (2000) for multiple relaxation techniques.

separation anxiety and possible fear of extinction, I often feel an almost irresistible pull to see them as often as possible. But I must remember that object constancy is not gained through the continual presence of mother but rather is learned through the consistent and predictable *return* of mother within a reasonable amount of time, based on a child's ability to cope with separation and absence. Object constancy is acquired through trust. A child is able to say to herself, *Even though I can't see Mom right now, I know Mom is not gone forever because she always comes back, just in time.*

I therefore establish myself as a constant and trustworthy object by my predictable return to our regularly scheduled appointments (and possibly midweek phone calls).[10] Eventually, my consistency will carry and soothe her even when she is outside of my office. As she assimilates my ongoing trustworthiness or constant psychological presence, she can begin to internalize a sense of inner stability and ultimately trust.

Because a woman's inner pain and anxiety thresholds may reach their limit during this phase, I will regularly

- *assess her stability and monitor her suicide ideation.*
- *develop an emergency plan and safety contract* involving several support people and local crisis resources,[11] if needed.
- *return her phone calls as soon as possible*, especially if she called and left a message during the height of a severe panic attack or a major depressive cycle. I process any reaction she may have had due to my unavailability and delayed response. Although she knows that I am not available on a twenty-four-hour basis, she may still feel frustrated or utterly abandoned. My attunement and empathy at this point supports her to remain open to my care while integrating that my care has limits.
- *monitor her dreams and possible flashback memories* of trauma and abandonment.
- *assess how well and how consistently she can care for herself.*

When appropriate, I will also

---

[10]"The predictability of three or four sessions per week was the external structure that permitted them to control and to confront themselves. Yet they had to assure themselves that the analyst was *concretely* [italics added] present between sessions. Therefore, the telephone calls became a compromise that helped [to stabilize and hold the woman in process] and could be analyzed later" (Siegel, 1988, p. 30).

[11]I am unable to provide 24-hour on-call services, so must rely on other caregivers.

- *increase the number or length of weekly sessions* for the purpose of stabilization if financially feasible for her. This decision is based on *my* determination of its necessity, not her felt need.

- *pace each session* according to her need for containment prior to closing. During this time it may become very difficult for her to say goodbye.

- *use even greater caution* in any counselor-client physical contact. Touch at this point will intensify her attachment, leading to possibly even greater turmoil. However, touch can also be powerfully regulating as I move my chair closer or hold her hand to reassure and comfort.

- *avoid canceling or changing regularly scheduled sessions.* I also make every effort to start sessions on time.

- *inform her weeks in advance if I am going to miss a session.* This will give us time to process her feelings and prepare her for my absence.

- *personally return a call in which she expresses her desire to cancel an appointment.* Cancellations during this phase are often defensive efforts to alleviate anxiety. If she does not have a scheduling conflict, I strongly recommend that she keep her regular appointment, promising we will discuss her disturbing feelings.

- *periodically check in* by making an unscheduled call or by sending a short e-mail letting her know that I was thinking about her.

- *record a reassuring message* on her voice mail so that she can listen to it over and over again.

- *encourage her to call my voice mail* so that she can simply hear my voice (and know that I am still there) or tell me how she is doing. I reassure my clients that I want to hear from them and that I *do* listen to their messages. Many women will not want to call because they are afraid of bothering me.

- *give her a token reminder* that she is loved, such as a small stuffed animal. Sight activates attachment. One of my clients describes how she kept a picture in her wallet of an adolescent girl friend well into her adult years. She felt good every time she looked at it, remembering that she had been liked. A woman can use a picture or transitional object to self-soothe when she is feeling nervous or alone.

- *receive her token gift* if it carries the sentiment of my client's gratefulness or is symbolic of her sense of a warm attachment or a milestone in her process (Schaffner, 2003; Zur, 2007). If the pattern of gift giving or the value of the gift becomes inappropriate, I will discuss its meaning with her, graciously declining the gift while affirming her thoughtfulness.

- *maintain professional boundaries*, expecting full cooperation with payment and cancellation policies.
- *regularly assess my overall caseload* and my potential for burnout.

In the first years of my practice, I worried that my clients would remain stuck in a regressed state of dependency. However, I have observed that by offering the above interventions, my clients are stabilized and supported to progress *through* their regressed dependent state. Siegel (1988) addresses this concern by recommending that at some point the therapist begin to explicitly discuss with the client the fact that she is using three sessions per week and still requiring a mid-week phone check-in, for example. This is not done in a shaming manner but in a way that encourages the client to integrate her primarily unconscious processes (emerging dependency, separation anxiety and habitual reliance on another) into her conscious awareness. I may ask her what she thinks of our current arrangements or how she thinks we might begin to change them, such as cutting back on sessions.

To progress through a dependent state, she must also integrate, and not just unconsciously take in, my acceptance, patience and attuned consistency into a conscious experience and understanding. This means that we will also explicitly debrief and reflect on our warm moments together. As we do so, she internalizes my care, storing up memories of being comforted and loved. It will become as if I, the "good enough mother," live inside of her. A woman is then able to experience herself as being constantly loved (I am always with her) *and* continuously equipped with an object of affection upon which to attach *her* love. In my absence, she can begin to self-soothe as she practices this inner loving relationship. This will allow her to eventually self-monitor her separation anxieties and even coach or nurture herself up and out of what would otherwise be a reflexive dependency.

I do not view a woman's regression as an opportunity to reparent her per se. I will never be able to meet all of her unmet needs. Throughout this precarious stage, I continue to respect and empower her adult self, calling on her to observe, own and pursue her own needs fulfillment. This means that I help her to acknowledge and integrate the childlike parts of her self that may be affecting her regressed or dependent states.

WELCOMING AND BLESSING HER "LITTLE ONE"

To further enhance a client's positive sense of self and integrated personhood, several therapists, including myself, have found that inner-child work[12] is extremely powerful and beneficial for women with SSA. The inner child is a practical psychological construct that has been effectively used and taught to help people overcome the effects of a troubled childhood, such as one that lacked nurturing.[13] A woman who lives disconnected from this innocent and vital part of herself, as many women with SSA do, will often find her identity and expression in a false or wounded self such as the "tough girl" discussed in chapter nine. For growth and recovery to occur, a woman will need to be reintroduced to her core *true self* and all of its natural longings, experiences, wounds and needs.[14] Helping a woman to connect with her inner-child voice allows her to connect with the unconscious feelings and needs that may have fueled her ongoing projections and transferences.

As I begin to introduce a client to the concept of her little one within, I might ask her to do one or more of the following exercises:

- *Bring in photographs of herself as an infant and little girl.* As we review each picture, I will ask questions like, "What was she [the little girl] feeling when this picture was taken? What made her happy? What made her sad?" I might begin to refer to her little girl by using one of her childhood nicknames.

- *Draw a picture of her little girl and her family when she was growing up.*

- *Draw a picture of her little girl's heart.*

---

[12]For an excellent synopsis of the historical contributions to the understanding of inner-child work, I recommend Price (1996).

[13]Whitfield (1987) defines the "child within" as our true or real self, the "part of each of us which is ultimately alive, energetic, creative and fulfilled" (p. 1).

[14]Post (1982), in her article on dependency conflicts in high-achieving women, shares a story of a client who was becoming aware of her inner conflict between her needs for warmth and closeness and the side of her that demanded self-sufficiency. She chose to call the needy side her "little one." Her voice would change as she alternated between these two parts of her. Post explains, "These were not dissociative episodes, but a creative way of bringing to the surface characteristics of herself that she had previously suppressed because she felt they were unacceptable" (p. 86). The therapeutic task, according to Post, is one of integration, which involved "the client accepting herself as a person with diverse abilities and feelings, including gentleness as well as strength" (p. 86).

- *Draw a picture of her little girl and the inner house in which she now lives.*

These exercises may initially raise suspicion or a defensive reaction in my clients, especially if they have disidentified with their gender or have practiced active self-rejection of all that is tender or vulnerable within. She may respond to my implication that she has a little girl with statements such as "What little girl? I don't have a little girl" or "Why do we have to talk about *her?* I locked her up a long time ago." These objections must be handled sensitively. It may take some clients many months to open themselves to this type of work.

If a client exhibits severe resistance to the thought of their own little girl, I might ask her to think of a little girl she knows (like a niece or a neighbor) and to tell me all about her.[15] We will focus on the girl's characteristics as a small person, such as needing help, love, encouragement and protection. I will ask my client how she feels at the thought of this little girl being needy or dependent on another's care. Typically my client will respond compassionately and warmly. I appeal to my client's affection for this child by telling her that this is how I feel about her and her inner little girl. I emphasize how important her little girl is to her ongoing process of healing. Her little girl still holds many thoughts, memories and feelings that she experienced when she was young.

When a client is ready, I may assign additional exercises such as these:

- *Make a chart of a little girl's characteristics (e.g., small, weak, helpless but fun, playful and free) and an adult woman's characteristics (big, strong, powerful).* This will help a woman begin to identify when she is regressing into a little-girl state or feeling the feelings of her little girl.
- *Play a game, color or read a children's story* during or outside of our sessions.[16]
- *Watch a little-girl movie at home.*[17]
- *Purchase a doll or teddy bear that represents her little girl.* When a client is feeling afraid or alone, I will encourage her to sit or rock her doll or teddy bear, speaking comforting words to assuage her anxiety.

---

[15]This can be a homework assignment in and of itself. If a client does not have nieces or regular contact with small children, she should be encouraged to place herself in settings where she can observe and befriend a little girl.

[16]Excellent books to read include *You Are Special* by Max Lucado (1997), *Love You Forever* by Robert Munsch (1995), *The Velveteen Rabbit* by Margery Williams (1991), *I'd Choose You* by John Trent (1994), *The Runaway Bunny* by Margaret Wise Brown (1991) and *The Missing Piece Meets the Big "O"* by Shel Silverstein (1981).

[17]Excellent movies include *Heidi* (Disney, 1993), *A Little Princess* (Warner Bros., 1995), *Mulan* (Disney, 1998) and *Anne of Green Gables* (Sullivan Entertainment, 1986).

- *Play lullaby music or deeply nurturing spiritual or classical music.*

As we continue, I will begin to speak *about* her little girl within a session, always using a soft, tender, motherly voice. I might say, "I am wondering what your little girl is needing or wanting right now. I want to make sure I understand her. Can you tell me what she needs?"

Then, as my client is ready, I speak directly to her little girl (her small and fragile ego state), possibly using her nickname: "Elizabeth, I am so sorry you felt alone as a little girl. It must have been very painful." Leaning forward in my chair and softening my voice, I will say "Elizabeth, would it be okay if I speak directly to little Elizabeth?" If she says yes, I help her to relax into the process by instructing her to close her eyes and take in a few deep breaths as she imagines herself at age four or five. I shift into an authentic and appropriately energized tone for a child. "Lizzie, I am so glad to be talking to you. You are such a special little girl, and I want to get to know you better. I would like to hear about your life, your thoughts and all of your feelings." Pausing again, I ask, "Lizzie, will you tell me what it was like for you when you were little? I so want to hear more of your story."

As a woman speaks, she may shift noticeably in her body posture or tone of voice to what looks or sounds girlish. Many women will, at this point, naturally and easily pour out childhood experiences or access deep emotions. However, I am not surprised that once a client begins to envision her little one, she defensively reacts, once again expressing dislike and contempt. One client announced, "My little girl is disheveled. She looks like a poor Appalachian girl. She's sort of lifeless and dead. She is locked away in a room, and that's where she lives even today. I don't think she can talk right now." Other clients have said things like "No one gets to see her. Hardly anyone knows she's there." "I do hate her. She's so pathetic and needy." "It's not safe to be her. I don't really like thinking about her. Do we really need to keep doing this?"

Besides bringing to the surface her self-hatred and self-abdication, little-girl work may also naturally usher a woman into her sense of loss and grief (Whitfield, 1987; Kneisl, 1991) and possibly uncover abuse and trauma. All of these reactions provide rich therapeutic material for our ongoing work.

As we continue in this process, I may ask her to write a letter to her little girl from her adult self. This is done using her normal writing hand. I will then ask her to write a letter from her little girl to her adult self. This is done using her nonwriting hand. As a woman becomes proficient in these processes, I may finally introduce her to an empty-chair exercise involving her adult and little girl. She is given a chance to communicate directly to her little girl or, as a little girl, speak directly to her adult self.

Ultimately, I want to cultivate a conscious, loving and respectful alliance between a woman's adult self and her fragile little-girl self. It is important that none of her "parts" be isolated from one another. When parts are fragmented or disavowed, such as her little-girl self, they often develop into an imbalanced false persona or remain unconsciously reactive and controlling. For growth and maturity, the adult woman must acknowledge, accept, understand and eventually show kindness and regard to her little one (Price, 1996).

Once a woman begins to accept the presence of her valuable and worthy little girl, I encourage her to daily

- respectfully listen to her little girl or inner self
- ask her *self* what she is longing for or needing
- be tender and nurturing
- offer herself grace, compassion and forgiveness
- speak hopeful and positive words[18]
- stop when she is calling a part of herself ugly or stupid
- let her *self* cry when she feels hurt or pain

I have found that women who have not done this special work of integration—entering and embracing the inner life of their little girl—often continue to struggle with a desperate need to be seen as special by other women. Many admit that they can recognize the innocent and beautiful little girl in another woman but not in themselves. As a woman pours her love into another woman, she herself remains fragmented, a victim to her little one's fears, anxieties and deep need. Cooperating with her own little-girl work and having the courage to see her own specialness will require the greatest humility and vulnerability on her part, but it will be well worth the discomfort and time spent.

Last night I practiced what my therapist had coached me to do whenever I start to spiral into a dark place when I am alone. I could feel it coming on so I got off the couch and told myself (actually my little girl), You will

---

[18]Some women will benefit from the book *Affirmations for the Inner Child* by Rokelle Lerner, which contains daily affirmations.

have to wait until the next time I see my counselor to deal with your pain and loneliness. I am not forgetting you, but I want you and me to be safe as we feel, together, all that you are feeling.

a client

REPROCESSING TECHNIQUES

I hope by now it has become clear that female SSA is much more than a trauma-based phenomenon. Trauma work, therefore, is only a piece of the overarching treatment plan. Memory or reprocessing work must be offered in the context of the experiential and integrating aspects of long-term interpersonal therapy.[19]

Many women with SSA are not prepared to address their abusive or trauma experiences until years into a therapeutic process.[20] A good friend of mine started attending a support group in 1988; she then worked with several therapists and continued to seek out ongoing accountability and support for her healing journey. It wasn't until 2000, within a professional counseling setting, that she began to deal with the trauma of her past. She was not able to fully face and grieve her losses until she was reassured she had someone who cared enough to grieve with her. She found this person in her therapist.

When I was first learning techniques such as eye movement desensitization and reprocessing (EMDR)[21] and theophostic prayer ministry,[22] attempting to

---

[19]Shapiro (2001), in her introductory book on eye movement sensitization and reprocessing (EMDR), notes that therapists must be responsible in assessing a client's history for the purpose of identifying not only potential target memories, but also the client's developmental deficits or milestones that were never reached or were never positively resolved or otherwise integrated into the client's personhood. She admits that developmental issues cannot be solely treated with EMDR but must be taught or attained through other aspects of a therapeutic relationship. In other words, EMDR cannot replace the *experiences* of attachment, love or unconditional acceptance afforded in a real relationship, but it can enhance these positive interactions.

[20]For women associated with profile 3 (see chapter 8), trauma material can often be introduced within the first year of counseling, but not always. For the remaining profiles, it may take 3 to 4 years or longer to even begin discussing an abuse memory.

[21]EMDR, pioneered by Francine Shapiro, is an information processing therapy integrating elements of many effective psychotherapies in structured protocols that are designed to maximize treatment effects.

[22]According to www.theophostic.com, "Theo (God) Phostic (light) is a ministry of prayer that is Christ centered and God reliant for its direction and outcome. Simply stated, it is encouraging a person to discover and expose what he believes that is a falsehood; and then encouraging him to have an encounter with Jesus Christ through prayer, thus allowing the Lord to reveal His truth to the wounded person's heart and mind." Retrieved October 22, 2007, from <http://www.theophostic.com/content.asp?ID=2>.

incorporate them into my existing practice, some of my clients found it confusing when I switched from more of a free-flowing, nurturing, empathic role to that of a technician, following what appeared to be rote therapeutic protocols. At that time, feeling a bit unsure about the benefits of EMDR, I often chose to forego the use of reprocessing techniques for the slower ongoing process of talk therapy or referred my client to an outside therapist trained and experienced in trauma work. However, now that I have more experience, I find that I can maintain the empathic alliance *while* I lead a client through a reprocessing experience. EMDR has been extremely powerful in assisting my clients with anxiety, core fears and relaxation as well as in altering negative core beliefs as memories are reprocessed.

Nevertheless, I still thoroughly assess for client readiness prior to proceeding with either of these techniques, especially with women who fit profiles 1 and 2 (see chapter 8). If my client has established a solid level of trust with me, she may be willing to try just about anything I suggest; however, she may also still have unconscious defenses that prevent her from meaningfully participating in the process. Many women with SSA have difficulty imagining or visualizing, or may experience adverse reactions, becoming frightened of and overwhelmed by the technique itself. Some cannot participate in any spiritual process, such as theophostic prayer, because they are not ready to directly talk to or receive from God. I must respect a client's request that we forego or stop using a technique for a time being. I return to attunement and empathy in helping her process difficult emotions or surfacing resistance.

As I introduce a client to EMDR or other reprocessing or Gestalt-like technique, I initially focus our work on her fear or anxiety associated with the thought of processing unhappy memories or using a new technique. At the beginning, I also help her to create and install a "safe place." Once we begin working with actual memories or historical material, I target thematic material or memories that do not contain severe trauma. I find that the cognitions and emotions tied to even the most simple of memories are much more intense for these women than other types of clients. I never allow the urge to speed up therapy to overtake my primary goal of providing an ongoing empathic environment in which my client can slowly heal and develop new aspects of her self and identity.[23]

---

[23]Vogelmann-Sine (1998) emphasizes that only as much material as the client is capable of processing should be accessed at any given point in time. "The therapist's job, therefore, is to pace the process

THE ONGOING NEED FOR GRIEF WORK

Mourning our losses assigns meaning to our existence and value to our stories and personhood. It restores and integrates a woman's true self. As a woman grieves, she will continually unlock the desires and longings for which she was truly made, restoring her dignity as a person made in the image of God.[24] As Solomon (2001) claims, "To be creatures who love, we must be creatures who can despair at what we lose" (p. 15). Women with SSA have much to mourn: the loss of childhood trust, attachment,[25] self-love and security as well as the pain of abuse, rejection or gender confusion. They often need to grieve the letting go of their former identity and mourn their relational losses, including the loss of former lesbian partners. Most will continue to grieve their ongoing struggle with depression, loneliness, singleness, unmet relational need and defensive patterns. Even though I am only making a token reference to the process of grief, the significance of grieving within a woman's life should not be minimized or overlooked.

I never attempt to speed up a woman's process of grieving. She is apt to cycle through all of the stages of grief, moving in and out of anger, bargaining, depression and sadness over and over again. The moments in which I simply sit with her and empathetically allow her to *be* in these important places are often memorialized as holy ground for us both. A woman's grief will produce scars that are a testament and memorial to her past. These scars become a part of her individuality as well as places from which she will eventually help and support others.

---

carefully so that the client can function appropriately at each new level of adaptation and to respect the client's inability or unwillingness to go further" (p. 175).

[24]Many women have been helped by Viktor Frankl's book, *Man's Search for Meaning* (1992), a beautiful piece of literature heralding the nature and benefits of redemptive suffering.

[25]Moberly (1983) suggests that defensive detachment or the repressed yearning for attachment is an avoidance of the normal process of mourning triggered by a separation or break in attachment between parent and child (p. 15). Essentially, "The unresolved 'mourning' process of a young child has persisted into adult years" (p. 16).

CHAPTER TWELVE

Finding the Feminine Within

Who can feel ugly when the heart meets delight?
It is as if, somewhere inside,
within the hideous face and bony limbs,
one is soft, fresh . . . and desirable.

C. S. LEWIS, *TILL WE HAVE FACES*

In her honest, heartwarming essay "Butch in a Tutu" (Cytron & Malinowitz, 1999), Sara Cytron, a self-identified lesbian, shared her shocking discovery that even though she was extremely comfortable with her butch or masculinized self, buried in her own psyche was evidence that she still ultimately wanted to identify herself as female. Cytron discusses several dreams in which she was facing a mirror. In these dreams, she would switch between the idealized images of a female, such as a ballerina, to a Greek, godlike man. Through the help of her therapist, she came to admit that she was searching for hidden parts of herself. She realized she had "anxiously submerged" the feminine or underlying essence of herself.

While not seeking to alter her sexual identity as a lesbian, Cytron reports that she nevertheless explored the many reasons and processes behind her escape or split from her feminine identity. For example, as a youngster, she felt sick and panic-stricken about wearing a dress or playing with dolls. She was much more comfortable dressing, acting and imagining herself as a boy. With an overly emotionally engulfing father, she associated femaleness with being invaded or overwhelmed; yet she had no sense of closeness with her mom, leaving her lost and alone. Cytron realizes that the striking relational contrast between her mom and dad led her to desperately want attention from women and distance from men. She notes that although she associated her femaleness with danger, she wanted to be near femininity but "dreaded inhabiting it" (p. 212).[1]

At 43, Cytron had another one of her telling dreams. She saw a little girl in a prison cell. This girl was in a pretty party dress but was slowly swinging, back and forth, from a noose connected to the ceiling. In her dream she heard a voice say, "A young girl is being executed" (p. 222). Cytron and her therapist wisely explored this young girl's death, what she suffered and where she went. Cytron describes how at one point in therapy, she felt like a transsexual—as if she, a feminine woman, was trapped in a butch's mind and body.

Cytron closes her article by wondering what her relationship to her own femininity would have been like if her father hadn't "filled that territory with land mines and if my mother had been able to meet my gaze and offer herself as the female mirror I kept searching for" (p. 224). She now reports that she is more relaxed and at peace with herself as a woman and has even slowly softened her wardrobe, allowing her female "figure to show." Cytron is comfortable being seen as the unique and distinctive female only Cytron herself could have become.

FACING HER FEMININE SOUL

As my clients continue in their journeys of integration and healing, filling and furnishing their own inner home, most will eventually be faced with the issue of their long forgotten or openly despised femininity. Gender identity difficulties within women with SSA can range from severe dissociation and profound hatred of their femaleness and female body parts to a prevalent desire to be female and feminine yet unable to fully integrate a feminine identity because of one or more of the following:

- a lack of knowledge and understanding of female subculture—such as female habits, accoutrements, or social expectations—which results in an insecurity about or absence of "gender self-confidence"[2]
- a lack of an acceptable definition of femininity or understanding of womanhood beyond mere restrictions or rigid gender roles

---

[1] Similarly, Kris, one of the women I interviewed for this book, also admits that she desired other women to nurture or "wash over" her with the feminine but refused to receive or integrate it into her self as a woman.

[2] Gender self-confidence refers to "one's genuine self-assuredness about being female or male—how much one accepts, respects, and values oneself as a female or male person" (Hoffman, 2006, p. 359).

- a lack of self-acceptance of her femaleness and her feminine characteristics
- the presence of distorted images of femaleness and negative core beliefs and attitudes about men and women in general
- the presence of unresolved abuse memories and negative emotional material associated with her femaleness

Women associated with profiles 3 and 4 (see chapter 8) are commonly far more integrated in terms of their feminine identity and appearance; however, many may still struggle with a negative gender image and deeply held negative cognitions about womanhood and the nature of men. Women associated with profiles 1 and 2 often exhibit the most profound splits and confusion within their gender identity. Regardless, each woman will have possible deep dissociations or self-rejections that may need to be resolved as they relate to her femaleness, especially if she desires to eventually build an intimate relationship with a man. Of course, not all women will have this as a stated goal. But for those who do, they must first become a "woman"[3] among women.

I have learned, however, to never assume that *every* client will eventually consider exploring this extremely threatening topic. Many of my long-term clients are still not ready to see themselves within a feminine light; many others have terminated counseling before they crossed this therapeutic threshold. Some have moved on to establish new professional and mentoring relationships, intentionally expanding their network of women (and men) with whom they trust and can connect. It has often been with these new therapists or mentors that they began addressing the issues associated with their femininity.

There are still others who, although sincerely committed to growth and change on all levels, will frankly not live long enough to fully deal with all of their inner fragmentation, developmental voids, woundings or identity confusions—let alone a possible dissociation from their inherent gender. To maintain a hopeful and optimistic stance, I affirm and applaud every step forward my clients take, always confident that each step will result in something new and rewarding, even if they do not quickly arrive at their final destination.

But when I sense that a client is ready, she and I will first discuss and mu-

---

[3]Siegel (1988) notes, "A woman whose body is her own, that is who has successfully integrated her sexual organ and her sexual self within her total inner self representation is able to meet a potential male partner without either resenting him or competing with his maleness. For the women I treated this was at first an insurmountable task because they had to acquire a more complete body image and sense of self" (p. 6).

tually agree that it is time to begin to address issues pertaining to her feminine identity. I am careful not to prematurely initiate conversations around this extremely sensitive and often shameful topic. Many clients invite me to help them embrace their femininity or change their external appearance but also warn me that they still feel tremendous inner resistance to the thought of becoming a "woman." At any point in our process, they can easily become consumed with terror, shame or disgust. I may discover that a woman needs to do further work around basic formation and stabilization of her core self before we can take on such a conflicted part of her fundamental identity as her femaleness.

WHO NEEDS THIS FEMALE THING?

Misogyny is defined as the hatred, devaluing and dishonoring of woman or the feminine. It has been commonly associated with the cultural and sociological oppression or subjugation of women as a whole and, of course, can take on many forms: sexual objectification, unequal pay for equal work, rigid gender roles, religious fundamentalism that promotes male superiority, family favoritism of boys, or the elevation of autonomy and productivity over connectivity and beauty. Sadly, most little girls have to face and eventually deal with the subtle and not-so-subtle misogynistic attitudes and patriarchal systems that still pervade our culture (and others). But as addressed in chapter three, little girls who may have higher IQs, attuned sensitivity especially toward injustice and inequity, and natural gender nonconforming interests and abilities may be more affected by misogynistic messages.

However, no matter how oppressive or violating the surrounding cultural messages about femaleness or her own experiences of sexual and gender abuse may be, when a woman rehearses a misogynistic mantra within her own mind, personally undertaking an active hatred and disavowal of her femaleness, she is essentially practicing a murderous attitude toward what may be the least changeable aspect of her life. Women with SSA often believe that to be female is to be weak and powerless, second-best and inferior, used and taken for granted, rejectable and contemptible, and devoid of value, substance, and directedness. Being female is not fun, rewarding or *safe*. Her self-contempt coagulates around what seems a logical and final conclusion based on reason and circumstance: *It is not good to be female.* In her article "My Path to Lesbianism," accomplished journalist Diane Mattingly (2005) writes, "I hated men. I hated women. I hated myself for being a woman. I had no more value for women than any women-hating man does, and yet no one was more surprised to discover that I, too, was a misogynist" (p. 64).

Many of my clients do not even *feel* like women. This is not necessarily a symptom of a transgender struggle but an indication of their alienation from their core feminine self. They came to believe that they *should* have been boys because they would have made a better boy. In fact, they often made vows to *become* the best boy possible. As a result, later in life they realized that they no longer felt like a female and had no idea what it meant to *be* female.

Yet chromosomally, they *are* female. And no matter how hard they try to distance themselves from this genetic fact, they can only do so at a great cost to their personhood, both emotionally and psychologically. As Cytron discovered, to be at strife with such a significant part is to maintain an ongoing and disintegrating attack on one's existential wholeness.

> *I hated the fact that I was a woman. I would mock that woman inside of me—to the point of death. I hated her enough to kill her. I discovered that some of this severe hatred came out of my sexual abuse as a kid. I responded to the touch and had no power. I thought being a female makes you powerless. So I decided I will not be a female. She must die.*
>
> *Jordan*

I believe that a woman's violent repression or her minimizing neglect of her femaleness (which is often seen in her reluctance to go to a gynecologist) contributes greatly to the vacuum within her core. Deep within her feminine soul, she houses a tomb, so to speak, permeated with a spirit of death and darkness. In order for a woman to walk in healthy relationship with her self and others, this deep-seated self-hatred must be exposed and her murderous attempts at self-annihilation stopped. But as one might imagine, altering these lifelong patterns of repression and rejection and restructuring her negative cognitions will require a tremendous amount of energy and commitment on a woman's part.

UNVEILING THE VALUE AND NATURE OF GENDER

To effectively work with women who dislike or are insecure with being female, I found that I needed to develop my own constructs for the abstract notions of femininity and masculinity. This was not something that my clients could teach me. They were overwhelmed by the basic questions, such as *What is a female? Who am I as a female?* and *What is femininity?* I had to do my own work—reading, assimilating and questioning the research and my own beliefs about maleness and femaleness. I also had to examine my own enculturation and beliefs pertaining to social constructs related to gender roles and appearances, so as not to project my expectations or standards onto my clients. I then had to find the words in which to enter nonthreatening dialogues with my clients as they also reflected, explored and consolidated new beliefs about themselves as feminine gendered beings.

I have to revisit and be honest about my own dislike of and frustration at being female and my residual mistrust and anger toward men. I do not want to unconsciously align with my clients' negative attitudes, failing to offer the objective support and intervention they need. Needless to say, I continue to work on my own life as a *woman,* proactively seeking my own healing and becoming more of who I was designed to be in relationship with other women and men. My clients look to me (similar to how daughters look to a mother) to cast a vision of femaleness that is both desirable and respectable, that is not just based in head knowledge but also illustrated through my living example.[4]

Ultimately, each therapist will have deeply personal, and most likely differing, experiences and viewpoints in this complex arena of gender. What is most important is that a counselor is at least *self-aware* in terms of his or her own process or difficulty in being male or female and that he or she can *articulate* some sort of working model of who is woman and who is man. Most women with SSA long to be free of the shame and confusion around this fundamental aspect of life. They will therefore unconsciously look to their female therapists as role models and will closely watch how their male therapists treat, feel or think of women in general.

I have found that the following psychological and theological presuppositions, offered in a spirit of openness, have proven to be helpful to both the women *and* the men with whom I have worked.

---

[4]This is perhaps the point where a male therapist might want to consider securing the aid of a female therapist or female mentor in his ongoing work with a woman with SSA. No doubt a woman's experience with a male therapist will play an indispensable role in healing her image of men, but it will be difficult for him to facilitate the intuitive understanding and role modeling that occurs between two females as they explore the deep world of the true feminine.

1. Biological sex. A woman's femaleness or biological sex is genetically determined and usually signified by female genitalia[5] and associated with unique brain, hormonal and physiological structures.[6]

2. Gender. Gender is an intrinsic, permanent aspect of a woman's internal *essence* and identity as a human being, it is directly tied to her biological sex, and it *may* manifest itself in sex-typed psychological or behavioral characteristics (sometimes referred to in psychological literature as gender roles).[7] In other words, a female is more than a body with female genitalia and brain; she is a *feminine being,* a being qualitatively different than a masculine being. I do not believe that we are gender neutral or blank slates at birth and therefore *only* a product of our socialization and education. While our affective sense of ourselves as either male or female is vastly influenced by our social experiences, beliefs, cultural values and so on, there remains an innate foundation for a solid gender definition that is inextricably linked with a person's biologic sex. In other words, there is an inherent blueprint to which a woman can return if she has actively rejected and now wants to search for and reassociate with her true essence as a feminine being.

The significance of this maxim lies within the corollary discussion of social gender roles. *Social gender roles* are the rules, standards, expectations and limitations placed on both men and women that arise out of political, social, cultural and religious systems. These roles have left many of my clients dissatisfied or confused with respect to their status as a female. I've come to realize that within many social settings, especially the church, more emphasis is placed on what a woman and man should or shouldn't *do*—in particular, what a woman can or can't do—than on who we *are* as distinct gendered beings.[8]

Besides, what I *do* as a female with an intact gender identity will not diminish or directly affect my inherent femaleness. Gender is constant. For example,

---

[5]Exceptions are those situations involving genital ambiguity or intersex conditions in genetic females with congenital adrenal hyperplasia (CAH) or genetic males with partial androgen insensitivity syndrome (pAIS), or 5α-reductase 2 deficiency (5-ARD).

[6]Biological sex includes chromosomes, gonads, in utero hormones, pubertal feminization or virilization, internal reproductive structures and external genitalia.

[7]Many women with SSA manifested gender nonconforming behaviors, not common sex-typed characteristics or behaviors. However, these manifestations did not minimize or negate their core feminine gender essence. For more information on the genetic underpinnings of gender, see the book website at www.ivpress.com.

[8]Based on trinitarian theology, Deddo (2006) emphasizes that since roles do not distinguish the unique persons of the Trinity, roles should not be the distinguishing factor in the relations between male and female.

I could, if I wanted to, work as a lumberjack. I may or may not be a good lumberjack, but nevertheless I will most certainly approach my job, relate to my fellow workers and process my life *as a female.* Donning overalls and slinging an axe does not make me less of a woman or more of a man. Based on the biological reality that every cell in my body is stamped with an XX chromosome pair, I assume that everything about my being is thoroughly and completely female regardless of my titles, roles or clothing.

These points are especially important for women with SSA who are presently working in male-dominated careers or regularly donning male clothing and masculinized haircuts. A woman does not have to change careers or appearance to take her first step in understanding her femininity. She can discover and even embrace her feminine identity as she continues to work in the field of her choice and dress comfortably. However, if she suffers regular sexual harassment or discriminatory abuse in the workplace, or if she believes her job or appearance no longer align with her internal changes and integrated feminine self, then transitions might be advisable on their own merits.

3. Gender identification. Gender identification is the process through which a female discovers, defines, embraces and integrates her femaleness and inner feminine essence into her broader sense of self and identity. This process is often disrupted or confused in many women with SSA, resulting in gender identity insecurity, confusion or what can be formally diagnosed as gender dysphoria.[9] While gender is fixed with a biological basis, gender identification is a fluid process and can be reopened at any point in a person's life. A woman can resolve deep insecurities and confusions related to her gender.

4. Harmony and flexibility. The greatest levels of psychological and emotional health are experienced when a woman's sense of self or gender identification is *harmonious* with her biological or genetic sex and yet flexible enough to accommodate her individual diversities of expression, behavior and natural gifting.

5. God's image bearer. In response to the unsettling religious dogma and discriminating theologies that many of my clients contend with, I enjoy pointing out a few perspectives from and implications of the creation accounts in Genesis.

---

[9]Gender dysphoria refers to the discontent with one's biological sex, the desire to possess the body of the opposite sex or the desire to be regarded as a member of the opposite sex. Extreme cases are diagnosed as transsexualism or Gender Identity Disorder (GID) in the *DSM IV-TR.* Some women with SSA do meet the criteria for GID.

Upon creation, humanity is differentiated into gendered beings, and *both beings, male and female, are made in the image of God* (Gen 1:27). This means that the essence or nature of a woman (feminine soul) reflects the nature or character of God just as much as does the masculine soul or core essence of man (Erickson, 2002). Therefore, the very existence of both woman and man is absolutely *essential* in portraying the full image or character of God.[10]

This may seem like splitting hairs, but these truths can bring a sense of relief to a woman who has felt continuously devalued and negated by her faith culture. That women and men were created in God's image imbues both with inherent dignity and value. For a woman who also struggles with deep resentment and hatred of men, these truths may also help her to distinguish between the good of masculinity, or the God-given *core essence* of men, versus abusive or disrespectful *behaviors* of broken men.

6. Equality under God. Males and females are *equal* in value, dignity, responsibility and purpose within the larger context of the world and cosmos (Erickson, 2002; Grenz, 1995). Recall that in Genesis 1:28 the first man and woman were *both* equally blessed and commanded to rule and subdue the outside world (garden and animals) and fill and multiply the realm of human relatedness and existence. Initially, God makes no distinction in his proclamation of blessing, commands and roles: men and women are to "exercise their powers and joint authority together" (Deddo, 2006, p. 14).[11]

7. Good by design. Maleness and femaleness are both equally seen as good. "God saw *everything* [italics added] that he had made, and indeed, it was *very good* [italics added]" (Gen 1:31 NRSV).

8. Unique differentiation. The concepts of *masculine* and *feminine* are best understood in terms of unique differentiation and special strengths and propensities that harmonize, balance and enhance the other (Balswick & Balswick, 1999).

An assertion that women are the same as men does nothing to promote a sense of value and significance for women, especially for women who do not know what it means to be female. Typically, within this assertion is the pre-

---

[10]The relationship between male and female is also meant to mirror the unity and diversity of the persons and relationships within the Trinity (Deddo, 2006; Balswick, King & Reimer, 2005).

[11]See also Hess (2004). For more material related to the creation order and the Hebrew word translated as "helper," see "Gender Differences and Special Uniqueness" on the book webpage at www.ivpress.com.

supposition that men (or the masculine) are the ultimate standard or measure of value and importance. Women, therefore, must measure up to men in order to find significance. An exclusive focus on the *sameness* of men and women neglects the particular and necessary value of the nuances, specialties and strengths of the two *differing* genders.[12]

The *second* creation account in Genesis does suggest uniqueness and diversification between the genders. Not only do the first man and woman's primal origins differ (earth versus living tissue), but so do their initial experiences and postures toward their new worlds. These differences may offer a clue to the ways in which women and men *uniquely* reflect aspects of God's nature or character. Instead of negating man and woman's fundamental *equality* in value, the text, by highlighting these differences, enhances the significance and necessity of each. As Deddo (2006) writes, "Woman is everything the man is except man, and man is everything the woman is, except woman" (p. 13).

9. Definitions. Any word or sentiment used to describe and distinguish the primal (innocent) inner essence of woman *(feminine)* and man *(masculine)*, made in the image of God, should be a word or sentiment, comparatively speaking, that is used to describe characteristics of God.[13]

Our culture, families, faith communities and even pop psychologies have used terms like *weak, manipulative, overly emotional,* or *second-best* to describe what it means to be female. Words like *violating, detached, isolated* or *dominant* have been used to describe what it means to be male. These words are inappropriate and unfair. They do not describe God, so they cannot be good descriptors of the image of God within us. Perhaps women *confused* in their true feminine identity and therefore living out of their fallen nature *act* controlling and manipulative, for example. Perhaps men confused in their true masculine identity and therefore living out of their fallen nature *behave* coldly and arrogantly. But these behaviors are a distortion of who we were truly made to be—beings who reflect the very image and dignity of their Creator.

10. Generalizations. Any words or symbols employed in defining the characteristics of femininity and masculinity should be considered as *generaliza-*

---

[12]For more information on gender differences and special uniqueness, see the book website at www .ivpress.com.

[13]Grenz (1995) states, "God's relationship to creation takes on both male and female dimensions. Therefore, God forms the foundation for the distinctively male and female dimensions of human existence" (p. 150).

tions and therefore not be used to form rigid expectations or roles for either gender.

Ruth Tiffany Barnhouse, professor emerita, ordained Episcopal priest, and author of several books focused on homosexuality and gender, stresses that

> the most damaging influence of [gender] stereotypes of any kind is that they single out *one* of these many factors and make it decisive for how a person should behave or be treated by others. This does violence to the true complexity of everyone's identity. . . . The more rigid the cultural views on what constitutes "true" masculinity or femininity, the harder the lot of those who are perceived as being too much like the other sex. (1984, pp. 44-45)

A woman does not need to curtail her "masculinized" behaviors and preferences to become a woman. Rather she needs to *internalize* a sense of her feminine identity and integrate it with her gender nonconforming attributes in order to live out of her true and unique feminine self.

11. Feminine strengths. The core of the true feminine is not one of weakness or subordination, but of the *power to be* and the *courage* to face the chaos and complexities of the *inner world* of human relatedness with the *strength* to birth, nurture and sustain life.[14]

True femininity is measured not in terms of hairdos, short skirts and makeup, but in terms of an integrated and consolidated sense of self and the capacity to psychologically and emotionally receive the presence of another without a loss of self or a dependent consumption of the other. Women with SSA commonly exhibit an external masculinized identity and posture in life, exerting physical strength and toughness within the outer world while experiencing a core emptiness and desperation within the inner world of relationship. Sadly, their toughness disguises their inner need. And their inner need, so often expressed in terms of dependencies, speaks to the depth of their gender confusion or brokenness. They are not living out of the fortified *inner strengths* of the true feminine. Within their same-sex relationships, they have simply been attempting to connect with and become the female they have always been.

12. Restoration. It is possible for a woman who has been cut off from her femininity to be *restored* by healing and reintegrating her feminine soul.

---

[14]For substantiation of this perspective of femininity, see the discussion of gender differences and special uniqueness on the book website at www.ivpress.com.

Indeed, restoration of a woman's feminine identity will help to complete the construction of her inner home. Relating out of the good and strength of her feminine soul will also transform her relationships, bringing greater stabilization and variegation.

DISCOVERING THAT WHICH IS LOST, RESURRECTING THAT WHICH IS DEAD

Restoration for a woman who struggles with her feminine identity commonly begins with a basic acceptance of her biological sex (femaleness). She will then need to engage in an ongoing process of confronting the facets of her deep gender confusion and self-hatred. It will be neither easy nor straightforward.

Below I have enumerated some of the many considerations and steps most women need to take in their pursuit of integration and wholeness. These steps are not given in a particular order and will require various levels of emphasis throughout a woman's recovery. Many of these steps parallel those set forth in chapter 9 for helping a woman through her initial process of self-discovery and self-acceptance. The protocols listed within that chapter may be useful at this point, with a focus on femaleness and her feminine features. Note that none of the following steps directly addresses a woman's external appearance. This will be dealt with in the following section.

Identify her current self-concept and beliefs about herself in terms of being a female/woman. If a woman cannot find words to articulate this, she might try to draw a picture of herself in comparison to other women. Some women will not be able to define themselves at all in terms of femaleness. They will have to begin with either a masculinized or an androgynous image. These initial images will begin to change as she slowly discovers aspects of femaleness or femininity that she can truly accept and embrace within herself.

Identify and challenge negative core beliefs about femaleness/women in general. These may include *Women are weak and powerless* and *Women are nothing more than refuse to be used and thrown away by men.* Many of my clients also believe that a woman cannot stand up for herself, that every woman is shallow, and that a woman will never experience life with the ease and notoriety afforded men. A woman's core beliefs about men are naturally intertwined with her understanding of women. It is interesting to observe how a woman's distorted definitions of male and female seem to complement or enhance the other, such as *Men can't survive without a woman,* and *Women will do anything to keep a man.*

Identify defining moments throughout her childhood that led her to dislike or re-ject her gender. Because we are not gender-neutral, most painful memories will be seen through the lens of our gender. A woman may have unconsciously thought, *When I was sexually abused, I was abused because I was a girl.*

Reprocess these defining memories, negative cognitions and arrested affec-tive inner states.

Accept that she has a body, accept she has a female body and accept all of the aspects and hormonal cycles related to a female body. McDougall (1980) quotes a woman, Sophie, who confesses that

> my body is repugnant to me, especially my breasts. Everything about me that is flabby is disgusting. I have always tried to have hard strong hands. My hands resemble my father's and help to cover up all that is moist or wrong with my body. (p. 111)

Sophie further explains that until she met Sarah, it felt like she had no body—only a head (p. 112). Many women with SSA are not healthily attached or connected to their physical body, let alone their female body parts. They often feel like an alien in their own skin. McDougall (1989) mentions another client who confesses that she does not possess her own female body, saying, "It's only through the body of another woman that I regain mine" (p. 217).

Many women are not able to discern when they are hungry, thirsty, tired or stressed or even when they need to go to the bathroom. Some women, when asked to scan their body for a visceral feeling or sensation, will not recognize any sensation. They are not only cut off from their emotions but also their bodies. They will require help to develop a pattern of listening to and integrat-ing with their bodies. Once a woman can connect, she might want to make lists of bodily sensations throughout a day, similar to how she would note her emotional states.

Touch, as discussed in chapter ten and provided by mentors, friends or therapeutic massage professionals, is another powerful medium to enable a woman to accept and connect with her body. Davis (1999) underscores that "the simple act of accepting someone for who they are in their body and caring for them physically through touch and massage can do wonders for a person's self-acceptance" (pp. 153-54). It is often only after a woman is able to accept and connect with her body that she can address possible body image issues or restructure her diet and overall treatment of her bodily self.

When a woman finally enters into the self-awareness of owning a body, she is more apt to recognize the fact that hers *is* a female body. I might suggest that, in the privacy of her home, she stand in front of a full-length mirror and look for any hint or indication that she is female. She is to report back to me with the results. At a later time, I suggest that she repeat the exercise with the added step of removing some of her clothing and continuing to observe and identify all that is female—including curves, bulges and body parts. I may instruct her to describe her body as she goes: for example, as she recognizes that she does indeed possess breasts, she would say aloud, "Yes, I have breasts." This second stage helps her process any negative reactions or emotions around her observations and then supports her efforts to eventually reach a place of acceptance, a point at which she could say, "Yes, I accept that I have breasts." In the final step, which is not quick in coming, she is coached to say, "I am thankful and glad that I have breasts." This last step depends on a genuine integration of the inherent value and blessing of her female body.

To assist in this latter level of integration, I have sometimes conducted an "initiation ritual" or ceremony for a client during which I speak affirmations and blessings over her femaleness and womanhood. I methodically name, describe and sanction each major aspect of her female body as a good and holy thing. For example, using deeply mystical and metaphorical language, I may communicate that as a woman she is blessed to have breasts. Her breasts are extremely special and are symbolic of her more mysterious capacity to offer rich and sweet sustenance to others out of the storehouses of her inner life. They provide a place of safety, rest and nurture. I light candles and play soft, beautiful music in the background. A woman might want to invite some of her closest friends to this special session, further integrating her into the broader world of women.

Share her story related to puberty. Ask her, "What was it like? Did your mother talk to you about periods, breasts or the facts of life?" I have had clients tell me that as adolescents they were completely caught off guard by the onset of menstruation. Many seriously believed they were dying. Some, because of severe mistrust of their mothers, suspected that their mothers were trying to kill them through poisoning. This time of their lives is often severely traumatizing and will contain voluminous material that will need to be discussed and processed.

The subject of puberty is, however, an excellent one to raise within a group setting. Since many of these women did not have same-sex peer groups or even close friends in early adolescence, they were deprived of the typical female camaraderie of discussing feminine cycles, which are simultaneously fascinating, frustrating and scary. As women realize there were others like them, often the shame and pain of their traumatic past is dissolved into laughter and further confession and storytelling. Essentially, the door to a very precious but heretofore internal silent dark room is flung wide open to the light of accepting others.

Distinguish between inherent and modeled (learned) similarities with her dad, her brother or other significant male figures. If a woman has identified with masculine role models, many of her behaviors, attitudes and even career choices may have arisen out of mimicking rather than out of reflection on her true self or gifting. A woman will need to sort through that which is true to her (such as a love for athletics, for example) and that which was assumed or developed (such as a masculinized style of clothing or appearance) as a means to fit in with the boys or be accepted by her dad. A woman may need to challenge her belief that she is just like her father and eventually find acceptable female role models.

A woman may also need to work through a disidentification or separation process with her father similar to what a boy has to do with his mom prior to entering into the world of men or identifying with his dad.[15] She must establish her autonomy and differentiation in terms of being female and a daughter rather than "daddy's little boy" or "daddy's best friend."

Break vows and challenge underlying fantasies about being male. The deeply seated conviction that she should have been a boy will not be quickly dismantled, but it can be whittled down as a woman reassesses the value of the feminine, heals her wounded heart, restores wholesome images of men and women, and seeks to align herself with her God-given, genetic feminine inheritance. If a woman has overidentified with the male sexual organ, it is important that she work toward curtailing wishful thinking or fantasizing about having sex with another woman as a man. These fantasizes, let alone sexual behaviors, will continue to block her self-acceptance as a woman.

Identify and curtail masculinized postures. This step does not require that she

---

[15]She may also need to work through the symptoms of emotional incest.

stop using hammers and screwdrivers or driving a truck. The masculine behaviors that block her development as a feminine being are behaviors or body postures that have internal meaning or are related to core affective states. For example, my clients have admitted that they "bow or bulk up" at times, especially when they sense danger or are experiencing a sexual attraction toward another woman. They literally tighten or flex their muscles (as one would in preparing for a physical altercation) and assume an aggressive body stance—leaning forward, spreading their legs, flaying their elbows and essentially hunkering down. They might purse their lips, squint and cock their heads. This, they say, gives them a sense of power and virility. It is my job to help them discover and embrace their truer *internal* feminine power to persevere the ups and downs of heart-to-heart connections instead of relying on mere external prowess. But until they make the switch, they may still rely on flexing muscles and a masculinized appearance to define and reassure themselves.

A woman may wear certain articles of clothing to invoke a butch-type emotionality and identity. For instance, a client may arrive to a session wearing a baseball cap pulled low over her eyes. Baseball caps are neutral items, but during these occasions, the cap accompanies an alter or masculine persona, as if the cap is used to warn others of her guarded, toughened or reserved affective state. (Or perhaps the cap was used to access this toughened affective state.) I view this type of externalizing as an acting out of her gender insecurity. In other words, I do not condemn or judge her behavior, but I do attempt to uncover the possible triggering emotions of fear, shame, loneliness or emptiness. As she connects with these emotions, she will naturally be more associated with and truer to her feminine soul.

Identify and confront internal hostile messages, judgments or labels about herself as a female or a woman. Many of her internalized voices are tied to actual statements spoken to her in the past, such as "You are so homely that you will never find a man," or "You would make a better boy than girl."

Identify and curtail minimizing or devaluing behaviors as they relate to her femaleness. These include refusing to take care of her body and health, begrudgingly buying new clothes or cursing herself each time she has a period.

Break all vows to disassociate with her femaleness. A woman with SSA probably told herself things like *I will never want to be a girl. I will never look like a girl. I will never let anyone treat me like my mom was treated. I will never get married or be a mom.* While a woman may *never* actually become a wife or mom, rehearsing these types of vows limits integration of the fullness of her *capacity as a feminine being*.

Develop a new inner construct of femaleness or femininity that is positive and desirable.[16]

Integrate and embrace (a valuing process) inner feminine attributes. I am very deliberate in listening for expressions of my client's feminine heart, such as her deep longing and vision for closeness or intimacy or her compassion for the weak or oppressed. I openly affirm her femaleness by making comments such as, "I love hearing your heart for relationship. You are *such a woman!*" I want to assign dignity and value to that which arises out of her innermost feminine being, not just to what she does. Those clients who have spent substantial time investing in their external roles will have to retrain themselves to look deeper to find the treasures of their inner feminine attributes.

Abandon the idealization of the feminine and the subtle (or not so subtle) arrogance of believing that women are better than men. Women with SSA often idolize and swoon over extremely idealized caricatures of "woman." Most of their female icons embody strength, sensual beauty and superior acumen when compared to men, such as Xena the warrior princess, Trinity in *The Matrix* or actress Angelina Jolie, known for playing Lara Croft in *Tomb Raider*. Ironically, as my clients admire these images of what they believe is pure female perfection, they negate and repress themselves even further, doubting they could ever measure up. This contemporary idol worship must eventually be exchanged for a deeply grounded sense of self-love.

Accept that she is a woman (not just a female or a girl, but a grown adult woman). When a client is engaged in inner-child work, the specific emphasis on her "little girl" lays the foundation for this later acceptance of womanhood. For a while, she may not feel old enough on the inside to be called a woman.

A large part of the process of dealing with my own misogyny was for me to be able to agree with God that being a woman was a good thing. It has taken me years to get to this point. First I started with, Okay, I am a girl,

---

[16]Literature that portrays rich and strong images of females—such as *The Secret Life of Bees* by Sue Monk Kidd (2002), *The Red Tent* by Anita Diamant (1997), *Jane Eyre* by Charlotte Brontë (2006) and *Anne of Green Gables* by L. M. Montgomery (1998)—may be useful in helping a woman regain a positive perspective of women and herself.

a woman. I am female. I can see that. But back then I still didn't like it.
Jordan

Confront patterns of defensive detachment with other women. The self-dismissing belief that she is not like other women will block a woman's ability to associate and identify with other women and her own femaleness. She may believe that she has nothing in common with dainty or beautiful women and, thus, nothing to offer or vice versa. In terms of helping a woman with her negative self-talk, I might suggest that she rehearse an internal script such as this: *I am a woman and I belong in the company of women. I'm no longer going to stand on the outside of the circle looking in. I am not excluded. I don't need to look just like the other women to fit in. I am special and unique in my feminine beauty. I also do not need to act or be just like the other women. I do not need to enjoy conversations about fingernail polish to gain a sense of belonging. I am an individual, and I bring unique interests and talents to share with other women. I am acceptable and valuable just the way I am. I choose to stop dispossessing myself of my identity as a woman and of my rightful place within womanhood.*

Select and develop a mentoring relationship or friendship with a few women who exhibit desirable qualities as women and who are comfortable with their femininity. My clients must eventually align themselves with other females more than with the males of their past and present. I offer myself as a model, but I also encourage them to identify several other women they admire.

Explore the broader world of average women with average lives. Because so many women with SSA have lacked the mirror of another woman, they often assume that other women automatically know how to put together a nice outfit, how to style their hair, how to be completely comfortable with their bodies and confident in their appearance, and know how to act in social gatherings with other women or men. Hearing that this is often not the case and that they are probably similar to most women is liberating news. A woman's need for supportive "real" women is further discussed in the following section.

ALLOWING HER FEMININITY TO BE SEEN FROM WITHOUT

Looking like a female does not usually substantially affect or reflect a woman's internal self-image or feminine identity. That is why I have learned to never assume a feminine-looking woman with SSA is more solid or further along in her work than she really is. On the contrary, many women who still carry a noticeably masculine look and gait are often women who have made incredible strides toward inner wholeness and integration. Dealing with a woman's external appearance is typically one of the last steps in her restoration process, and this step should only be taken if the woman truly desires to address her external appearance. This may not be essential for a woman's ongoing sense of femaleness. However, when a woman desires to "feel" more like a woman and seeks to align and identify with her inner feminine beauty and value, her external appearance can be a powerful symbolic means to arrive at her goal.

Initially, a woman may be uncertain about the extent to which she wants to alter or affirm her external styles and appearances to match her internal feminine self. She may again be flooded with a mixture of emotions including excitement, terror, residual shame, fear and insecurity, hope and delight. She may be asking herself, *Am I special or valuable enough to be treated as special or to look special?* She may experience a heightened ambivalence or resistance to external changes, unveiling a deep inner protest to accommodating what she believes to be rigid (such as pink or lacy clothes) or inappropriate (such as revealing clothing) social and cultural expectations for female beauty. Yet for most women, a growing desire to "take off" the old masculinized or androgynous styles and "put on" the new remains a driving force. But it is not so easy to determine the "new."

Here are additional suggestions for supporting a woman in her process of integrating an *external* feminine identity:

Gather the help and support of other women who are knowledgeable and sensitive to a woman's internal and external struggle with her femininity. If a woman has not been able to secure intimate friendships and supportive female mentors up until this point, it is absolutely imperative that she do so now. She will need guidance and protection during this very vulnerable process.

Mentoring and initiating her into the world of the feminine is important, *but it must be done slowly.* As she requests, she might be given tips on basic hygiene and self-care, shopping strategies, stores and clothing styles, clothing budgets, nature of fabrics and color coordination, hairstyles, hair salons, hair maintenance and hair products, body products, body treatments or undergarments. She should not be merely told about all of these products and services; she should be literally and sensitively escorted to a store or through a manicure, for instance, by her trusted friend.

It is not uncommon for a friend or mentor of a woman with SSA to get carried away in her excitement to help. If a woman becomes too overwhelmed or frightened by the foreign nature of these new things and places, she will necessarily retreat and defend against the very thing she needs to feel at home and comfortable with. Patience, once again, must be a directing virtue. In summary, it is more important that she be introduced and initiated into the broader subculture of women than that she embrace and use every technique for eyebrow shaping, for instance. She needs the opportunity to find her unique path within the general female milieu.

Slowly experiment with a variety of clothing and styles in order to determine her unique tastes and preferences. For a season, Rhonda was completely dependent on her church friends to help her shop, coordinate outfits and even get dressed. But during this time she grew in confidence. First, she switched from a backpack to a purse. Next she bought shoes with a little bit of a heel. She then added scarves and jewelry to her wardrobe. Eventually, Rhonda had other women asking *her* how to tie scarves or put an outfit together. After several years of experimenting and learning, Rhonda admitted, for the first time in her life, that she felt attractive. She also felt confident. She knew she could look good.

Most of the women with SSA that I know do not want to wear anything too fluffy, too pink or too stereotypically female. They often start with high-quality basic or sporty clothing. Bright colors may not feel safe; neither will apparel that feels too exposing.

> For my birthday a friend gave me my first pair of hoop earrings. I am 42 and have never owned hoop earrings. It took some getting used to, but they are small and not real shiny or bright. So after the initial shock, I did better. It only took 10 minutes to get them on the last time. The simple things in life that some people take for granted are major milestones for others.
>
> *Abby*

If a woman has a contemptuous reaction toward *everything* that appears feminine, then I suspect that there is still an underlying problem with core beliefs or gender acceptance. However, if a woman simply decides that she prefers a natural or sporty style to her appearance and therefore does not want to wear gold and rhinestones, then I affirm her preference and give her the freedom to look like herself.

Protect her from too much attention or affirmation for donning female attire. When some of these women were girls, they dressed exclusively as a tomboys. When they then attempted to dress like the other girls, kids laughed at them. Many now fear that they will be exposed and shamed once again. Cytron, whose dreams were discussed above, contemplated wearing female attire to work but concluded she and her coworkers weren't quite ready: "I know that my waking self could not cope with my own shock at such a transformation, much less the shock of those who have become so used to my particular brand of self-presentation" (Cytron & Malinowitz, 1999, p. 223).

I have had clients tell me that in public settings their friends have insensitively cackled, "Ooooh, look at Susan. She's wearing a skirt. Can you believe it? She's in a skirt!" Again, this type of acknowledgment will humiliate a woman who is already extremely self-conscious in a skirt. Further, this mocking and teasing will come at the very moment when she has dared to step into the innocence of her tender little-girl, desirous of reinstigating her own growth process as a feminine being.

However, when my client arrives to a session wearing a new outfit or having curled her hair, it would be a mistake for me to not notice or not mention her pleasing appearance. Yet if I pay too much attention, I might leave her feeling awkward and incredibly exposed. So I attempt to offer very quick and simple affirmations, looking into her eyes (versus scanning her body), saying, "You look very nice today. Your hair looks beautiful curled that way" or just "Hello. You look very nice today." I smile and wait for a reply, and if there is none, I immediately proceed as usual. A pregnant silence at this point is not beneficial. If she is unable to respond, I might bring up this exchange during the next session to explore her feelings and possible fears, but I do so very gently; her confidence at this point is extremely fragile.

As a woman continues to appropriate and integrate her full feminine self, she may also want to consider changing jobs, careers, vehicles or even living situations. I allow her to initiate all conversations in this regard and to process in a way that gives her complete freedom to either defer or instigate a change.

TESTIMONIES OF HOPE

Like all the other processes described herein, the process of finding herself as a woman will continue throughout a woman's life. I have been amazed as I've witnessed among my clients and other women whom I have known some of the most profound transformation that I have ever seen within a human being. Having journeyed a lengthy road of healing and growth, some of these women are now in positions of leadership, speaking to groups of women on healing and restoring the feminine soul. Some have discovered that they have special giftings in fashion and design. Others have recognized and stepped out in the power of the mother's heart inside them, volunteering to work with children or serving as surrogate step-moms or aunts to their friends' kids. They often develop a deep sense of common purpose with others concerned with women's issues, often participating in international efforts to stop oppression and subjugation.

These women are a living testimony to the depth of redemption that is available to any broken, confused or wounded soul.

CHAPTER THIRTEEN

Venturing Out
The World of Men and Closure

Psychotherapy is not a substitute for life
but a dress rehearsal for life.
In other words, though psychotherapy requires
a close relationship, the relationship is not an end—
it is a means to an end.

IRVIN YALOM, *THE GIFT OF THERAPY*

FOURTH STAGE OF THERAPY: CONSOLIDATION AND MATURITY

As a woman continues her journey, she may want to consolidate her newfound identities and relational capacities around a new understanding and appreciation of men. Joining a therapy group[1] or working with a male therapist[2] can be beneficial in this stage of a woman's process. Ultimately, however, a woman will need to establish herself within a safe, unconditionally accepting and loving community of both men and women that can bridge the progress a woman makes in individual therapy and the consolidation that needs to occur within a broader context of relationships. Once a woman is settled within these communities, she may no longer require the support of a professional therapist. The end of therapy, though, does not mean the end of a woman's journey. Now solid and confident, a woman can launch herself into new beginnings and life-long dreams.

---

[1]For more information on group therapy with women with SSA, see appendix A.
[2]For more information on male therapists and women with SSA, see appendix B.

EXPLORING THE "OTHER" SEX

Before I turn my attention to my clients' common issues and struggles pertaining to men, I want to say that I believe that every woman who has commenced a journey of growth and has determinedly pressed into the concerns and topics previously addressed in this book deserves a medal of honor. Truly, few other people would make such a sacrifice of time, energy and money to grow or change even a small aspect of their lives. These women display immeasurable integrity and tenacity. They are an inspiration and a statement of God's grace and endless compassion—even if they never expereince the world of romance with a man.

Dating or marrying a man is *not* their ultimate prize of victory. Jeannette Howard (2005), in her book *Into the Promised Land,* eloquently pronounces that the "reward for a faithful walk away from homosexuality is not marriage and children, unambiguous heterosexuality or even a powerful life of ministry. *Our reward is resting in God's perfect plan for our life* [italics added]" (p. 17). I couldn't agree more. While Elaine Siegel (1988) claims that many of her clients experienced the "psychological birth of [their] full womanhood" (p. 15), she also admits that some women, even after years of work, insight and growth, never fully eradicated "the scars life had inflicted" (p. 15). They were not able to enter into heterosexual relating. Yet even these women deserve our admiration and applause. *Never* should one of these women be shamed for not being able to date or romantically relate to a man. But for those who desire to explore the world of heterosexual relating, I offer my wholehearted support. However, many issues may still need to be addressed.

ARE MEN REALLY NECESSARY?

A woman with SSA is likely in an unconscious cycle of disqualifying, misunderstanding or avoiding *emotional* closeness with males; she restricts her opportunities to genuinely know the true heart or soul of a good man. Existing relationships with men in her life may be primarily based on intellect, activity (performance) or pretense.[3]

Once a woman discovers the warmth and gentleness of a relationship with

---

[3]It is important to understand that even a woman of faith who struggles with unwanted SSA and who has committed herself to the therapeutic process may wrestle with or be uncomfortable with the concept of God being male. She may transfer her negative feelings and experiences with men onto her relationship with God.

a female, men may appear even more irrelevant or unnecessary. She knows women and is comfortable with them. She may relive the pattern established when she was a little girl, unconsciously looking exclusively to her mom (or females) to meet the many needs that were not perceptively being acknowledged or adequately met by her dad (or males). She may no longer notice men's social cuing (if she ever did). She may unknowingly develop a defensive posture *(I am not available)* or a deliberate cold stance with men in general. Men remain an unknown, undesirable and unavailable commodity.

> *Most of my life men were like furniture. They were just there. I didn't know how to relate to them. I didn't hate them, but I just felt they were another species.*
> *Margaret*

She may come to believe that if she can't have a woman, then she will have no one. Her deepest fear is not being loved or being alone for the rest of her life. She cannot bear the thought of the aloneness, especially in light of her legitimate and ongoing intimacy needs. It is this fear that often sends a woman back into another woman's comforting embrace, unintentionally validating her SSA while invalidating men and her heterosexual potentiality.

This may be one of the hardest cycles to break. Many of my clients are well beyond becoming emotionally enmeshed with another woman, but they still find themselves facing temptation because of the normal cycles of reflective loneliness as single women. They are in what many describe as a plateau or neutral zone. They are not attracted, so to speak, to either sex. And to the extent that their ability to ever relate to men remains curtailed, they will indeed be vulnerable. This is where supportive communities and surrogate families can have a lasting impact on women in conflict with SSA.

OPENING UP TO THE POSSIBILITIES

Unsurprisingly, in order to assume an accepting and open posture toward men, a woman will need to be supported by safe and caring men *and* women as she

- identifies and challenges her negative beliefs and internalized images of men
- identifies and challenges her negative beliefs about sexuality

- explores and reprocesses historic material that fuels her beliefs and negative emotional reactions toward men and sexuality
- confesses and resolves her self-destructive attitudes and feelings toward men (e.g., hatred, bitterness, disgust)
- curtails her dismissive or distancing behaviors toward men (in thought, word, or deed)
- forgives men[4]
- breaks vows and promises to never get close to a man
- gains a broader understanding of wholesome masculinity
- accepts the reality and value of men
- grieves her real losses as they pertain to dad, brothers or men in general
- presses into her shame and fear surrounding sexuality
- opens herself to experiential healing opportunities with men
- builds trust

> *The thing that changed my mind most about men was finally meeting some healthy guys who had been taught how to respect a woman. I also developed some friendships with married people whose relationships were pretty healthy. I watched how a good man treats his wife and kids. For years, I got to see men in action who were different, a lot different, from what I had perceived men to be.*
> *Shari*

IS IT WORTH ALL THIS PAIN?

In addition to finding many of the above tasks difficult, a woman may be further blocked or confused in her process with men due to the following:

An ongoing primary need to repair and build a healthy relationship with self and other females. For example, it may take years for many women associated with profile 1 (see chapter 8) to establish and stabilize their core self and healthy relational patterns in general. They should never be rushed or pressured through these primal processes or prematurely directed to examine their issues with men.

---

[4]It is very powerful for these women to actually hear a man confess, on behalf of the men in her past, the sins and violations against her and to ask for her forgiveness. Experiential moments of healing will have the greatest impact on her heart and life.

Delayed sexual development. Many women associated with profile 1 or 2 are often delayed in their sexual development. They must continue to progress in their feminine gender identification so that they can experience and pass through the "boys have cooties" stage. This normal developmental stage, albeit difficult to identify, should not be misconstrued as a woman's hardness or refusal to deal with a fear or hatred of men. Developmentally, she is not yet an adolescent, and so she should not be expected to swoon over the opposite sex. Because of these subtle nuances in a woman's process and the heightened danger of misintrepretation, I remain committed to a nonjudgmental stance throughout this step in therapy.

Unresolved childhood sexual abuse and trauma, incest or adolescent rape. As well as dealing with trauma memories, a woman with SSA may have to challenge the platonic feelings that seem to surface whenever she does pursue closeness with a man, blocking any possible romantic or sensualized feelings. This may be a consequence of her "friendship" with her father or her history of primarily relating with boys as brothers as a young girl.

Faulty beliefs around sex or sexuality. Some girls are raised to fear boys because of the possibility of getting pregnant. Others are informed by their mothers that as women they too will have to learn how to endure sex with their future husband. Parents who are not comfortable with their own sexuality may inadvertently shame their daughter's blossoming sexuality through their own peevishness, embarrassment or avoidance.

Disappointment in current marriage. In addition to overcoming past negative experiences with males, many of my married clients face the challenge of ongoing unhappiness, difficulty and unhealthy relational patterns with their husbands, entrenching their general disillusionment with men.

Fear and pain surrounding a deep longing to be in relationship with a good man. One night in group, a woman shared about a new relationship with a very amazing man. She was both apprehensive and excited as she spoke. I noticed that another group member became very quiet as she listened. Her face reflected her pain. I turned my attention to her and asked what was going on. She could only look down and shake her head in unbelief. I remained patient but coached her to share. She teared up. When she finally spoke, she shared her deep pain over the realization that there are indeed some decent men out there. In agony she implored, "Why haven't they been in my life?"

Lack of experience of emotional closeness with men. Not all women with SSA hate men. Tragically, some have never had even a single opportunity to connect with a man on any meaningful level whatsoever. They simply have no idea where to begin. And short of a man's taking the time to invite her into a friendship, she will probably remain in her isolation.

Arrogance and overriding contempt of men. For some women, especially those associated with profiles 2 and 4, the failure to humbly assess the significance or value of the opposite sex stems not from their negative core beliefs about men but rather from their narcissistic beliefs about themselves. As long as they assume that women are entirely self-sufficient and perhaps the superior gender, there is no logical reason to bother with the pettiness of knowing or needing a man.

Hopelessness or depression. Many women with SSA struggle with chronic depression or episodic major depression. Throughout therapy, they may also cycle in and out of grief. I try to remain sensitive to the times that my clients need a break from threatening therapeutic processes such as dealing with issues related to men.

Exhaustion with the recovery process. Need I say more? Moberly (1983) defines heterosexuality as the "fulfillment of certain psychological needs, and not just a potential for sexual activity." It is the capacity for relating to people "as a psychologically complete member of one's own sex" (p. 22). It does not necessitate sexual involvement with the opposite sex. I quote this in support of the many women who reach a point in therapy where they feel confident and content with offering their singleness to God, knowing that they are more available to God as single women than they would if they were married. They are not content with the thought of spending several more years in therapy, attempting to uncover every possible issue yet uncovered, for the bleak possibility of entering into a relationship with a man. They instead need overt affirmation of their value and ongoing encouragement as a single woman.

> *Some of the women I've known who have come out of lesbianism were married within three years. Here I am going on 11 years out. I am really tempted to ask myself, What's wrong with me? Do men not see me as attractive? Am I not healed? But then I remember all that God has done and how much I have changed and grown. Reverting back into those old questions is not a good place for me to be. I also remind myself that he is in control of my life. Much of life is not up to any of us. I don't have the power*

to make things happen like I used to believe I did. Not having a husband
is no indication of my lacking beauty, femininity or an open heart.

Kris

A NEW HORIZON: DATING AND MARRIAGE

I wholeheartedly support those women who do desire marriage and a family and therefore choose to exert more energy and effort in an attempt to resolve all outstanding issues related to intimacy with men. They will need several close female and possibly male mentors with whom to ask questions (How do I know if he likes me? How should I act?), get reality checks (Is this normal? Is he normal?) and discuss their reactions or concerns.

Generally, a woman who has struggled with SSA will not necessarily be sexually attracted to every man that comes along. If she begins to date or marry, it is because she is interested in *one* man.[5] And that is all that is required. After she identifies this one special man, she will first want to get to know him as a friend only. My clients tell me that they need to know a man's heart and begin to feel comfortable interacting with him.

Once a sense of mutual affection and trust is established, a woman may feel ready for the next step: offering greater levels of vulnerability and commitment. If he shows physical affection too quickly, especially before discussing it with her, he may lose his chance. She must be reassured that he loves her for who she is and not what she can give, especially in the sexual realm. Dating opens up an entirely new process for these women and may revive old issues such as those surrounding trust, fear or shame. I recommend that her male friend also seek personal counseling if he has not already done so, find wise mentors and move slowly and patiently in the relationship. Many fear that a man will not have the patience for this type of relationship building. But often many do. I have been amazed at the quality of men who have fallen in love with and married women who have faced the many struggles described in this book.

"BUT THEY ARE SO DIFFERENT!"

The most common complaint I hear from my clients as they seek to relate with men is their extreme difficulty *sensing* an emotional connection. These women—like many women *without* SSA—testify to the pleasure of friend-

---

[5]For more information on dating, marriage and parenting, see Paulk (2003).

ships in which two women can "read each other's minds" or in which they "get" what the other woman is feeling, saying or experiencing without even speaking. It can be frustrating to realize that although emotional connection is certainly available with men, it looks and feels different. Furthermore, to *have* a relationship with a man, he must necessarily *be* or act and behave like a man—not a former female lover.

> *When I started dating Steve, I had only been with women. I really had no clue about men or being with a man. I remember the first time we kissed there was something poking my leg. I thought it was his keys. I didn't know any of that! I was just totally shocked about it all. His kissing was a lot more aggressive and he had facial hair. He felt different. He wasn't soft. That was something I had to work through, but I loved touching his strong arms, feeling his strength.*
> *Nicole*

This new journey becomes something akin to a crosscultural experience as these women navigate heterosexual relating and what they might call men's quirks. It will not be easy for some. After experiencing one "bad date," a woman may be tempted to believe that she could never be happy with a man, resigning herself to the belief that she will be lonely for the rest of her life. Other women might find themselves constantly comparing men to women, only to discover that men still pale in comparison. Should a woman want to continue on this journey, she will need ongoing support and encouragement to do so. But if she has done the deeper work of maturing and solidifying so that she can cope with the ups and downs of intimate relationships, then she has just as good of a chance as other women, if not better, to grow old as a wife, mother and grandmother, assuming an available good man enters her world.

SINGLE OR MARRIED: ONWARD THEY GROW

I have heard it said that an unhealthy soul is one that is bent downward and inward, energized by miserliness and greed, confused in its attempts to resolve and fill the emptiness within. Sadly, many people remain trapped in this posture throughout their lives. In contrast, a healthy soul is one facing upward and outward, energized by generosity and openness, living out of a sense of fullness and continuous infilling. This latter picture is how I see many of my clients at this stage of therapy. No longer shrouded in shame, they rise and confidently take their place at the banqueting table of life.

As a woman progresses through these developmental stages

- attachment and formation
- self-awareness
- self-differentiation and individuation
- self-empowerment and transformation
- self-acceptance and integration (which necessarily includes the work of healing, grieving and rebuilding)
- self-solidification and consolidation

she will mature in her expressions and experience of

- self-disclosure, leading to authentic relating and deep intimacy
- self-sacrifice, resulting in a sense of personal meaning
- self-fulfillment

A woman is exhibiting a consolidated self when she proclaims to herself, *I know who I am and who I am not. I know what I feel, what I want, what I desire, what I like and why I do some of the things I do. I know my talents and strengths, weaknesses and limits. I can distinguish another's feelings, thoughts and likes or dislikes from my own. I can respect another person's differences.* Expanding her identity to include dimensions other than her sexual preference,[6] she will naturally continue to grow in health and intimacy as she negotiates an increasing number of variegated relationships.

As a woman approaches this phase, she may be filled with excitement and anticipation. Not only is it time for her new life to be celebrated (hopefully her friends will help her celebrate throughout her long journey), but it is also time for her to take hold of life and her adulthood—whether single or married. She might want to pursue unfulfilled dreams such as educational or career aspirations, revamp her living arrangements or start a new hobby. Ultimately, it is important that she exercise the freedom to follow her unique interests or call and purpose in life.

Moving on may also mean terminating with her counselor or emancipating herself from the center of others' accountability or support. It is now time for her to become the person who offers accountability and support. She will have

---

[6]On sexual identity reconstruction, see Ponticelli (1999).

much to give. Naturally, she may feel a sense of loss or perhaps fear and doubt mixed in with her expectancy and hope. Launching herself does not mean that she will be without struggles.

> *I feel better not being so emotionally enmeshed. I don't throw myself at people. I definitely don't talk to them six times a day—maybe only once every other day. However, I know I can't be naive and think there won't be temptation. I met someone recently. She was so open and honest. My heart broke for her as she shared about her abuse. I so wanted to comfort her and be that nurturer. That's why I need to be very careful. It still feels so good to be needed.*
>
> *Karen*

As a self-aware and healthy woman, she will most certainly continue to recognize additional areas of her life that need more healing and growth, but she will have the core strength to be able to face the reality that neither she nor life is perfect. Before reaching this stage, most women will have established certain disciplines within their daily routines related to self-care, reflective processing (including quiet times for meditation or journaling) and protocols for ·handling temptation or difficult situations. She will have also established a sense of her own power and responsibility for the direction of her life.

For instance, one day Shari decided to read the entire Bible and mark everything that God said he would do and everything that she needed to do. She explained, "If something falls within my realm of responsibility, then I can't expect God to magically take it away or make something else happen. I need to step up to the plate and make the choices that *I* am supposed to make."

A woman often finds great comfort in knowing she can methodically, rather than fearfully, address a surfacing same-sex attraction, for example.[7] She might follow a brief protocol such as this:

1. Honestly admit what she is feeling and own her temptation and thoughts.

2. Ask herself what she really wants or needs *on a deep level* and remind herself that, for instance, getting special attention from another woman is not going to

---

[7]For more suggestions in specifically managing same-sex attractions, especially for women of faith who do not experience a complete change in their sexual orientation but remain committed to sexual purity, see Yarhouse & Burkett (2003) and Howard (2005).

resolve the anxiety she feels because of a disagreement with a work associate.

3. Accept the reality that she still has needs. She can talk to God about her needs and show herself compassion.

4. Explore whether this is a need that she can meet for herself or whether she needs to involve supportive others.

5. Uncover any negative beliefs or thought patterns that may be driving her in unhealthy directions. She might ask herself, *Are there any underlying fears or disturbing emotions that I have neglected?*

6. Remind herself of certain truths about life, self, God and others, such as *Life does not always feel good. I do not always have to feel good. I can make it with God's help.*

I am thrilled when a client begins to use our counseling hour as a time to report her discoveries and commitments made as a result of going through a process such as the one just described. I know that our season together is drawing to a close.

A woman at this point has usually discovered that she has a *choice* in the type of pain she endures: she can choose the pain of caving into old habits or self-destructive patterns or the pain of foregoing immediate gratification for the sake of long-term growth or obedience to God. Maturity is about understanding that life cannot progress without some sort of pain.

SAYING GOODBYE

Terminating therapy is a mixed blessing. Even though I practice firm professional boundaries, my clients and I experience a heartfelt and authentic relationship within the therapeutic setting; they have been a part of my personal journey perhaps as much as I have been a part of theirs. I care about them and will continue to care about them even after we end our professional relationship.

By the time we reach formal closure, a client has usually already explored the possibility of becoming my friend outside therapy. I am honored by her request, but I am also very honest about my busy schedule and full life. While I cannot offer ongoing relationships to my clients, I do leave the door open in terms of periodic future correspondence or phone calls. I do not believe that it is in my client's best interest to offer her a nurturing environment for several years and then abruptly cut her off by refusing any further contact.

Janine Puls has pointed out to me that "as kids, we would never want to leave home if we knew we could never come back. As long as there is a sense that we have a home and a place to which we can return, we have freedom to leave and build our own life." Upon termination, she reassures her clients that, barring an unforeseen accident or disaster, she intends to remain in the city in which she currently lives and would, from time to time, love to hear from them. This gives her clients a grounding point of the home that they established with her.

In offering this sort of grounding point, I clearly communicate and discuss all criteria for and expectations of any future contact with each client. A woman should never be left guessing or stressing over what is appropriate or inappropriate. If a former client is *not* able to handle or appropriately understand the nature of informal periodic contact, then this type of contact should *not* be considered or continued. I want to protect our professional relationship even if we are not regularly engaged in therapy. Many of my clients seek additional assistance years after an initial termination. Again, I keep my client's best interest in mind when negotiating termination sequences.

It often takes months to process and prepare for bringing therapy to a close. I believe that goodbyes with these women are as important and meaningful as hellos. I want my clients to integrate the reality that most relationships are transient. Whereas some last for decades, others last for a short season. But both are important. Obviously, some relationships are easier to let go of than others. I believe it is appropriate to honor all relationships that have been deeply meaningful or significant by celebrating the relationship and the other person in some act of heartfelt closure or ritual.

A woman may experience separation anxiety at the first discussion of closure. She will need time to stabilize and regain a sense of enduring *emotional* connection with me in spite of our impending physical distance. I encourage her to be intentional throughout the season of closure. Across several sessions, she and I will both share our reflections and observations of how she has changed. We may want to discuss the high points and the low points or the most meaningful seasons. I want her to feel honored as I reflect on my memories, and I want her to further integrate her warm experiences by sharing her own. As a woman who has played an extremely important role in her life, I often bestow a small token gift such as a small jewelry box or piece of jewelry as a memorial to our time together or as a reminder of my ongoing care and emotional support.

And if I'm lucky, six months or a year down the road, I will be blessed in return by receiving a treasured note such as this:

> I just wanted to send you a quick note to let you know that I spoke with my parents last week. It went really well. I felt that God was pressing on my heart to not be such a kid but to behave like an adult and ask for forgiveness and take some ownership in some of my choices. So since you have been a vital part of my life, I wanted to share with you yet another testimony of his faithfulness—all just to say thank you many times over for being one of a few during a very difficult time to show me devotion, consistency and unconditional love. As a professional counselor, you know your stuff. As a godly woman who exercised strength, love, gentleness and godly wisdom, you penetrated a heart that had died. May you be blessed!

Epilogue

In the Bible we learn that David was a man after God's own heart and that because of his love, he wanted to build a permanent home for God's presence. God thanked David for his concern but reassured him that he didn't need a permanent home, at least not at that time. God was fine moving from place to place. However, God informed David that it *was* time for David and God's special people, Israel, to stop moving from place to place. God promised to provide a safe place for his people and to plant them there so that they could have a *home of their own* (2 Sam 7:10).

I believe this is the same promise that God extends to each woman with whom we work. He does not expect her to first carve out a place for him. He wants to carve out a place for her, so that one day, she can rest and proclaim, *I am home.* And surprisingly, she will find that he is fully present there.

David's son Solomon did finally build a home for God. There are many parallels between how Solomon's people built this house, or temple, and how God constructs and prepares an inner home within a woman's soul. First, the construction of the temple could not begin until there was peace and rest in the land. The wars had to stop. The temple could not be built if the workers were still holding onto their weapons for defense. They needed to work in a safe environment, grounded in a sense of trust that it was all right to lay down their weapons and pick up their tools. This cetainly made them vulnerable.

Similarly, a woman with SSA will not be able to commence the deep inner work of repairing or building her inner home without having first established a place of trust and safety with a therapist. She also needs to drop her defenses so that she can put her hands to the task of healing, repair and growth. This step may be as important as the actual construction itself.

God gave very meticulous instructions about the temple's design and decor. It was to be stunningly beautiful, made of the finest wood and stone and precious metals. The smallest detail mattered. Skilled craftsmen were recruited and the people of Israel committed themselves to support the building project in any way they could. The workers labored for seven years to complete the temple and all its inner furnishings. It was a lavish work of art.

In the same way, the process of building and rebuilding of a woman's inner dwelling place is so special and important that it is worth every expense of time, skill and loving care. And indeed, for a woman to journey through all the stages of healing, growth and change, she must have the help and support of a caring and skilled community. She cannot do it alone. The skill required is not clinical or technical training as much as an artful ability to see and affirm a woman's unique and inner beauty—to hear her special melody. God has placed an exceptional song within her and has designed every detail of her being. We are to discover the distinctive design of her individual blueprints.

God was neither impatient nor disappointed with the time it took to complete and dedicate the temple, nor is God impatient or disappointed with the amount of time it may take for a woman to finally settle into her new home. Like the temple that is to house the very presence of our living and eternal God, she is to be filled with her own very valuable and glorious self, created in the image of the one who loves her and chooses to dwell with and inside her for eternity.

Appendix A

Group Therapy

GROUPS PROVIDE CORRECTIVE EXPERIENCES

A professionally facilitated therapy group will give a woman the chance to discover she is not alone in her journey.[1] Surrounded by others of like mind and heart, she may feel safe to take new risks in connecting with her self and others. She can learn and practice new communication skills and relational behaviors; integrate and consolidate her private and public self within relationship; grow in trust, empathy and mutuality; and find mirroring support, validation, accountability, camaraderie and love.

As in individual work with women with SSA, in the group setting I am always weaving in and out of an experiential here-and-now process.[2] In "process groups" such as mine, we primarily focus on what is happening in the room in the present moment rather than on outside stories or even the actual content of a discussion. Here-and-now process or asking "What are you feeling or sensing right now?" encourages women to remain connected to their bodies and emotions. Asking, "What are you noticing about the woman on your right? On your left?" encourages women to be aware of others. Process groups invite authenticity and intimacy.

Yalom (2002) stresses that "we learn best about ourselves and our behavior through personal participation in interaction combined with observation and analysis of that interaction" (p. 63). He goes on to say that "effective therapy consists of an alternating sequence: *evocation and experiencing* of affect followed by *analysis and integration* of affect" (p. 71). This alternating sequence

---

[1] For a review of the historic literature on group therapy with homosexual strugglers, see Rogers, Roback, McKee & Calhoun (1976).

[2] Corey, Corey, Callanan & Russell (2004) is an indispensable guide to structuring and managing process groups.

becomes the heartbeat of my therapy groups. Interactions and even evocation of affect come natural to most group settings. But as mentioned in chapter nine, many women with SSA have difficulty assigning meaning to what are often warm memorable moments and have even more trouble integrating the actual warmth and love being offered by others in the moment. When a woman seems to be missing out on these warm moments in group, I invite her to reflect on the interaction she just had (or is still having). For this type of reflection, group members need to objectify their experience for the purposes of integrating it as a potentially corrective experience.

REVISITING RESPECT AND TRUST

To engage a group on this level of vulnerability and process, the atmosphere of the group must be one of mutual respect and trust. This does not mean that group members must always show respectful and trusting behaviors. It means that *I* must consistently exhibit respect for each woman, no matter where she is at in her process or how she initially behaves. I must also create enough of a sense of safety that each woman will be able to *trust* in *my* ability to care for her and to facilitate and manage the group. For example, I must be able to protect a "victim" without slaying the "perpetrator." I must be comfortable with discomfort and thick tension. I must not be compelled to fix conflict or require that all the loose ends be neatly tied up. I need to allow these women to process their experiences of unresolved tension or unsettled issues within the group according to their time frame and ability. My mannerisms and therapeutic attitude are what will set the mood for my groups.[3]

During a group's opening stage, a woman may not be able to make eye contact with anyone other than me. For a time, I allow her to use me as a home base as much as she needs. However, this pattern will eventually disrupt her ability to connect with others in the room. When I determine that she is ready, I begin to casually break eye contact (especially when she is speaking), more or less forcing her to find at least one other group member with whom she feels

---

[3]Gershman (1975) agrees that it is the therapist that establishes the atmosphere within a group setting. He therefore warns that if a therapist does not have compassion and perceptivity about the kinds of problems common to many women with SSA, he or she should not be in this line of work. He shares, "The mood I try to create in my group relates to my feeling of openness, compassion, and honesty in trying to understand the people in the group. There is an atmosphere of acceptance toward every member of the group. . . . The group atmosphere must also be an atmosphere of positive possibilities" (p. 307).

safe. Exercises requiring eye contact among group members (or role-playing no eye contact) are extremely valuable.

GROUPS ARE A MICROCOSM AND INTENSIFY RELATIONAL ISSUES

Group settings tend to re-create a woman's past or present worlds. For instance, within the first month or so of a new group, one brave woman usually steps forward and begins to admit her jealousy of the other group members. She had always thought that she was my special client, but now she can clearly see that I have many special clients (children). She had never considered the possibility of needing to share her "mom" or of having to contend with "siblings." Most of the other group members happily chime in, admitting that they thought and felt the same way. Almost immediately, the symptoms of jealousy and sibling rivalry are dispelled.

What makes most process groups so powerful, then, is that in the midst of a woman's sense that this group is her "family," group members' responses are typically *not at all* like her dreaded family members'; in fact, they tend to be slanted toward the positive rather than the negative. For example, when one of the women is insecure and unsure whether she fits into the group, I'll ask the other members to share how they view her and to respond to her concern about fitting in. Of course, the insecure woman becomes almost paralyzed with the fear of what she thinks she is about to hear. But as she listens, she begins to relax under the group's kind and insightful words. She may cry as she admits that no one has *ever* shared such affirming and encouraging sentiments. Even when the group members confront one of its own, it is usually done from an affirming stance, with members asking a woman, for instance, "Why are you so quiet? We want to hear from you. We care about you and want to know what is going on. You matter to us."

GROUP STRUCTURE

In my experience, groups work best when they have a maximum of eight members and when they meet for two hours. I have also found that the best groups have mixed membership. When placed with women who do not struggle with SSA, women with SSA have the chance to identify with and gain a sense of belonging in the broader context of womanhood. This seems to far outweigh the benefits of forming a group around a single focus such as SSA or emotional dependency. In fact, a more homogeneous group of this nature tends to become psychoeducational and often weighed down with unhealthy relational patterns.

Requirements and Expectations of Group Members

Over the years, I have discovered that these criteria are beneficial for recruiting appropriate group members.

Members must be receiving individual therapy. While I prefer to be the primary therapist for my group members, I will accept a woman who is not my client if she provides a written release for me to speak to her individual therapist as I deem necessary. Further, each potential group member must have adequate ego strength to handle the exposure and pressures of a group experience and must be able to self-regulate and manage anxiety.

Members respect confidentiality. I insist on strict confidentiality that includes all group members' names, identifying information and personal stories.

Members make a twelve-week commitment. Every twelve weeks, women may enter or exit the group. Initially, most women will be unable to commit to anything more than twelve weeks. The group itself is *perpetual,* so a woman can remain for up to two or more years. Two years is the average length of stay.

Members are punctual and attend consistently. If a woman is unable to attend, she must call me in advance. Group members will worry about an unannounced absence, fearing the worst for the missing woman or fearing their own abandonment.

Members are honest about their personal process. This may mean that the most a woman can process is that she is unable to participate in the process. *Being* is emphasized over *doing.* In other words, completing a group task is not as important as articulating her inner experience.

Members do not have contact outside of the group setting. The only permissible contact is either prearranged to include the entire group or is in the context of a dire emergency. This rule is repeatedly analyzed, challenged and objected to by group members, but given my experience with exceptions to this rule, I no longer budge on this criterion. When a woman believes that she has been excluded from an "outside" get together or when she begins to be sexually attracted to the woman from group with whom she just had coffee, for example, an otherwise safe and working group can deteriorate into subversive jealousies, dissension, clandestine meetings and destructive suspicions. To further protect against these types of counterproductive effects, any individual contact made outside of group must be reported to and processed by the entire group.

Members follow a consistent weekly agenda. I want to provide group members with a predictable enough environment that they can weather the unpredictability of relationships within the environment. Following are common features of my standardized agenda:

- *Processing last week's absences.* This is extremely powerful for women who have never realized their own value or impact on others. It is important for them to hear how they were missed and what they missed so they can maintain an overall sense of attachment and belonging.

- *Sharing thoughts, feelings, reflections and reactions from last week.* This encourages women to process their group experiences throughout the week rather than disconnecting from or avoiding such processing. It also secures a sense of continuity and ongoing connection.

- *Following up on any difficult or significant interaction.* If a group discussion was left pending, now is the time to continue reflection and processing.

- *Presenting psychoeducational material or topic for discussion.* I always come prepared with a discussion topic, but I neither force this part of my agenda nor cling to it if a deeper process is arising organically within the group. The following topics are beneficial for mixed groups of women: safety, trust, life stories, sexual abuse, puberty, masturbation, communication skills, defense mechanisms, false selves, negative self-talk, femininity, self-image, relationship building, codependency, emotional dependency, boundaries, sexual attractions and "falls," and men.

- *Conducting formalized closure.* I give group members time to reflect on their experiences across the evening, to identify things that still need to be said, or to share their final thoughts and feelings as they leave.

- *Formally exiting the group.* Whenever a woman terminates her group involvement (at the end of a twelve-week session), significant time—often up to two full groups—and effort are spent processing her impending departure. It is possible that the group has become the closest thing to a family that she has ever had. Group members celebrate her involvement by sharing their special memories of her, observations on how she has grown or reflections of what her presence has meant to them. She is also given time to share her memories, including her most positive and negative experiences, what she has learned, or her observations of other group members. The group discusses guidelines for future contact, and members are reminded that their present participation in the group does not obligate them to entertain future friendships. Tearful members exchange formal goodbyes and token gifts or written cards and express their hopes for a wonderful future.

Ultimately, a group's success is related to the therapist's ability to be creative and sensitive as he or she enters into the dance of a real human encounter with their clients.

Appendix B
Male Therapists

Just as groups can pave the way for a woman to confidently enter other safe and healing communities, so too can male therapists offer a way for a woman to consider building relationships with trustworthy men. In general, male therapists, clergy, friends and relatives can have a tremendously positive influence on women with SSA.[4] Many women can progress through multiple stages of therapy with the support and guidance of a sensitive male counselor.

In preparation for this book I separately interviewed two male therapists, Eddie Traughber, a licensed marriage and family therapist and private practitioner who offers individual and group therapy to men and women with SSA, and James B. Lewis, a licensed clinical social worker, former clinician with Latter Day Saints Family Services, private practitioner and support-group leader for Evergreen International. Lewis has also worked with men and women with SSA in both an individual and a group setting. Both Traughber and Lewis had worked with men with SSA for several years prior to working with women, and both initially started working with women in a therapeutic group setting.

When I opened the interviews, I asked each of them what was it like when they first started working with women with SSA. They both quickly replied, "Different!" Traughber further explained that when he started facilitating women's groups, he met with a lot of skepticism and sometimes even overt hostility. They contemptuously asked, "What are you doing here?" "At the beginning I chose to have a very respectful attitude toward them. I didn't walk in and presume to know everything that was going on. I went in and did a lot

---

[4]Siegel (1988) agrees that male therapists can effectively work with women with SSA: "They appear to have little difficulty projecting paternal transferences onto a female analyst or maternal transferences onto a male analyst" (p. 204).

of listening," he said. He added that he never made *any* overture to initiate physical contact: "I made appropriate eye contact and never joked inappropriately. I treated them as very special, precious people, probably how I would treat my own daughter—not with physical affection, but with the same level of sensitivity and respect."

Traughber also indicated that he was careful not to do anything that might be misinterpreted as overtly aggressive.[5] "They start out assuming that since you are a man, you have no clue what they've been through or what their life is like. So I decided to be transparent about my life," he explained. "If they had questions, I answered them. I didn't have any problem letting them know a little bit about myself. In my mind, if I became real with them, then they'd allow me to enter into their life—to help them see what needs to be changed—and then to help them effect the change."

Traughber went onto say that if the women started talking or joking about men, he would laugh right along with them. "I wouldn't be offended. 'You are right,' I would say. 'We are jerks sometimes. We do have problems.'" He admitted that this required a large amount of humility on his part. But he stressed that as the women experienced his humility and respect, they began to realize that not all men are abusive and self-serving. He shared that he had several women tell him that he had given them hope and that they realized that they didn't have to be scared of "every guy out there."

Lewis said that in the beginning he had women "in his face." "I immediately recognized the powerful transferences that were occurring. Many of these women had histories of extremely negative experiences with men. Their feelings and reactions toward me were potent," he recalled. He explained that he had to keep reminding himself that their reactions were not about him. "I took a lot of heat, but I stayed with them. It took a long time, but I made a choice to ride through whatever they sent my way." Lewis said his consistency helped the women to eventually form a sense of trust. "I was willing to prove my commitment to them. At times I had to put some extra energy in and give on an emotional level. These women knew that if I wasn't willing to put my heart into it, then I wasn't really willing to have a relationship with them."

---

[5]The main reason that these women often prematurely terminate with male therapists is their perception of anger or hostility. They are extremely sensitive to a raised voice or a simple gesture such as leaning forward or pointing a finger. Most women will not be able to identify their trigger or transference nor regulate their resulting fear and anxiety. They will simply never return.

When I asked him what he thought male therapists needed to know about working with women with SSA, Traughber said:

> I think a male therapist needs to be committed to the long haul in order to work with women with SSA. If he isn't or can't be, then he shouldn't agree to take them on as clients. Also, you need to educate yourself on this issue. Female SSA is a complex issue. You are not going to be able to walk in, as you might in a marriage counseling session, with your normal toolbox and just whip tools out and "fix" this thing in six weeks or less. It is more about growth for these women than fixing a problem. Familiarize yourself with the core issues, like emotional dependency, and begin to build a framework of understanding female SSA. Seek out consultation. If you aren't willing to learn about this population, then you will have little chance of having a lasting impact.

When I asked Lewis the same question, he answered,

> For these women to ultimately benefit from therapy, the therapist must do a lot more preparatory work in loving and caring for them than he would for other clients. I usually don't allow my clients to call me in between sessions, but with these women, I have to. It's more time consuming for me but absolutely essential for them to develop that connection. Also, they have challenged my sense of confidence as a therapist, even though I had had over 30 years experience under my belt.

In conclusion, both stressed that these women ultimately need men who can model something different from what they have experienced in the past.

References

Only those sources that have been directly quoted within this text are listed here. All other sources are listed on the book's website under "Bibliography."

Ahrens, C. (1991). Childhood trauma and female sexuality. In J. Dallas (Ed.), *Desires in conflict* (pp. 185-212). Eugene, OR: Harvest House Publishers.

American Psychiatric Association. (2000). *Diagnostic and statistical manual of mental disorders* (4th ed. text revision). Washington, DC: Author.

Anthony, B. D. (1982). Lesbian client-lesbian therapist: Opportunities and challenges in working together. In J. C. Gonsiorek (Ed.), *Homosexuality and psychotherapy: A practitioner's handbook of affirmative models. Journal of Homosexuality* 7(2/3), 45-57. New York: Haworth Press.

Baars, C., & Terruwe, A. (2002). *Healing the unaffirmed.* New York: St. Pauls.

Bailey, J. M., Dunne, M. P., & Martin, N. G. (2000). Genetic and environmental influences on sexual orientation and its correlates in an Australian twin sample. *Journal of Personality and Social Psychology, 78*(3), 524-36.

Barnhouse, R. T. (1977). *Homosexuality: A symbolic confusion.* New York: Seabury Press.

Bartholomew, K., Kwong, M. J., & Hart, S. D. (2001). Attachment. In W. J. Livesley (Ed.), *Handbook of personality disorders: Theory, research and treatment* (pp. 196-230). New York: Guilford Press.

Batgos, J., & Leadbeater, B. J. (1994). Parental attachment, peer relations and dysphoria in adolescence. In M. B. Sperling & W. H. Berman (Eds.), *Attachment in adults: Clinical and developmental perspectives* (pp. 155-61). New York: Guilford Press.

Baumgardner, J. (2007, March). Why more girls are dating . . . girls. *Glamour,* 174-75.

Bayer, R. (1987). *Homosexuality and American psychiatry: The politics of diagnosis.* Princeton, NJ: Princeton University Press.

Bearman, P. S., & Bruckner, H. (2002). Opposite-sex twins and adolescent same-sex attraction. *The American Journal of Sociology, 107*(5), 1179-1205.

Beckstead, A. L., & Morrow, S. L. (2004). Mormon clients' experiences of conversion therapy: The need for a new treatment approach. *The Counseling Psychologist, 32*(5), 651-90.

Bell, A. P., Weinberg, M. S., & Hammersmith, S. K. (1981). *Sexual preference: Its development in men and women.* Bloomington: Indiana University Press.

Bergin, A. E., Payne, I. R., & Richards, P. S. (1996). Values in psychotherapy. In E. P. Shafranske (Ed.), *Religion and the clinical practice of psychology* (pp. 297-25). Washington, DC: American Psychological Association.

Bergner, M. (2004, Autumn). Watching the Lord heal lesbian attractions. *Redeemed Lives News, 5*(3), 3-6.

Bowlby, J. (1988). *A secure base.* New York: Basic Books.

Brodzinsky, D. M., Schechter, M. D., & Henig, R. M. (1992). *Being adopted: The lifelong search for self.* New York: Anchor Books.

Burch, B. (1987). Barriers to intimacy: Conflicts over power, dependency and nurturing in lesbian relationships. In Boston Lesbian Psychologies Collective (Eds.), *Lesbian Psychologies* (pp. 126-41). Chicago: University of Illinois Press.

Byne, W., & Parsons, B. (1993). Human sexual orientation: The biologic theories reappraised. *Archives of General Psychiatry, 50,* 228-39.

Byrd, A. D. (2005, August). *Special report* [Review of the book *Destructive trends in mental health: The well-intentioned path to harm*]. Narth Bulletin, 13(2), 3-10.

Cloud, J. (2005, October 10). The battle over gay teens. *Time, 166*(15), 42-51.

Cox, S. E., & Dant, D. R. (1999). *Developing genuine friendships: A guide for women struggling with same-sex attractions.* Salt Lake City: Evergreen International.

Dallas, J. (1996). In defense of clinical treatment for homosexuality. *Journal of Psychology and Christianity, 15*(4), 369-72.

Davis, P. K. (1999). *The power of touch.* Carlsbad, CA: Hay House.

Deddo, G. W. (2006). *Why we're gendered beings—a trinitarian perspective: The difference difference makes.* Paper presented at the meeting of the Evangelical Theological Society, Washington, DC. Retrieved October 22, 2007, from the Trinity Study Center website: http://www.trinitystudycenter.com/topical/trinityandgender.pdf.

Eckleberry-Hunt, J. G., & Dohrenwend, A. (2005). Sociocultural interpretations of social phobia in a non-heterosexual female. *Journal of Homosexuality, 49*(2), 103-17.

Edelman, H. (1994). *Motherless Daughters.* New York: Dell.

Eldridge, E. (1994). *Born that way? A true story of overcoming same-sex attraction with insights for friends, families and leaders.* Salt Lake City: Deseret.

Erikson, E. H. (1980). *Identity and the life cycle.* New York: W. W. Norton.

Falco, K. (1991). *Psychotherapy with lesbian clients.* New York: Brunner/Mazel.

Fogel, A. (2002). Remembering infancy: Accessing our earliest experiences. In G. Bremmer & A. Slater (Eds.), *Theories of Infant Development.* Cambridge: Blackwell.

Friedman, R. C., & Downey, J. I. (1993a). Neurobiology and sexual orientation: Current relationships. *Journal of Neuropsychiatry and Clinical Neurosciences, 5,* 131-53.

Frisch, M., & Hviid, A. (2006). Childhood family correlates of heterosexual and homosexual marriages: A national cohort study of two million Danes. *Archives of Sexual Behavior, 35,* 533-47.

Gartrell, N. (1981). The lesbian as a "single" woman. *American Journal of Psychotherapy, 35*(4), 502-9.

Gilligan, C. (1982). *In a different voice: Psychological theory and women's development.* Cambridge, MA: Harvard University Press.

Goode, E., & Haber, L. (1977). Sexual correlates of homosexual experience. *The Journal of Sex Research, 13*(1), 12-21.

Grenz, S. J. (1995). *Women in the church: A biblical theology of women in ministry.* Downers Grove, IL: InterVarsity Press.

Gundlach, R. H., & Riess, B. F. (1968). Self and sexual identity in the female: A study of female homosexuals. In B. F. Riess (Ed.), *New directions in mental health* (Vol. 1, pp. 205-31). New York: Grune & Stratton.

Gundlach, R. H., & Riess, B. F. (1973). The range of problems in the treatment of lesbians. In D. S. Milman & G. D. Goldman (Eds.), *The neurosis of our time: Acting out* (pp. 147-69). Springfield, IL: Charles C. Thomas.

Haldeman, D. (2002). Gay rights, patient rights: The implications of sexual orientation conversion therapy. *Professional Psychology: Research and Practice, 33*(3), 260-64.

Hall, J. M. (1994). Lesbians recovering from alcohol problems: An ethnographic study of health care experiences. *Nursing Research, 43*(4), 238-44.

Hawley, G. A. (1988). *Measures of psychosocial development* (MPD). Odessa, FL: Psychological Assessment Resources, (800)331-TEST.

Hogan, R. A., Fox, A. N., & Kirchner, J. H. (1977). Attitudes, opinions and sexual development of 205 homosexual women. *Journal of Homosexuality, 3*(2), 123-36.

Howard, J. (1991). *Out of Egypt: Leaving lesbianism behind.* Tunbridge Wells, UK: Monarch.

Howard, J. (2005). *Into the promised land: Beyond the lesbian struggle.* Grand Rapids, MI: Monarch.

Hughes, D. A. (2004). *Attachment focused therapy for children, adolescents and families.* Santa Rosa, CA: R. Cassidy Seminars.

Jones, S. & Yarhouse, M. (2007). *Ex-gays? A longitudinal study of religiously mediated change in sexual orientation.* Downers Grove, IL: IVP Academic.

Jordan, J. V., & Surrey, J. L. (1989). The self-in-relation: Empathy and the mother-daughter relationship. In T. Bernay & D. W. Cantor (Eds.), *The psychology of today's woman: New psychoanalytic visions* (pp. 81-104). Cambridge, MA: Harvard University Press.

Jordan, J. V., Surrey, J. L., & Kaplan, A. G. (1991). Women and empathy: Implications for psychological development and psychotherapy. In J. V. Jordan, A. G. Kaplan, J. B. Miller, I. P. Stiver & J. L. Surrey (Eds.), *Women's growth in connection* (pp. 27-50). New York: Guilford Press.

Kaplan, A. G., Gleason, N., & Klein, R. (1991). Womens' self development in late adolescence. In J. V. Jordan, A. G. Kaplan, J. B. Miller, I. P. Stiver & J. L. Surrey (Eds.), *Women's growth and connection* (pp. 122-40). New York: Guilford Press.

Kaplan, H., & Sadock, B. (1991). *Comprehensive glossary of psychiatry and psychology.* Baltimore: Williams & Wilkins.

Kaufman, P. A., Harrison, E., & Hyde, M. L. (1984). Distancing for intimacy in lesbian relationships. *American Journal of Psychiatry, 141*(4), 530-33.

Koh, A. S., & Ross, L. K. (2006). Mental health issues: A comparison of lesbian, bisexual and heterosexual women. *Journal of Homosexuality, 51*(1), 33-57.

Krestan, J., & Bepko, C. (1980). The problem of fusion in lesbian relationship. *Family Process, 19*(3): 277-89.

Levy, T. M., & Orlans, M. (1998). *Attachment, trauma and healing.* Washington, DC: Child Welfare League of America Press.

Lewis, C. S. (1960). *The four loves*. New York: Harcourt Brace Jovanovich.

Lindenbaum, J.P. (1985). The shattering of an illusion: The problem of competition in lesbian relationships. *Feminist Studies, 11*(1), 85-103.

Manning, B. (2000). *Ruthless Trust*. San Francisco: HarperCollins.

Mara, J. (1983). A lesbian perspective. In J. H. Robbins & R. J. Siegel (Eds.), *Women changing therapy* (pp. 145-55). New York: Haworth Press.

Masterson, J. F. (1985). *The real self.* New York: Brunner/Mazel.

McCandlish, B. M. (1982). Therapeutic issues with lesbian couples. In J. C. Gonsiorek (Ed.), *Homosexuality and psychotherapy: A practitioner's handbook of affirmative models* (pp. 71-78.) New York: Haworth Press.

McDougall, J. (1970). Homosexuality in women. In Chasseguet-Smirgel (Ed.), *Female sexuality: New psychoanalytic views* (pp. 171-212). Ann Arbor: University of Michigan Press.

McDougall, J. (1980). *Plea for a measure of abnormality.* New York: International Universities Press.

McDougall, J. (1989). The dead father: On early psychic trauma and its relation to disturbance in sexual identity and in creative activity. *International Journal of Psycho-Analysis, 70,* 205-19.

Miller, A. (1981). *The drama of the gifted child.* New York: Basic Books.

Miller, J. B. (1991). The development of women's sense of self. In J. Jordan, A. Kaplan, J. Miller, I. Stiver & J. Surrey (Eds.) *Women's growth in connection* (pp. 11-26). New York: Guilford Press.

Millon, T., Millon, C., Davis, R., & Grossman, S. (1994). *Millon clinical multiaxial inventory-III* (MCMI-III). Minneapolis: Diacandrien. Available from Pearson Assessments, (800)268-6011.

Minuchin, S. (1974). *Families and family therapy.* Cambridge, MA: Harvard University Press.

Moberly, E. (1983). *Homosexuality: A new Christian ethic.* Greenwood, SC: Attic Press.

Mullins, H. (1995). Evolution of a tomboy. In L. Yamaguchi & K. Barber (Eds.), *Tomboys: Tales of dyke derring-do* (pp. 40-49). Los Angeles: Alyson.

Nichols, M. (1982). The treatment of inhibited sexual desire (ISD) in lesbian couples. *Women & Therapy, 1*(4), 49-66.

Nichols, M. (1988a). Low sexual desire in lesbian couples. In S. R. Leiblum & R. C. Rosen (Eds.), *Sexual Desire Disorders* (pp. 387-412). New York: Guilford Press.

Nichols, M. (1990). Lesbian relationships: Implications for the study of sexuality and gender. In D. P. McWhirter, S. A. Sanders & J. M. Reinisch (Eds.), *Homosexuality/heterosexuality: Concepts of sexual orientation* (pp. 350-64). New York: Oxford University Press.

Nicolosi, J. (1993). *Healing homosexuality.* Northvale, NJ: Jason Aronson.

Nicolosi, J., Byrd, A., & Potts, R. (2000a). Retrospective self-reports of changes in sexual orientation: A consumer survey of conversion therapy clients. *Psychological Reports, 86,* 1071-88.

Paulk, A. (2003). *Restoring sexual identity.* Eugene, OR: Harvest House.

Payne, L. (1984). *The healing of the homosexual.* Westchester, IL: Crossway Books.

Pearlman, S. (1989). Distancing and connectedness: Impact on couple formation in lesbian relationships. In E. D. Rothblum & E. Cole (Eds.), *Loving boldly: Issues facing lesbians* (pp. 77-88). New York: Harrington Park.

Phillips, G., Psych, M., & Over, R. (1995). Differences between heterosexual, bisexual and lesbian women in recalled childhood experiences. *Archives of Sexual Behavior, 24*(1), 1-20.

Post, R. D. (1982). Dependency conflicts in high-achieving women: Toward an integration. *Psychotherapy: Theory, Research & Practice, 19*(1), 82-87.

Prescott, J. W., LaFortune, M., Levy, J., & Wallace, D. (1980). Affectional deprivation in childhood and adolescence in the United States and Quebec, Canada: A cross-cultural study of sexual alienation and violence. In R. Forleo & W. Pasini (Eds.), *Medical sexology: The third international congress* (pp. 169-81). Littleton, MA: PSG Publishing.

Quinodoz, J.-M. (1989). Female homosexual patients in psychoanalysis. *International Journal of Psychoanalysis, 70,* 55-63.

Rand, M. L. (1996). As it was in the beginning: The significance of infant bonding in the development of self and relationships. *Journal of Child Care and Youth Care, 10*(4), 1-8. Retrieved October 22, 2007, from the Association for Prenatal & Perinatal Psychology and Health website: http://www.birthpsychology.com/birthscene/ppic5.html.

Rentzel, L. T. (1990). *Emotional dependency.* Downers Grove, IL: InterVarsity Press.

Ross, C. (2000). *The trauma model.* Richardson, TX: Manitou Communications.

Roth, S. (1984). Psychotherapy with lesbian couples: The interrelationships of individual issues, female socialization, and the social context. In E. S. Hetrick & T. S. Stein (Eds.), *Innovations in psychotherapy with homosexuals* (pp. 90-114). Washington, DC: American Psychiatric Press.

Satinover, J. (1996a). *Homosexuality and the politics of truth.* Grand Rapids, MI: Baker Books.

Schaffner, B. (2003). Questioning some traditional "rules" in psychotherapy. In J. Drescher, A. D'Ercole & E. Schoenberg (Eds.), *Psychotherapy with gay men and lesbians: Contemporary dynamic approaches* (pp. 237-48). New York: Harrington Park.

Schneider, M. S., Brown, L. S., & Glassgold, J. M. (2002). Implementing the resolution on appropriate therapeutic responses to sexual orientation: A guide for the perplexed. *Professional Psychology: Research and Practice, 33*(3), 265-76.

Sheehy, S. (2000). *Connecting: The enduring power of female friendship.* New York: William Morrow.

Siegel, D. J. (1999a). *The developing mind.* New York: Guilford Press.

Siegel, E. (1988). *Female homosexuality: Choice without volition.* Hillsdale, NJ: Analytic Press.

Smalley, S. (1987). Dependency issues in lesbian relationships. *Journal of Homosexuality, 14*(1/2), 125-35.

Solomon, A. (2001). *The noonday demon.* New York: Simon & Schuster.

Spitzer, R. (2003). Can some gay men and lesbians change their sexual orientation? 200 participants reporting a change from homosexual to heterosexual orientation. *Archives of Sexual Behavior, 32*(5), 403-17.

Stevens, P. E. (1992). Lesbian health care research: A review of the literature from 1970 to 1990. *Health Care for Women International, 13,* 91-120.

Surrey, J. L. (1991a). The relational self in women: Clinical implications. In J. V. Jordan, A. G. Kaplan, J. B. Miller, I. P. Stiver & J. L. Surrey (Eds.), *Women's growth in connection* (pp. 35-43). New York: Guilford Press.

Thomson, P. (2004). The impact of trauma on the embryo and fetus: An application of the diathesis-stress model and the neurovulnerability-neurotoxicity model. *Journal of Prenatal and Perinatal Psychology and Health, 19*(1), 9-63.

Toufexis, A. (1995, November 13) New evidence of a "gay gene." *Time.* Retrieved October 22, 2007, from http://www.time.com/time/magazine/article/0,9171,983713,00.html.

Tozer, E. E., & McClanahan, M. K. (1999). Treating the purple menace: Ethical considerations of conversion therapy and affirmative alternatives. *The Counseling Psychologist, 27*(5), 722-42.

Tronick, E. Z. (1989). Emotions and emotional communication in infants. *American Psychologist, 44*(2), 112-19.

Van Wyk, P. H., & Geist, C. S. (1984). Psychosocial development of heterosexual, bisexual and homosexual behavior. *Archives of Sexual Behavior, 13*(6), 505-44.

Vogelmann-Sine, S. (1998). Healing hidden pain: Resolving the effects of childhood abuse and neglect. In P. Manfield (Ed.), *Extending EMDR* (pp. 167-90). New York: W. W. Norton.

Walant, K. B. (1995). *Creating the capacity for attachment.* Northvale, NJ: Jason Aronson.

Ward, A. J. (1991). Prenatal stress and childhood psychopathology. *Child Psychiatry and Human Development, 22*(2), 97-110.

Whitfield, C. L. (1987). *Healing the child within.* Deerfield Beach, FL: Health Communications.

Wilbur, C. B. (1965). Clinical aspects of female homosexuality. In J. Marmor (Ed.), *Sexual inversion: The multiple roots of homosexuality* (pp. 268-81). New York: Basic Books.

Winnicott, D. W. (1965). *The maturational processes and the facilitating environment.* New York: International Universities Press.

Yalom, I. D. (2002). *The gift of therapy.* New York: HarperCollins.

Yamaguchi, L., & Barber, K. (Eds.). (1995). *Tomboys: Tales of dyke derring-do.* Los Angeles: Alyson.

Yarhouse, M. A. (1998). When clients seek treatment for same-sex attraction: Ethical issues in the "right to choose" debate. *Psychotherapy, 35,* 248-59.

Yarhouse, M. A., & Throckmorton, W. (2002). Ethical issues in attempts to ban reorientation therapies. *Psychotherapy: Theory, Research, Practice, Training, 39*(1), 66-75.

Zucker, K. J. (2001). Biological influences on psychosexual differentiation. In R. Unger (Ed.), *Handbook of the psychology of women and gender* (pp. 101-15). Hoboken, NJ: John Wiley.

Zucker, K. J., & Bradley, S. (1995). *Gender identity disorder and psychosexual problems in children and adolescents.* New York: Guilford Press.

Janelle Hallman can be contacted at

Janelle Hallman, M.A., L.P.C.
8771 Wolff Court, Suite 210
Westminster, CO 80031
303.429.2100
www.janellehallman.com